QUICK ACCESS CONTENTS

D0150668

Writing Research Papers

A Guide to the Process

Writing Research Papers

A Guide to the Process

SIXTH EDITION

Stephen Weidenborner
Domenick Caruso

Kingsborough Community College,
The City University of New York

Bedford/St. Martin's   Boston ◆ New York

For Bedford/St. Martin's

Editor: John Elliott
Editorial Assistants: Belinda Delpêche, Gregory S. Johnson
Senior Production Supervisor: Dennis Conroy
Marketing Manager: Brian Wheel
Project Management: Books By Design, Inc.
Cover Design: Robin Hoffman
Composition: Pine Tree Composition
Printing and Binding: R. R. Donnelley & Sons

President: Charles H. Christensen
Editorial Director: Joan E. Feinberg
Editor in Chief: Nancy Perry
Director of Marketing: Karen R. Melton
Director of Editing, Design, and Production: Marcia Cohen
Manager, Publishing Services: Emily Berleth

Library of Congress Catalog Card Number: 99-62182

Manufactured in the United States of America.

6   5   4   3
f   e   d   c

For information, write: Bedford/St. Martin's, 75 Arlington Street, Boston, MA 02116 (617–399–4000)

ISBN: 0-312-40085-3

Acknowledgments

The authors and the editors would like to acknowledge the invaluable assistance of Lawrence Thompson (Kingsborough Community College) in the collection of electronic source materials for the student search in Chapter 7 and for the sample paper "Solenopsis invicta: *Destroyer of Ecosystems" in Chapter 21.*

"Cotton Mather" entry from *Encyclopedia Americana,* 1992 edition. Copyright © 1992 by Grolier, Inc. All rights reserved.

"Emma Goldman" entry from *Notable American Women,* Volume II, edited by Edward T. James, Janet Wilson James, and Paul Boyer, Harvard University Press. Copyright © 1971 by the President and Council of Radcliffe College. Reprinted by permission of the publisher.

Figure 5-1. *Readers' Guide to Periodical Literature, 1984–1985.* Copyright © by the H.W. Wilson Company. Material reproduced with permission of the publisher.

Figure 5-2. Excerpt from *Magazine Index*™. © 1996 Information Access Company. Reprinted by permission.

Figure 5-3. From *The New York Times Index* (fig. 3-10), October 28, 1995. Copyright © 1995 by The New York Times Company. Reprinted by permission.

Figure 8-1. Netscape Netcenter Web site. Copyright © 2000 by Netscape Communications Corp. Screenshot used with permission.

Figures 8-2 & 8-3. Lycos screen shots. Copyright © 2000 Lycos, Inc. All rights reserved. The Lycos™ "Catalog of the Internet." Copyright © 1994, 1995, 1996, 2000 Carnegie Mellon University. All rights reserved. Used by permission.

Acknowledgments and copyrights are continued at the back of the book on page 336, which constitutes an extension of the copyright page.

Preface

We live in what is commonly called the Information Age. Along with traditional, pre-electronic information outlets, students can now tap into a rapidly growing number of electronic sources that provide access to both long established and recently defined categories of knowledge. However, the increased emphasis on information-gathering in our society causes confusion for many students learning to carry out a research project. Given the flood of information—and misinformation—available to them on- and offline, many students equate the gathering of raw data with the process of doing research. They have yet to learn that a successful research project involves more than just collecting information.

Writing Research Papers: A Guide to the Process will help students to understand that writing a good research paper requires planning, being organized, and making careful choices about what topic to research, which sources to consult, what kinds of notes to take, and how to put these notes together in a coherent, purposeful paper that reflects not only the quality of the research but also the writer's thoughtful interaction with his or her material. When the writer has only a sketchy knowledge of the field in which he or she is working, the step-by-step approach of *Writing Research Papers* can be the key to mastering the fundamental skills of research paper writing. In addition to this proven method, the sixth edition of the book retains all of the other features that have made it work for so many students and instructors over the last two decades: a clear and friendly writing style, a handy spiral-bound format, and attention to the kinds of difficulties first-time writers of research papers are likely to have.

New to This Edition

In revising *Writing Research Papers* for this edition, we have concentrated on making the book easier to use as a reference. To help students find the material they need more quickly and efficiently, we have made the following changes:

- a new organization of 6 parts and 21 chapters, which divides many of the longer chapters of previous editions into smaller units
- color tabs on the outsides of the pages to identify each part of the text and each major documentation system
- more prominent running heads
- more bulleted and numbered lists within the text

We have also made the following additions and changes to bring the book's content up to date, especially in the area of technology:

- expanded and updated treatment of the Internet and the World Wide Web
- the latest MLA and APA guidelines for citing Internet and other electronic sources, with more examples
- replacement of the MLA endnote/footnote system with the more widely used Chicago style
- a new chapter on formatting final manuscript, including advice on choosing type fonts and using color and visuals
- the inclusion of more electronic sources and visuals in the sample student papers

The review questions and exercises, which have been revised and updated, now appear at the end of each part. The two appendices, "Glossary of Internet Terms" and "Reference Sources," have also been updated.

Overview of the Book

The first two parts of *Writing Research Papers* (Chapters 1–8) guide students through the process of finding a workable topic and searching for information about the topic, using the library as well as online sources and field research where appropriate. We demonstrate how a tentative thesis, or *hypothesis,* can be a powerful tool for evaluating the potential usefulness of sources and for taking effective notes, steps that are covered in Part Three (Chapters 9–13). Here we include detailed guidelines for deciding when to use direct quotations and for avoiding plagiarism, along with an extended example of effective note-taking.

The next major stage of writing a research paper involves turning a collection of notes into a coherent whole. We devote Part Four (Chapters 14–16) to strategies for developing the paper—organizing, drafting, and rewriting—including detailed advice about revising paragraphs, sentences, and wording, as well as instruction on writing abstracts.

Part Five (Chapters 17–19) presents a fully updated discussion of documenting sources, including additional emphasis on documenting electronic sources. Chapter 17 provides a thorough explanation of what kinds of material require documentation. Chapter 18 is a complete description of the MLA style of parenthetical notation, incorporating a wide range of sample notes and Works Cited entries as well as guidelines for inserting references effectively within the text. In Chapter 19, we illustrate the endnote/footnote system of the *Chicago Manual of Style*, the author/year format of the American Psychological Association (APA), and the number style used in the sciences. Students are also directed to sources of information about the various styles they will need for specific disciplines across the curriculum.

Part Six (Chapters 20 and 21) contains the new chapter on document design and four sample student research papers showing the leading documentation styles in practice. In this edition, we have changed the documentation in the Cotton Mather paper from the MLA endnote/footnote system to the Chicago system. Throughout the book, we illustrate each step in the research process by following the work of these four student writers and others as well.

Acknowledgments

In making these revisions, we have benefited greatly from the thoughtful, constructive advice we have received from instructors across the country. In particular, we wish to thank Judith Angona (Ocean County College), Christopher Bursk (Bucks County Community College), Kim Brian Lovejoy (Indiana University at Indianapolis), Brian E. Michaels and Nora S. Michaels (St. Johns River Community College), Jack Scanlon (Triton Community College), Lolly Smith (Everett Community College), and Carl Waluconis (Seattle Central Community College). Nick Carbone (Colorado State University) provided useful comments on the discussion of the Internet and the World Wide Web, and Denise Quirk helped to update this and other material on finding sources, as well as the appendix of reference sources.

Stephen Weidenborner
Domenick Caruso

Contents

Part Three   Working with Sources

Part Four   Writing the Paper

Part Five   Documenting Sources

19 Using Other Documentation Systems   *227*

Part Six   Preparing the Manuscript

20 Following Format Requirements   *251*

Writing
Research
Papers

A Guide
to the Process

Part One

Laying the Groundwork

1

Understanding the Research Process

As you think about writing a research paper, you may wonder how this assignment differs from other kinds of papers you have written. The fundamental difference has to do with the major content of each. Research papers do not grow out of your personal experiences and opinions to the same extent that other compositions do. Instead, they require that you use your critical thinking skills to evaluate information and ideas that you uncover while learning about a topic through research.

Sometimes, virtually all the information and ideas will come from books, magazines, newspapers, and nonprint sources like the Internet or personal interviews. In these cases, your work will consist mainly of finding the information and organizing it into a coherent *report* of your findings. More often, however, you will be encouraged to go a step further and make judgments about the information you discover—that is, to *evaluate* it.

For example, if you chose to investigate the controversy over the effect of acid rain on forests and lakes, you would be expected to evaluate (as an intelligent citizen, not as an expert, of course) the arguments put forth by both sides. You might conclude that the environmentalists have made the better arguments, or you might decide that the experts working for the smokestack industries have provided good reasons for doubting the accuracy of their opponents' charges. Or you might feel that it is impossible to choose between the two positions, but that, too, would amount to a judgment on your part.

Producing a good research paper is no easy task. But completing this work has its reward, not only in the beneficial effect a good paper will have on your course average but also in the satisfaction you will get from having met this formidable challenge. Furthermore, as you increase your

3

knowledge of a topic and begin making judgments as to which sources are most believable, you rapidly become an "expert" on the topic—someone who knows the subject well and whose opinions other people will listen to. This means that when you write your paper and share it with your instructor or other students, you are fulfilling an important goal of research paper writing: adding your voice to an academic "conversation" about a meaningful issue.

Basic Steps in the Process

Before you examine the research process in detail, it is important to grasp these three essential operations:

1. **searching**   You must search harder than most people realize for a good topic; rarely can you find a topic merely by thinking about the matter. Once you have a topic, you must learn how to find the information you need, starting at the library or the Internet.
2. **reading**   This operation involves more than understanding the materials you are reading. You must learn how to recognize what information is likely to be truly relevant to your research goals and what can be safely skimmed over or ignored.
3. **writing**   Because you will be handling a great deal of information, most of which will have come from your sources, the ability to organize intelligently may count as much as a fine writing style. But that does not mean that style doesn't count, as you well know.

All three of these operations demand constant exercise of good judgment as well as competence in dealing with language. And neatness counts—not just from the instructor's point of view, but from your own, for carelessness can prove costly when you are working with large amounts of information.

Mastering these skills and developing your judgment will take time and experience, so you should plan to spend several weeks—more likely a month—completing your first full-length research assignment.

Some Essential Definitions

Be careful to note the specific ways in which the following terms are used here, for they are often tossed around much more loosely in daily conversation. You will need to understand their precise meanings if you are to benefit fully from the discussions that follow.

- **subject**   a broad area of interest that can be narrowed down to a suitable topic. Subjects themselves are either too broad or too loosely defined to serve as topics for research papers. For example, entire books have been written on the following subjects:

  - addictive behavior
  - Russia's economic troubles
  - Jane Austen's novels
  - prehistoric animals
  - rain forests
  - cancer cures
  - early childhood education
  - illegal immigration

  To develop a workable topic from one of these subjects, ask yourself what you would be looking for in your readings on the subject. What questions would you be answering?

- **topic**   a reasonably narrow, clearly defined area of interest that could be thoroughly investigated within the limits set for a given research assignment. Here are some topics that might work quite well for a paper of seven to ten pages:

  - the effect of parental attitudes on teenage alcoholism
  - the role of U.S. policies in the collapse of the Russian economy
  - the relationship between young women and their fathers in three novels by Jane Austen
  - the role of humans in the extinction of large prehistoric mammals
  - the effect of U.S. policies on the depletion of rain forests in South America
  - the role of emotions in the cure of certain cancers
  - the effectiveness of Head Start programs in preparing children for grade school
  - the effect of illegal immigration on unemployment in the Southwest

- **thesis**   a general statement that announces the major conclusions you reached through a thoughtful analysis of all your sources. This statement appears near the beginning of your paper; the main body will then explain, illustrate, argue for, or in some sense "prove" the thesis.

- **hypothesis**   a prediction, made sometime before you read the sources, as to what conclusions your research will produce. That is, a *hypothesis* is an attempt to predict what the paper's *thesis* will be. As you will see, this "educated guess" helps you find exactly the information you need, as quickly and efficiently as possible, by keeping your attention focused on several specific aspects of the topic.

A More Detailed Look at the Research Process

Now that you have these definitions clearly in mind, we can examine the process more closely. Here is a brief summary of the steps you need to follow:

Step 1: Finding a Topic and Forming a Hypothesis

- Choose an interesting *subject*, if the choice is left to you.
- Read about this subject in a textbook, encyclopedia, or general reference work, either in print or online.
- Find a workable *topic* in this background reading.
- Form an opinion (*hypothesis*) as to what your research is likely to reveal.

Step 2: Finding Useful Sources

- Keep your hypothesis in mind as you look for titles of what seem to be valuable sources.
- Make sure to collect more potential sources than you will need.
- Skim these sources, weeding out those of little or no relevance to your hypothesis.

Step 3: Taking Stock of What You Have Found

- Decide whether you have a sufficient number and variety of sources.
- Decide whether or not your hypothesis is clearly focused and still seems valid.
- Construct a brief preliminary outline for the paper based on what you have seen so far.

Step 4: Reading Sources Closely and Taking Notes

- Keep your hypothesis and preliminary outline in mind to save time and avoid taking too many notes.
- Be ready to revise the hypothesis and preliminary outline in light of what your research turns up.
- Fit your notes into the preliminary outline to make sure you have covered each subtopic fairly well.

Step 5: Arriving at the Thesis

- Analyze your findings to see how closely they support the hypothesis.
- State the thesis clearly, setting it within a well-developed introduction.

Step 6: Preparing to Write

- Write a brief summary of the content, often called an abstract.
- Construct a full outline.
- Assign each note to its position in the outline.

Step 7: Writing the Paper

- *Rough Draft:* write fairly rapidly, worrying about formalities later.
- *Revised Draft(s):* reorganize for greater effectiveness; improve style.
- *Completed Version:* edit for correctness, use of language, positioning of documentation.

Step 8: Documenting the Sources

- Carefully place notes within parentheses at the appropriate places.
- Construct the Works Cited, or References, list at the end of the paper.

Step 9: Preparing the Final Version

- Proofread the paper and correct any errors.
- Format the paper appropriately, incorporating any visuals.
- Make a copy for your files.

A glance at this outline might lead you to believe that a fine paper can be produced by following a simple, step-by-step prescription — moving from subject to topic to hypothesis to thesis. In actual practice, however, you must be ready at every step to revise your earlier decisions in light of the new information you are continually discovering. This advice applies in particular to the hypothesis, which is, after all, only an educated guess as to what conclusion your research might reach.

Much of the discussion so far has been rather abstract. To get a good idea of what an actual research paper looks like, read the sample student papers in Chapter 21. Note how the writers of the first three papers state,

Laying the Groundwork

early in the paper, the thesis they intend to "prove." (Although the writer of the fourth paper does not state a thesis, he does state the purpose of his paper.) As you go through the body of a paper, think about the way in which the writer presents the ideas and information that led to the thesis. Finally, notice the parenthetical (or numbered) notes that indicate where the various pieces of supporting information were found. After you finish looking over the sample papers, return to Chapter 2, where we begin discussing each step of the process in detail.

2

Deciding on a Topic

At the heart of a successful research paper lies a clearly expressed thesis, which tells the readers the major conclusions you reached after a thorough investigation of your topic. For example,

Topic: "New immigrants: Are they an asset or a burden?"

Thesis: If these recent immigrants do as well for themselves and the economy as earlier immigrants, they will prove to be more of an asset than a burden to the United States.

Topic: "Emily Dickinson's reluctance to publish her poems"

Thesis: Dickinson felt that her poetry was ahead of its time, so she kept her poems from the public, waiting for the day when they would be fully appreciated.

Topic: "Cotton Mather's role in the Salem witch-hunts"

Thesis: Mather thought he and the Puritan colony enjoyed a special position in God's plan for humanity, and this belief led him to purge the community of what he saw as evil influences, namely, the witches.

Topic: "Fire ants: Destroyers of whole ecosystems in the South"

Thesis: Perhaps, in time, evolution and ecological changes will exert control over the ants.

In the research paper's body, you attempt to "prove" the thesis by explaining, illustrating, and arguing the case. Evidence to support the case consists of information gathered from a reasonable number of sources representing various points of view on the issue at hand.

One of the pitfalls awaiting someone doing a research paper is to think that all that is needed is a good topic, and then everything will easily fall into place. *Cotton Mather's role in the Salem witch-hunts* was a good topic, but with only this topic as a guide, Fred Hutchins could have ended up producing a short history of Mather's actions as judge and commentator. That, however, would have been only a "report" because historians do not disagree to any great extent on *what* Mather did. The interesting question concerns *why* he played such an active role. Was he a woman hater? A thoughtless conformist? A politically motivated crowd pleaser?

Once Fred had thought of an interesting question about his topic, he had a goal for his research—to answer that question. His research would consist of finding various historians' theories about Mather's motivation. The results of the investigation would be his thesis.

Having a question to investigate compels you to think about possible outcomes of your research. A bit of preliminary research should provide a basis for your making a reasonable guess as to what the answer to your question will be. This "reasonable guess" is called a *hypothesis.*

Moving from Subject to Topic

Step 1 of the research assignment consists of deciding just what question the research will answer—what problem will be worth exploring. Your first thoughts, however, are likely to be very general, only indicating the direction of your immediate interest. "I want to write about the trouble in the Middle East." "I want to know more about dinosaurs." "I am interested in UFOs and alien abductions." "I've always been fascinated by the flower children of the 1960s." You don't yet know what to say about the subject, or even whether it will lead to a satisfactory topic, but you are moving in the right direction.

The question now becomes: "How do I know whether the subject is any good?" To help you decide, consider whether or not the subject meets these criteria:

1. You must like the subject well enough to spend a good many days and nights working on it.

2. The subject must lead to a good topic, one that raises some questions that have not been answered to the satisfaction of all the authorities in the field.

3. The best subjects are those that suggest several interesting topics to choose from. If your first choice does not work out well, you then have several alternatives ready about which you already know something.

Finding the Best Topic

Although you should start thinking about finding a topic as soon as you know a research paper is required and not wait for the instructor to push you into action, never choose a topic hastily. Many people make the mistake of picking the first attractive topic that comes along, then rushing to the library (or the computer) and taking piles (or files) of notes, all before they have defined a problem to be solved. After days or even weeks of work, they come to realize that they have no control over the project, no clear sense of direction, and, worst of all, no time to go back and begin again.

Good Topics

A good topic raises questions that have no simple answers. When a question has no single accepted answer, the experts (your sources) will disagree to some extent, which is just what you want. This means you must avoid topics that can be fully covered by reading just one or two brief sources. For example, the question "Why is the sky blue?" has been answered to everyone's satisfaction. Any general science book or encyclopedia provides the same general explanation. The same holds true for seemingly more complex questions such as "How does vitamin C help the body fight disease?" "Why did the popes leave Rome for southern France in the 1300s?" or even "Why did Guiteau shoot President Garfield?" (Perhaps no one really knows, but historians—the experts—agree on one view of the event.)

As you search for a topic, remember that research should take you beyond mere reporting, beyond just finding information. Be prepared to demonstrate your ability to evaluate the information and ideas that you discover and to arrive at a clear, well-thought-through conclusion that gives the reader something to think about.

Topics that grow out of disagreements tend to fall into two categories:

1. *highly controversial current issues* the causes of alcoholism; the success of privatizing prisons; the effectiveness of affirmative action; the effect of new immigrants on the U.S. economy
2. *less well-known questions* the reasons behind Cotton Mather's involvement in the Salem witch trials; Emily Dickinson's reasons for not publishing her poems; the role of Jefferson Davis in the defeat of the Confederacy

Some excellent topics do not concern issues as such; they pose the general question "What is currently happening or being done in this area?" If you have chosen such a *data-driven topic* (as opposed to the *hypothesis-driven topics* we have been discussing thus far), your goal is not to make a judgment as to which side of a debate seems to carry more weight. Instead, the research consists of assembling information from various sources in order to present readers with a composite picture of the topic as it currently stands.

This kind of topic almost always deals with very recent events, such as

- the use of genetic engineering to detect and cure disease
- the use of computers in education
- the status of AIDS research

When the topic is so current, you are unlikely to find a single source that describes all the work being done, much less all the possibilities being investigated. Therefore, you will need to locate a fairly large number of articles in magazines, journals, newspapers, and online sources if you are to cover the topic thoroughly.

David Perez's paper "*Solenopsis invicta:* Destroyer of Ecosystems" (in Chapter 21) is an example of a data-driven paper.

Topics to Avoid

Avoid topics in which the controversy derives solely from personal opinion. For example, these questions are poor topics because they would *not* lead to the kind of research you are expected to perform:

"Is professional hockey too violent?"

"Was Ali the greatest boxer ever?"

"Should gay marriages be allowed?"

"Should abortion be banned?"

We are not saying that these issues are not important. Some of them may be more important to more people than any topic you will write about. But such questions can only be resolved by each individual in light of his or her personal values.

Similarly, beware of topics involving the paranormal (UFOs and ESP, for example). The problem here is that almost all the "sources" consist of personal accounts of occult phenomena or weird experiences. That is not to say that good topics cannot be found in these subject areas. However, you must choose the topic carefully to avoid simply reporting the fanciful opinions and accounts of the kind frequently published in popular magazines. The subject *UFOs* could lead to a reasonable topic such as *the Air Force's response to reports of UFO sightings.* (Question: "Are they hiding something, perhaps to avoid public panic or to keep new weapons secret?")

And the subject *ESP* could lead to the topic *scientific techniques for investigating ESP.* (Question: "Have scientists found any reason to consider parapsychology a valid field of study?")

Doing Background Reading or Preliminary Research

Until you feel certain that you have a good topic, take time to do some background reading in the subject area. Look up your subject or topic in such general reference works as these:

- encyclopedias
- biographical dictionaries
- surveys of wide areas such as Eastern religions, Native Americans, or English literature
- textbooks in broad areas such as business administration, abnormal psychology, or U.S. history

For example, if your subject is *astronomy* and your idea for a topic is *the beginning of the universe,* you could

- Look up "universe" in the *Encyclopedia Americana* or an encyclopedia of science.
- Read the section on astronomy in an atlas such as *Earth and Man.*
- Read ahead, or reread, the section on astronomy in your textbook if you are writing the paper for an earth science course.

The purpose behind preliminary research, or background reading, is to make sure you have the best topic within your subject area. A number of possibilities are likely to appear during your background reading. The student who wrote about Cotton Mather discovered several reasonable topics in the *Encyclopedia Americana,* as we shall see in Chapter 3.

Even if your original idea for a topic was a fine one, do not skip this preliminary step. It is important to refresh your knowledge of the subject in order to give yourself a strong handle on the many facts and ideas your research will uncover.

Tips for Effective Background Reading

- *Do not read entire books* during preliminary research. For instance, if your subject is *Martin Luther King Jr.,* do not begin by reading a full-length biography. Because you have not yet settled on a topic, most of the book will not be directly relevant to whatever topic you eventually choose. Even if you have a definite topic in mind, such as *King's relationship with militant black leaders,* you should first review King's career as a civil rights activist in an encyclopedia or a biographical dictionary.

- *Look for a list of sources for further reading* at the end of encyclopedia articles. Jot these titles down for future reference. They may be useful as sources for your paper.

- *Take notes you can refer to later* if you need to revise your topic and/or hypothesis. In taking these notes, avoid recording detailed factual information. Concentrate instead on major ideas and possible topics. You do not want your search for a topic to become lost in a flood of facts.

Brainstorming to Find a Topic

Another approach to finding a strong topic is an exercise called *brainstorming.* If you are already fairly familiar with your subject area, a little brainstorming may turn up several good possibilities for research. Brainstorming consists of wide-open, no-holds-barred thinking about some subject, in which your mind is free to generate many ideas, some good, some not so good. Because you are looking for a problem to investigate, these ideas may well come to you as questions. You may want to find a partner for this exercise; brainstorming with someone else can be especially helpful.

Tips for Effective Brainstorming

1. Record every thought, large or small, either in shorthand notes or, better yet, on a tape recorder. Do not reject any idea, even if it sounds irrelevant or silly or otherwise useless.

2. Stop after ten or fifteen minutes and review your notes or the tape. Decide which ideas seem most promising.

3. Put all the material aside overnight and review it again in a fresh light the next day.

Let's look at an example of what one student produced when she unleashed her mind on what was for her a fairly familiar subject, *dinosaurs.*

What exactly was a dinosaur? How do we know what it was, aside from the bones? When did people first find dinosaur bones? Where did dinosaurs live? What did they eat? Did any other creatures prey on them? What caused dinosaurs to die out? How long were they around? Did they evolve from earlier life forms? From sharks? From little lizards? Are crocodiles really modern dinosaurs? Are there any other dinosaurs around now, possibly in some unexplored jungle or on a deserted island? Someone said birds evolved from dinosaurs—are they right? What caused the extinction of dinosaurs? Did they just become too big? But what about the smaller ones? Did they run out of food? If so, how could that happen? Did they become unfit for survival? How? Were other creatures smarter than they were? How could we know how smart they were? Their brains were probably larger than ours. How do we know about these long-gone beasts? Or don't we know? Is it all guesswork? Do we find each skeleton all in one spot, or do we assemble possible skeletons from a mixed heap of bones? How come no animals are that big today (except whales)? Why are today's lizards and other reptiles no larger than alligators?

Obviously, this student had to know something about this subject or she couldn't have produced so much specific material. Notice that she returned to some points but that others led to dead ends.

Did you see several themes recurring throughout the notes?

- Why did dinosaurs become extinct? Topic: *cause of extinction.*
- What exactly was (or is) a dinosaur? Topic: *their place in evolution.*
- How do we know what we say we know? Topic: *the basis of our knowledge of prehistoric creatures.*

Any of the three topics would do just fine because these questions have no simple, uncontroversial answers.

Four Students Find Their Topics

We asked the writers of the four papers in Chapter 21 to describe how they went about getting started. Their approaches were not identical, but all four led to worthwhile research projects. The only thing they had in common was a consultation with their teachers.

Fred Hutchins

While in high school, Fred Hutchins had seen a television program dealing with the Salem witch-hunt of 1692. The half-hour program was, of necessity, superficial, and it managed to provide little more than an overview of the witchcraft hysteria and trials. Nonetheless, the program sparked Fred's interest in Cotton Mather, a powerful Puritan minister involved in the witch trials.

Several years later, Fred enrolled in a history course called Witchcraft in America that included a unit on the Salem witch-hunts. From the first day of class, Fred mulled over the possibility of doing research on Cotton

Mather. When his instructor asked for possible topics for research papers, Fred saw an opportunity to learn more about Mather.

In an after-class discussion, the instructor asked Fred what he particularly wanted to learn about Cotton Mather. Fred realized that "Cotton Mather" was far too broad to be considered a workable topic, so he narrowed that down to "Cotton Mather and the Salem witch trials." The instructor said that although this topic still seemed too broad, it did provide Fred with a starting point for his background reading.

The instructor then offered Fred some advice: "I think you need to do some reading about Mather that uncovers a controversy or some other angle that you can dig into—maybe a specific question about Mather's character that you'd like to answer for yourself." The instructor suggested that Fred begin his background reading with the *Encyclopedia Americana*. Here is the encyclopedia's Cotton Mather entry, reproduced in its entirety. Marginal notes point out how Fred used the article to help him find an interesting and workable topic.

Fred notes that Mather was a theologian as well as a minister. He wonders about the connections between Mather's religious beliefs and his involvement in the witchcraft hysteria.

MATHER, math or Cotton (1663–1728), American clergyman, theologian, and author. The eldest son of Increase Mather and the grandson of Richard Mather, he was born in Boston, Mass., on Feb. 12, 1663. He graduated from Harvard in 1678, received his M.A. in 1681, and in 1685 joined his father at the Second Church in Boston, where he served until his death.

Fred realizes this paragraph deals with matters about which he knows little. He doesn't expect this paragraph will be useful.

Mather was active in the rebellion in 1689 against Sir Edmund Andros, royal governor of Massachusetts, and wrote the manifesto of the insurgents. He vigorously defended the new Massachusetts charter of 1691 and supported Sir William Phipps, appointed governor by King William III at the request of Increase Mather.

Fred reads carefully here because the material refers to the subject of his interest. He also jots down "spectral evidence" because he wants to learn what it means. Fred notes Mather's humane attitude toward accused witches and considers exploring the reasons why Mather took this position. After reading about Mather's "popular reputation," Fred notes how this seems to contradict evidence of Mather's humane attitude.

During the witchcraft excitement of 1692, Cotton Mather wrote the ministers' statement exhorting the judges to be cautious in their use of "spectral evidence" against the accused, and he believed that "witches" might better be treated by prayer and fasting than by punitive legal action. In spite of this, Mather's popular reputation is that of a fomenter of the witchcraft hysteria who rejoiced in the trials and the executions. He was ardently interested in what he believed to be witchcraft, and his writing and preaching may have stimulated the hysterical fear of "witches" revealed at Salem, Mass., in 1692. In writing about the trials he defended the judges and their procedure more than seems consistent with his earlier warnings against "spectral evidence." He was no doubt unwise in helping to keep the witchcraft excitement alive, but the idea that he was a ruthless tormentor of the innocent is not justified by the evidence. If the court had paid more attention to his advice some lives might have been saved. The witchcraft trials ended before he was 30; most of the achievements that made him the most famous of American Puritans came later.

Fred notes Mather's defense of the witchcraft judges: Was Mather confused about how he regarded witches?

Renowned as a preacher, man of letters, scientist, and scholar in many fields, he read widely and wrote more than 450 books. The most celebrated is the *Magnalia Christi Americana* (1702), an "ecclesiastical" history of New England and the most important literary and scholarly work produced in the American colonies during their first century. It shows an amazing range of erudition and great stylistic skill.

Fred is impressed by Mather's accomplishments. Was it unusual for a person of such learning to believe in witches?

Mather's interest in science is revealed principally in other books, notably *The Christian Philosopher* (1721). He admired Sir Isaac Newton, advocated inoculation for smallpox when it was generally regarded as a dangerous and godless practice, and wrote one of the earliest known descriptions of plant hybridization. He was one of the few American colonists elected to the Royal Society of London and probably was better known abroad than any of his countrymen before Jonathan Edwards and Benjamin Franklin.

From the mixture of characteristics given in this paragraph, Fred concludes that Mather was a complicated person. Is it possible that his fascination with witches had something to do with his erratic personality?

Mather was vain, ambitious, hot-tempered, and sometimes a pedant, but had genuine piety and worked tirelessly for moral reform. His tolerance increased with age, and his later thinking moved somewhat away from the strict Puritan orthodoxy of the seventeenth century toward the rationalistic and deistic ideas of the eighteenth. He died in Boston on Feb. 13, 1728.

KENNETH B. MURDOCK
Author of "Literature and Theology in Colonial New England"

Fred now turns to the bibliography that followed the article to get a head start on his search for sources.

Bibliography

Breitweiser, Mitchell R., *Cotton Mather and Benjamin Franklin* (Cambridge 1985).

Holmes, Thomas J., *Cotton Mather: A Bibliography of His Works,* 3 vols. (1940; reprint, Crofton Pub. 1974).

Levin, David, *Cotton Mather: The Young Life of the Lord's Remembrancer* (Harvard Univ. Press 1978).

Middelkauf, Robert, *The Mathers: Three Generations of Puritan Intellectuals,* 1596–1728 (Oxford 1971).

Silverman, Kenneth, *The Life and Times of Cotton Mather* (Harper 1984).

Wendell, Barrett, *Cotton Mather: The Puritan Priest* (1981; reprint, Arden Library 1978).

Wood, James P., *The Admirable Cotton Mather* (Seabury 1971).

After finishing the article, Fred saw that he had several good potential topics:

- a possible connection between Mather's religious beliefs and his attitude toward witches
- Mather's humane stance toward accused witches

- the origin of Mather's popular reputation as a bloodthirsty witch-hunter
- Mather's intense interest in witchcraft and the possibility that this interest may have fanned the hysteria
- Mather's possibly confused attitude toward witches
- Mather's erratic personality as a source of his fascination with witches
- Mather's change of view toward the outbreak that came later in life

In the end, Fred decided that the question he had asked himself several times—"What did Cotton Mather believe about witches and witchcraft?"—held the most interest for him. Looking ahead to further reading, Fred submitted *what the Salem witches actually meant to Cotton Mather* as his topic.

Note the short list of titles under the heading "Bibliography" at the end of the encyclopedia article. Always be sure to note this information during background reading because it can give you some good leads on finding potential sources. Fred used several of the books on this particular list for his paper on Cotton Mather.

Shirley Macalbe

Shirley Macalbe found her topic during a sociology class discussion of immigration. Although the discussion revolved around the great waves of immigration during the early part of the twentieth century, several students commented on the large influx of foreigners into the United States during recent years. Some students described the changing characters of their neighborhoods. Others questioned the ability of the country to absorb so many new people. A few students defended the right of the newcomers to be in the United States, arguing that everybody in the room had immigrant roots of one sort or another.

The instructor informed the class that the recent upsurge in immigration was indeed a controversial issue in the United States today. She also said that similar controversies about the wisdom of allowing great numbers of people to immigrate to America had arisen during earlier periods in the nation's history.

Shirley, who had not had much luck thinking about a topic for the required research paper, found herself interested in the spirited discussion of the new immigrants. She wanted to draw a topic for her research paper from the controversy, but she wondered whether the subject was too current for her to find enough authoritative sources. Consulting her instructor after class, she learned that experts were already studying the newcomers' impact on the country and their prospects for success. Satisfied that the project could prove fruitful, she settled on the topic *are the new immigrants an asset or a burden?*

Susanna Andrews

Finding a topic consumed less time in Susanna Andrews's case. While taking a course in American literature, she had been excited by Emily Dickinson's rather mystical poetry. In thinking about a possible topic for her paper, Susanna remembered reading in the introduction to her textbook that Dickinson "did not write for publication and was easily discouraged from it." Only eight of her nearly eighteen hundred poems appeared in print during her lifetime. This point had also been made (with *eight* changed to *six*) in *The Oxford Companion to American Literature,* a standard background resource that Susanna consulted.

In lectures, her instructor had painted a fascinating picture of this remarkable woman, and Susanna had no trouble finding an account of Dickinson's life in the biographical dictionary *Notable American Women.* Once Susanna thought she knew a fair amount about her subject, she reviewed her notes and discovered that one idea for a topic persisted in her thoughts about the poet and her work: *her failure to publish her poetry.*

Susanna naturally wondered why such a great poet had published so few of her works. Consulting her instructor, she learned that the question had not been decisively resolved, so Susanna confidently chose as her topic *Emily Dickinson's reluctance to publish her poems.*

David Perez

David Perez was taking a course called Current Issues in Ecology, for which the instructor assigned several "research essays," giving students a rather limited set of subjects from which to choose. The papers were expected to run from four to seven pages. David's choice, *the disruptive effects of a transplanted species on its new environment,* left just one point undefined — which species to investigate.

While reading his textbook, David had found ants, especially army ants, very interesting. His instructor pointed out that army ants cannot be considered "transplanted" when they march across the jungle floor, destroying everything in their path. But the instructor thought that, nevertheless, ants were a good species to examine for this project. Reading an encyclopedia on CD-ROM in the library led David to a ferocious ant species that was likely to have received a good deal of attention for the way it disrupted the ecosystem to which it had been accidentally transplanted.

As you can see, no hypothesis was needed because the scope of the research had been so clearly defined by the instructor's wording of the

Laying the Groundwork

subject. David's topic had to be *the harmful effects of (his species of ant) being introduced to a foreign environment.* (The guiding word for his research would be *harmful*.)

Notice that if David had begun with a broader subject—for example, *introducing species to new environments*—he would have had to consider various possible results, good and bad, of such transplantings. Some species become extinct in their new habitat; some destroy parts of it; some improve conditions; some make an interesting adaptation. But David's instructor had cut through all that background research and produced a list of subjects that were easily converted to topics.

This assignment was certainly easier to research than those completed by the other students whose work we have been following. We include this kind of research assignment because it is different, although not unusual, and because it illustrates the APA style of documentation (described in Chapter 19).

3

Moving from Topic to Thesis

We have been discussing the choice of a topic as though you had to complete this step before moving on to the next one: forming a hypothesis. In practice, however, you should be thinking about a hypothesis while you are looking for your topic. This is only natural when you consider that *the topic raises unanswered questions, and the hypothesis predicts possible answers.*

Research can be made easier if you form a hypothesis as early as possible because the topic alone will not be strong enough to guide you through this complex process. The main problem is that the topic by itself offers little help when you are trying to decide whether or not a potential source is useful. Your research will uncover a great deal of information that touches on your topic in some way or other, but unless you have some idea of where you're going with the topic, it will be hard to tell which ideas and facts will play a definite role in the paper. Your notes will begin to look like a very long grocery list. If you tried to write a paper based on such loosely related materials, the result would lack focus and direction. It would be impossible to form a thesis that could make sense of all the information. Such a paper would do little more than show you had spent a lot of time doing research.

Benefits of a Hypothesis

There are two good reasons for starting out with a hypothesis, even if it may prove to be more or less inaccurate when you have completed all the research. As for possible inaccuracy, you can always modify the hypothesis as you read your sources and learn more about the topic. In fact, you should plan to review the hypothesis periodically throughout the research.

1. *The hypothesis points you in the right direction.*   It indicates the specific questions you need answers for. As you look for information that either agrees or disagrees with your hypothesis, you move closer to the "truth," which will become your thesis.

2. *The hypothesis tests the thoroughness of your research.*   If your conclusions are to be considered reasonable, you must consult a *variety of sources* representing *different viewpoints*. You should not try to defend your original hypothesis by using only those sources that support it. Your mission is to present readers with a balanced picture, giving them enough information to evaluate your conclusions intelligently.

If you are investigating the theory that intelligence (IQ) is inherited, for example, you cannot restrict your search to *The Bell Curve* plus the writings of E. O. Wilson, Arthur Jensen, and other advocates of this theory. You need to find experts such as Steven Rose and Stephen Jay Gould, who are less convinced of, if not downright opposed to, this theory.

Of course, your thesis might eventually conclude that:

1. Jensen and his supporters seem to be right,
2. Rose and other critics have proved them wrong, or
3. the issue has not yet been satisfactorily resolved.

But the paper would have to show that you weighed all sides of the question before reaching your conclusion. For some topics, you will find that expert opinion is divided into more than two camps, in which case you must present a balanced assessment of all sides of the debate.

Arriving at a Hypothesis by Brainstorming

Brainstorming can be as useful for arriving at a hypothesis as it can for deciding on a topic. Here are two examples.

Example 1: Dinosaurs' Extinction

The student who had brainstormed about dinosaurs was able, after a little background reading, to reject several potential topics. She discarded *the basis of our knowledge* and *what dinosaurs really were* because she was not very interested in either one, but the extinction problem seemed likely to lead to some exciting ideas, some of which had been mentioned in her background reading.

After she had settled on *causes for the dinosaurs' extinction,* another brainstorming session helped her form a hypothesis. Here are her notes.

Did the evolution of smaller, smarter animals somehow lead to the extinction of the slow-witted dinosaurs? Were these new creatures mammals? Or did major climatic changes bring about the extinction by eliminating the tropical swamplands in which the dinosaurs thrived? How fast might such changes take place? Could a meteor striking the Earth cause such a change? Or did deadly radiation from an exploding nearby star do them in? In either case, wouldn't some have survived? Or did dinosaurs become so large they could not find enough food in their environment? Were they the victims of a deadly virus? Or a fatal genetic mutation?

All these ideas made sense; her background reference materials did not take a stand on the question, and without reading all the sources, she could not judge the relative merits of the theories. She decided, therefore, to go with the newest idea: "Radiation from an exploded star caused the Great Extinction." This became her hypothesis.

(Her *thesis,* however, took another turn. After reading all her sources, she decided that equal support had to be given to the theory that a meteor had hit the earth 65 million years ago, drastically cooling the atmosphere and killing off the dinosaurs.)

Example 2: Alcoholism Therapies

After some background reading, another student narrowed the subject *alcoholism* to the topic *treatment of alcohol addiction.* A bit of brainstorming at that point produced the following notes:

How well do support therapies such as Alcoholics Anonymous work in their efforts to treat alcoholism? Does the addict have to be religiously inclined for such therapies to work? How successful are aversion therapies that use chemicals to make liquor repellent? Doesn't the effect wear off? How effective are cognitive therapies that try to get alcoholics to stop drinking by showing them films of their own drunken behavior? Is psychotherapy able to treat alcoholism by helping the patients understand the unconscious reasons for their drinking? How would knowing why you drink help you stop?

Again, we find someone faced with several possible answers to his research question. However, this student could see no grounds for choosing any one of them while still in the preliminary research stage. Also, he had personal reasons for doubting whether any method offered successful treatment. So he took a neutral position that expressed his intuition: "Of the four most common alcoholism therapies, none seems to have convinced its critics that it offers a strong likelihood of success."

The student did not feel committed to this pessimistic view; he hoped that his sources would show him good reason to believe that one of the approaches was definitely on the right track. Considerable research into this problem, however, did not fulfill this hope. Eventually, his *thesis* read: "The success of a particular alcoholism therapy depends almost entirely on the personality of the individual addict."

By the way, other students who chose the same topic of alcoholism therapies arrived at somewhat different conclusions (theses). Your thesis will depend on what sources you find and what you, as an individual reader, discover in them.

In short, you have a limited amount of time to spend finding sources, reading them, and taking notes. You will need a hypothesis to help you decide which ideas and facts in each source will be most useful in your effort to cover the topic thoroughly, intelligently, and efficiently.

Four Students Form and Revise Their Hypotheses

What about the writers of our sample research papers? They moved from topic to hypothesis in different ways.

Fred Hutchins: Finding a Hypothesis through Skimming Sources

Although Fred Hutchins was happy with his topic, *what the witches meant to Cotton Mather*, he could not see a reasonable hypothesis in the encyclopedia article or his textbook. So he took to skimming a few of his sources, looking for comments about this question.

The first few writers tended to agree that Mather's belief in witches was not at all unusual, considering the times in which he lived. In late-seventeenth-century America, almost everyone, intellectuals included, believed in witches. True, Mather's interest in witches was particularly intense because he liked to delve into subjects that challenged his intellect and imagination. This led Fred to the following hypothesis: "Cotton Mather accepted the existence of witches because such a belief was deeply embedded in the culture of his time."

Shirley Macalbe: Finding a Hypothesis through Interviewing

Shirley Macalbe's topic, *the new immigrants: asset or burden?*, grew out of a class discussion in which students expressed strong opinions about the impact the newest wave of immigrants was having on their city and on the United States as a whole. Because it had been her fellow students who had aroused her interest in the subject, Shirley decided to interview a number of them, with the idea of gathering impressions related to her topic. She thought the interviews might also help her develop a hypothesis to test against the sources she would find in the library.

After analyzing the results of her interviews, Shirley leaned slightly toward the hypothesis "the immigrants were becoming a burden to the country." Of course, she knew full well that the students' opinions might not hold up in the face of expert research, opinion, and theory.

Once she began reading sources, Shirley found that her interviewees had touched on several issues that the experts also discussed in some detail. However, the experts gave less weight to the students' greatest concerns and provided insights into other issues that seemed more likely to determine the answer to Shirley's question, "Are immigrants an asset or a burden?" She moved fairly soon to a revised hypothesis: "If we look at the history of U.S. immigration, we can believe that these people will be just as successful as earlier immigrants."

Susanna Andrews: Finding a Hypothesis through Brainstorming

Susanna thought she had a good topic, *Emily Dickinson's reluctance to publish her poems,* but her background reading offered only a vague suggestion that the poet's not publishing her poems grew out of her eccentric character. If that was the only answer to the question, Susanna's topic was too weak to pursue. So she brainstormed a bit to see whether she had good reason to continue. Finding a better hypothesis would indicate that the topic was worth the effort. Here are a few notes from her brainstorming:

Why didn't Dickinson publish most of her poems? Why would any poet do that? Did she think they weren't good enough? Didn't she know how great her poems were? Or did she write them for her own pleasure only? Was she too shy to let other people see her thoughts? Who did she let read them? Her family, her friends, or other writers? What did these readers say? Did she ever *try* to have the poems published? Why did she write poetry anyway? What did writing mean to her? What might publication have done for her, or her poems? How did the poems eventually get published?

These notes did not immediately yield a satisfying hypothesis, but as Susanna reviewed her lecture notes, she recalled her professor's talking about Dickinson's idealistic attitude toward the art of poetry and toward herself as an artist. When Susanna read some of the poems, these lines caught her eye: "The Soul selects her own Society / Then—shuts the

Door—. . . ." Remembering her background reading notes, which said the poet was extremely shy, Susanna decided on the hypothesis "Emily Dickinson chose not to publish most of her poems because she was a shy, reclusive person, more interested in her art than in winning public praise." This hypothesis forced Susanna when reading literary criticism to focus on those comments and facts that shed light on the poet's character and her deep concerns regarding publication.

David Perez: Using Data-Driven Research as a Hypothesis

David Perez, the student who wrote about ants, had no problem finding a hypothesis because of the nature of his assignment. Being so sharply focused, his assigned topic did the work of a hypothesis.

In short, as you can see from reading the full papers in Chapter 21, each student's hypothesis was only a beginning. In each case, research into specific sources disclosed additional information and persuasive reasons for coming to a somewhat different conclusion (thesis). Nevertheless, the students' hypotheses served them well as guides through the difficult steps of finding sources and extracting useful information from them.

Reviewing Part One

Questions

1. Explain the difference between a subject and a topic, as the terms are used in this book.
   - What is your primary concern when choosing a subject?
   - What must be your first concern when looking for a topic?
2. Which of the following items seem likely to work well as topics for research papers? Explain why you reject each item that seems to have poor potential. (Some are too broad for a paper seven to ten pages long; others would require no more than reading an encyclopedia to complete a full investigation; yet others are too deeply involved with personal values or deal with areas about which there is no concrete knowledge.)
   - working women in the United States today
   - the way FM radio signals are sent and received
   - the effect of robot machines on workers in heavy industries
   - the invention of gunpowder in China
   - treatments for breast cancer
   - the role of the pharmaceutical industry in AIDS research
   - the history of the Congo since independence
   - programs for prevention of child abuse
   - the role of parents in teenage alcoholism
   - the use of computers in small businesses today
   - the effectiveness of capital punishment in reducing violent crime
   - the solution to Russia's economic woes
   - the effect of illegal immigration on the economy of the Southwest
   - the effect of high salaries on the quality of major-league baseball
   - the ability of some people to see the future in their dreams
3. What is the value of brainstorming? At which point(s) in the research process is this activity likely to help you?
4. What is the purpose of background reading? If you know your topic from the start, should you skip this step?
5. Why is it a good idea to look for a controversy of some sort when trying to come up with a topic?
6. Why do you need to form a hypothesis if you have an excellent topic? How does a hypothesis help at various stages of research?

Exercises

1. Read the following article on Emma Goldman, which comes from *Notable American Women,* an excellent background resource for topics in women's studies. Take notes, much like those described in the margins of the Cotton Mather article earlier in this chapter, identifying several potential topics suitable for a seven-to-ten-page research paper. For each topic, think of a reasonable hypothesis.

GOLDMAN, Emma (June 27, 1869–May 14, 1940), anarchist rebel, lecturer, and publicist, agitator for free speech and popularizer of the arts, feminist and pioneer of advocate of birth control, was born in Kovno, Russia (Kaunas in modern Lithuania). Born to ride whirlwinds, as someone once said, she appropriately came from the Baltic, a region notorious for its political and social tensions, and from a ghetto Jewish family in which all these tensions were intensified. She was the first child of the marriage of Abraham and Taube (Bienowitch) Goldman. Taube Goldman, who had two girls from a previous marriage, responded coldly to her new husband and looked on her infant daughter as an additional burden. Abraham Goldman, a lower-middle-class shopkeeper, was embittered by his wife's attitude, by an initial business failure, and then by the birth of a daughter instead of a son. Even after he subsequently had two sons, he could not forgive his daughter her sex. His choleric disapproval and her mother's unsympathetic brusqueness clouded Emma's earliest experiences in Kovno and later in the small village of Popelan, where her father kept the inn and managed the government stagecoach.

After her family, dogged by failure, moved to Königsberg, Prussia, Emma Goldman attended *Realschule* for a few years. Her teachers successfully instilled in her a distaste for their own cruel pedantry. Only a teacher of German took an interest in her, helped develop her taste for literature and music, and guided her preparations for the Gymnasium examinations. Her justifiable pride in passing these was cut short by the refusal of her religious instructor to give her the requisite certificate of good character. In St. Petersburg, where the Goldmans moved in 1881, her formal schooling lasted only six months more. But even her work in a cousin's glove factory did not keep her from meeting nihilist and populist university students and reading widely in the new radical literature which had the capital in a ferment. The free-spirited Vera Pavlovna, heroine of Nicolai Chernyshevsky's *What Is To Be Done?* (1863), became the model for her own life.

In 1885, gladly escaping her father's demands that she submit to an arranged marriage, she emigrated to America with her half sister Helena Zodokoff. She settled in Rochester, N.Y., with another half sister and found work in a "model" clothing factory at $2.50 a week. She soon became a critic of the capitalism which prompted German Jews, like her employer, to welcome their Eastern brethren to Rochester only to exploit them in their factories and shops. In early 1887 she was married to Jacob Kersner (also Kershner), a fellow factory worker and naturalized citizen, and was shocked to discover that he was impotent. Each passing month made more obvious the hopelessness of their relationship, which, after a divorce and a reconciliation, ended finally in a permanent divorce.

In later years she always said that her life really began in August 1889 when she moved to New York City, met Johann Most, editor of the inflammatory paper *Freiheit,* and Alexander Berkman, a young émigré Russian revolutionist, and joined them in the anarchist movement. Her experiences had indeed prepared her for this moment: the harsh parental authority of her home; the rich ethical demands of the prophetic strain in Judaism; brutal Russian anti-Semitism and her vantage point on the margins of two cultures; her contacts with radical literature and students in St. Petersburg; the gap between the ideality and the reality in America; the judicial murders in 1887 of the so-called Haymarket rioters in Chicago; her own native intelligence, which led her to seek intellectual solutions to her problems—all readied her for her role as one of America's outstanding rebels. The anarchism of Peter Kropotkin, the brilliant Russian scientist and social philosopher, had an appeal which she could hardly resist, for it promised to replace authoritarian social hierarchies, the coercive political state, and supernaturalistic religion by a society of equals, a polity of small organic organizations in free cooperation with each other, and a warm humanism rooted in a concern for decency and justice in this world. Never a seminal social or political thinker, she made only one serious attempt to contribute to anarchist theory: at the Amsterdam Anarchist Congress of 1907 she presented a paper wherein she maintained that true anarchism meant both Kropotkin's emphasis on the community and Henrik Ibsen's emphasis on the strong, independent individual.

Her most serious mistake was an early acceptance of the tactic of individual acts of violence. During the Homestead conflict of 1892 she helped Berkman prepare to kill Henry Clay Frick and regretted that a lack of funds prevented her from being at her comrade's side when the attempt was made. Although Frick survived, Berkman disappeared for fourteen years behind the heavy gates of Pennsylvania's Western Penitentiary. In 1893 Emma herself began a one-year term on Blackwell's Island in New York, convicted of advising a Union Square audience of unemployed men that "it was their sacred right" to take bread if they were starving and their demands for food were not answered. Her prison work as a practical nurse led her to study midwifery and nursing at the Allgemeines Krankenhaus in Vienna in 1895–96. Meanwhile her ideas on individual violence were gradually changing as she came to reject the fallacy that great ends justify any means. By 1901, when President McKinley was shot by

Leon Czolgosz, a demented young man possessed by the delusion that he was an anarchist with this particular personal mission, she could sympathize with both the pathetic assassin and the stricken president. Notwithstanding the most energetic efforts of the authorities, no evidence was ever unearthed to establish her complicity. Aside from a few chance remarks on another occasion, Czolgosz had heard her talk only once, and then she had vigorously maintained that anarchism and violence had no necessary connection.

In the opening decades of the new century, Emma Goldman involved herself in a wide range of activities. Perhaps the most accomplished, magnetic woman speaker in American history, she crisscrossed the country lecturing on anarchism, the new drama, the revolt of women. Subject to stubborn and sometimes brutal police and vigilante attempts to censor her remarks or to silence her completely, she joyfully waged countless fights for free speech. As the editor, along with Berkman, of the radical monthly *Mother Earth* (1906–17) and the publisher of numerous pamphlets, her own book *Anarchism and Other Essays* (1911), and Berkman's important *Prison Memoirs of an Anarchist* (1912), she aroused the concern of radicals and liberals over threats to freedom of expression and such causes célèbres as the Tom Mooney case. Roger Baldwin, whose professional interest in civil liberties dated from the influence of her lectures, hardly overstated the case when he said: "For the cause of free speech in the United States Emma Goldman fought battles unmatched by the labors of any organization."

As an integral part of her libertarian message she discussed the works of Ibsen, Shaw, Strindberg, and other playwrights. Her lectures, begun as early as 1897, were published in 1914 under the title *The Social Significance of the Modern Drama*. Although she was not primarily responsible for making Shaw known in the United States, as Rebecca West has suggested, nor a "distinguished critic of the drama," as the *New York Times* once observed, she was a great popularizer of new literary currents.

Her concept of the New Woman owed something to Ibsen's influence, as seen in her attacks on the "conventional lie" of marriage and her advocacy of "free love." By the latter she did not mean a promiscuous "wild love," as some of her critics seemed to think, but the uncoerced mutual regard and affection of two mature persons for one another. She agreed with such feminists as Charlotte Perkins Gilman in rejecting for women the role of a mere "sex commodity," but criticized their "narrow, Puritanical vision" which sought to banish "man, as a disturber and doubtful character, out of their emotional life." The suffrage demand she dismissed as a mere fetish. For over two decades a public advocate of voluntary motherhood and family limitation, in 1915 she was moved by Margaret Sanger's arrest to lecture on preventive methods; one such lecture the following year brought her fifteen days in jail. Her efforts influenced Mrs. Sanger and prepared the way for a systematic birth control campaign. With some reason, then, the *Nation* insisted in 1922 that the name of Emma Goldman should be on any list of "the twelve greatest living women."

Government officials had long had a quite different view. In 1908 they deprived her of her citizenship by denaturalizing the missing Jacob Kersner. It was decided not to make her a party to the court proceedings against Kersner, for that, as Secretary of Commerce and Labor Oscar S. Straus confidentially wrote the Attorney General, "would too obviously indicate that the ultimate design . . . is not to vindicate the naturalization law, but to reach an individual . . ." (Feb. 11, 1909, National Archives). In June 1917 she and Berkman were arrested for their leadership of the opposition to conscription and sentenced to two years in prison. After her release from Jefferson City Penitentiary in September 1919, immigration officials, with the energetic aid of J. Edgar Hoover, took advantage of wartime legislation to order her deported to Russia. Three days before Christmas 1919 Emma Goldman and Alexander Berkman, along with 247 other victims of the postwar Red Scare, sailed back past the Statue of Liberty aboard the transport *Buford.*

Two years later she expatriated herself from Russia. An early supporter of the Bolsheviki, she had soon discovered their suppression of all political dissent. From Sweden and later Germany she lashed out at the emergent totalitarianism in newspaper articles and in her book *My Disillusionment in Russia* (1923). The egregious myopia of the liberals and radicals who cried out against the suppression of civil rights in the West and remained silent about much worse in Russia was the target of her sharpest attacks. In 1925 she married James Colton, a Welsh collier, to obtain British citizenship. Fearful of economic dependence, she sought to establish herself through her lectures and royalties from her autobiography, *Living My Life* (1931). When she was not touring England or Canada, she lived in Saint-Tropez, France, where friends had helped her buy a small cottage. In 1934 she was granted a ninety-day stay in the United States, but her visit made her return to exile more a torment than ever. In 1936 Berkman, seriously ill and despondent over his forced inactivity, committed suicide. Emma Goldman was saved from utter despair over his death by an urgent request from Barcelona that she come help combat Franco and help advance the social revolution. Apart from three visits to Catalonia during the Spanish Civil War, she stayed in London to enlist understanding and support for her Latin comrades. In 1939 she went to Canada to raise some money for the lost cause. As she had wished, she went out fighting: in February 1940 she suffered a stroke, and three months later she died in Toronto. Since she was now merely a dead "undesirable alien," United States officials allowed her body to be returned for burial in Chicago's Waldheim Cemetery, near the graves of the Haymarket martyrs.

When "Red Emma" was in her twenties, reporter Nellie Bly (Elizabeth Cochrane Seaman) was surprised to discover that she was attractive, "with a saucy turned-up nose and very expressive blue-gray eyes . . . [brown hair] falling loosely over her forehead, full lips, strong white teeth, a mild, pleasant voice, with a fetching accent." Four decades later the English novelist Ethel Mannin saw her as "a short thickset scowling elderly woman with grey hair and thick glasses." Throughout her life, Emma Goldman had an extraordinary capacity for close, lasting friendships, although she could be imperious and, on occasion, insensitive to the feelings of others. Offering an invaluable counterstatement to the pragmatic faith of progressives and socialists in the omnicompetent state, she fought for the spiritual freedom of the individual at a time when the organizational walls were closing in. When she died, radicals had almost unanimously rejected her message, but hers was, in the words of the novelist Evelyn Scott, "the future they will, paradoxically, hark back to in time."

[The principal holdings of Emma Goldman's papers are in the Labadie Collection, Univ. of Michigan Library; the N.Y. Public Library; and the International Institute for Social Hist., Amsterdam. There is important material also in the files of the Dept. of Justice, Dept. of State, and Post Office Dept. in the National Archives, Washington. For a fuller description and bibliography, including a list of her own writings, see Richard Drinnon, *Rebel in Paradise: A Biography of Emma Goldman* (1961). See also Frank Harris, *Contemporary Portraits, Fourth Series* (1923); Eunice M. Schuster, *Native American Anarchism* (1932); Margaret Goldsmith, *Seven Women against the World* (1935); Ethel Mannin, *Women and the Revolution* (1939) and *Red Rose: A Novel Based on the Life of Emma Goldman* (n.d.); Van Wyck Brooks, *The Confident Years* (1952).]

2. Choose a subject area from the following list, and then do enough background reading to find two or three potential topics for a seven-to-ten-page research paper.

- alcoholism
- endangered species
- China-U.S. trade relations
- environmental controls on large industries
- safety and the auto industry
- group therapy for emotional problems
- problems in the U.S. prison system
- Mexican immigration to the United States
- religious movements in the United States since the 1960s
- artificial intelligence
- genetic experimentation
- the role of government in medical care

- preschool education
- toxic-waste disposal
- the new global economy
- U.S. government treatment of Native Americans
- ethnic conflicts in the former Yugoslavia
- legalized gambling
- South American rain forests
- the ozone layer and ultraviolet radiation
- U.S. immigration policy for Caribbean peoples
- the Arab-Israeli prospects for peace
- the U.S. economic boom of the 1990s
- affirmative action programs
- the U.S. embargo of Cuba
- IQ studies
- the war on drugs
- the use of special effects in movie making
- government involvement in issues concerning parents' rights
- the use of force by police in minority neighborhoods
- the tobacco industry
- problems with capital punishment
- Harry Truman, controversial president
- Helen Keller, social activist of the early 1900s
- Malcolm X, militant African American leader of the 1960s
- Martin Luther King Jr., civil rights leader of the 1960s
- Eleanor Roosevelt, world leader in humanitarian issues

3. Start your own research paper now, following these steps:

    Step 1: Choose a subject—one of the above or any other that meets the requirements of this course (also see the list in Question 2).

    Step 2: Go to three or more background sources and find two to five potentially workable topics. (Record the titles of the sources, and take some notes as you read through them.)

    Step 3: Choose the topic that seems most interesting and/or most workable.

    Step 4: Try your hand at forming a hypothesis.

Part Two

Searching for Sources

Searching for Sources

4

Using Library Resources

After choosing a research topic and forming a hypothesis, you are ready to take the next step: compiling a list of sources. Your background reading may have yielded a few sources in the brief bibliographies attached to encyclopedia articles. Now you need to search for sources on a wider scale, and this operation requires you to become familiar with the resources and services offered by your library. Of course, your search may well extend beyond the walls of the library. You may want to consult specialized archives, or examine television or radio programs, or collect information from various people through interviews and surveys. In addition, if you have access to the Internet via a computer in your home or at school, you will discover a rich array of information sources online.

In short, your research assignment will require you to explore at least one of the following avenues, and perhaps all three: library research, hands-on investigation in the outside world (often called *research in the field,* or *field research*), and online research on the Internet and the World Wide Web. This chapter focuses on the first of these options.

Working with Librarians

One of the most valuable sources of information in a library is the reference librarian. It is a good idea to introduce yourself to this person early in your research and to describe your project briefly. Librarians are professionals. They are trained not only to manage libraries but also to keep abreast of existing sources. Their job is to help people with research projects on any subject. They can tell you about any special resources your library offers and can often help you solve problems quickly that might take hours to solve on your own. The research librarian may even have helped someone else working on a topic related to yours and may be able to give suggestions leading to valuable sources you might otherwise miss.

Nevertheless, you must remember that although most librarians are quite willing to assist you with your research, they are not obliged to do the research for you. Do not go to the librarian and announce, "I have a paper to do for my American history course, but I don't know what to write about. Can you help me to get some books?" The librarian has not attended your classes nor read your textbooks and is therefore in no position to provide you with a topic. If you are at a loss for a topic, see your instructor, not your librarian.

Kinds of Library Sources

In your library research, you will be working mainly with printed books and periodicals, and occasionally with the Internet, to which most libraries now provide access. (A periodical is a publication that appears regularly under the same title: *Washington Post, Newsweek, Science News, Publications of the Modern Language Association [PMLA],* and so on.) Books are cataloged and shelved in one way, periodicals in another, and the Internet has its own methodology.

In planning your library research, do not forget how useful an *encyclopedia* can be. In Chapter 2, we showed how reading an encyclopedia entry might help you refine your topic. Remember that encyclopedia entries end with a list of the sources from which the information in the entry has been drawn. (For an example, return to Chapter 2 and review the Cotton Mather entry that our student Fred Hutchins read when he was working on his topic.) Authors of encyclopedia articles are usually acknowledged experts in their field. By consulting general as well as specialized encyclopedias, you can find references to sources that can provide a good starting point for your research. Many encyclopedias are now published online as well as—or instead of—in print.

In addition to books and periodicals, your library may contain *unpublished sources* such as manuscripts, letters, and business and personal diaries that can prove valuable in certain kinds of research projects. Furthermore, most libraries carry *nonprint and multimedia sources* such as sound recordings, video materials, and CD-ROMs. The reference librarian knows the special sources the library holds and can tell you whether these sources will help in your particular research project.

We begin this chapter with an overview of today's typical academic library, then describe systems for locating books and other materials through the library catalog. In Chapter 5, we discuss finding periodical articles through indexes and electronic sources of information available in libraries; in Chapters 6–8, we describe other resources inside and outside the library, including the Internet and the World Wide Web.

The Library Catalog

Although it is still possible to encounter a traditional card catalog in some academic libraries, you are far more likely to find instead a space outfitted with computer terminals. Some of these terminals connect to the library's online catalog, allowing the same kind of searches people used to do in card catalog drawers, searches that can be performed with computers more quickly and efficiently. Other terminals allow access to electronic databases. Before starting to search for sources, try to determine— perhaps with a librarian's advice—which terminal or databases are most likely to lead to good sources for your subject.

Often the catalog terminals also allow access to all of the library's electronic resources, frequently through the library's main Web page. You can search periodical indexes and view full-text databases, including government publications. It may also be possible to access the Internet, send e-mail, and even make interlibrary loan requests. If the college is extensively computerized, you may even be able to use these resources and services remotely from a dormitory or home computer.

You have undoubtedly used library catalogs before this, but it helps to review the way they are organized. Most libraries have computerized their catalogs, although they may still retain their card catalogs. Online systems afford greater flexibility than card catalogs, by showing whether a source has been checked out and by making it possible to print out an entry rather than copy it by hand. Keep in mind, though, that an online catalog may be limited to materials in the library acquired after a certain date. If you cannot locate an item that was published more than ten years ago, go to the card catalog, if it still exists, or consult a librarian.

When using an online catalog, read the directions posted near the computer terminals or made available as pamphlets at the library's information desk. Note that every library follows its own set of directions or commands for conducting a search. If none is readily visible, ask a librarian for help.

Searching the Catalog

After you log on to the library's online catalog, the computer will ask what type of search you want it to perform. Any book in the library can be found using the *title,* the *author,* or the primary *subject* of the book, or a *keyword* likely to appear in the book's catalog record. For example, these are the headings under which Ralph Phillip Boas's *Cotton Mather: Keeper of the Puritan Conscience* can be found:

author	Boas, Ralph Phillip
title	*Cotton Mather: Keeper of the Puritan Conscience*
subject	Mather, Cotton
subject	Massachusetts—History—Colonial period, ca. 1600–1775
keywords	Cotton Mather; Boas, R; Puritans

Authors can be individual authors or editors of books, or institutions or corporations that sponsored or published the source.

Keywords can be parts of titles, or they can be names, subjects, concepts, ideas, or dates related to your topic.

When you are beginning to compile a list of potential sources, it seems natural to start with a *subject* search. For his paper on Cotton Mather, Fred found several items under "Mather, Cotton." If you start your search with just a topic (or subject), be forewarned that even though the library has compiled a subject catalog, it will not include every subject you might think of. If the subject heading you input into the computer does not result in any entries, try a *keyword* search. (If you are working on relatively recent topics, you will do better to search for sources in periodicals rather than books, a process described in Chapter 5.)

Keyword searches seek out all instances of a word, whether it is an author's name, a title, a subject, or, in some online catalogs, a term in the table of contents or abstract of a book. A problem arises when the search yields many more findings than could possibly be useful. This happens when many of the titles that turn up happen to contain one of your keywords, although the books are unrelated to your subject. An advantage to keyword searches, however, is that you can search for sources even if you are unsure about the exact wording of a title or the author's full name; you can also use keywords to broaden your search to include books on related topics.

Here are some time-saving hints for searching a library catalog:

1. In searching by author, enter personal names, last name first.

2. In dealing with titles, ignore the words *A, An,* and *The* at the beginning of titles.

3. For keyword searches, you can use AND between keywords to tailor your search. For example, a search for "*environment* AND *laws*" will find only sources containing or related to *both* of those terms. Similarly, you can use OR between keywords to search for related terms, synonyms, and different spellings (*theater* OR *theatre; rats* OR *rodents*).

In his search for books on Cotton Mather, Fred had heard of an author who had written about Mather, so he looked for other possible sources under the author's name, Silverman, Kenneth. This search produced five books:

1	Silverman Kenneth	UW COE	1968
	Colonial American poetry,	PS 601 .S5	
2	Silverman Kenneth	UW COE	1976
	Cultural history of the American revolution:	NX 503.5 .S54	
3	Silverman Kenneth	UW COE	1991
	Edgar A. Poe: Mournful and never-ending	PS2631 .S525 1991	
4	Silverman Kenneth	UW COE	1984
	Life and times of Cotton Mather	F 67 M43 .S57 1984	
5	Silverman Kenneth	UW COE	1969
	Timothy Dwight	PS 739 .Z5 S5	

The computer asked Fred to choose the line number of the entry he was interested in. Fred chose entry 4, and the computer displayed the information shown in Figure 4-1.

Understanding a Catalog Entry

The organization of information in a catalog entry—whether in an online catalog or on a catalog card—is standard throughout all libraries. Thus, if you understand the format and the significance of the various

```
AUTHOR(s):   Silverman, Kenneth.
TITLE(s):    The life and times of Cotton Mather /
             Kenneth Silverman. 1st ed.

             New York : Harper & Row, c1984.
             x, 479 p., [8] p. of plates : ill. ; 25 cm.
             Includes bibliographical references and index.

OTHER        Mather, Cotton, 1663–1728.
ENTRIES:     Puritans  Massachusetts  Biography.
             Massachusetts  History  Colonial period,
             ca. 1600–1775.

LOCN: COE            STATUS: Not checked out--
CALL #: F 67 .M43 S57 1984
```

Figure 4-1   An online catalog entry.

pieces of information, you can readily use any library. On the entries shown in Figures 4-2 and 4-3, key pieces of information are identified. Three of these key pieces of information—call number, author, and title—are essential to locating the book on the library shelves. The other items in Figures 4-2 and 4-3 may also prove useful when evaluating sources for the paper. (See Chapter 10.)

Note that in an online catalog, you will see the same entry for a book whether you search by author, title, subject, or keyword. In a card catalog, however, separate cards are arranged alphabetically by author, title, and subject(s). Figure 4-4 shows the variations in these cards for the same book.

Locating Other Materials in the Library

Many libraries include sources in their collections—such as videos, audio recordings, or films—which can be located through the online catalog (see Chapter 6). Follow the same basic principles in conducting searches for these materials as you would for books. Keep in mind that when you do a keyword search, the computer returns both print and nonprint sources that match your keyword.

Articles in periodicals are generally not listed in library catalogs. To find articles, you need to use guides known as *periodical indexes* and *abstracts* (see Chapter 5). Indexes list the title and author of articles and identify the name and issue of the periodical that contains each article;

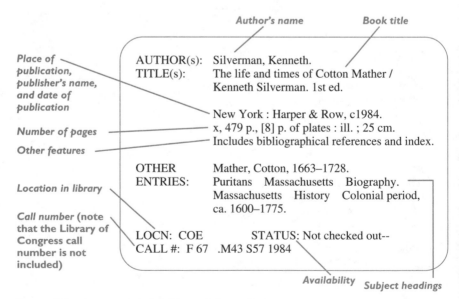

Figure 4-2   An annotated online catalog entry.

Searching for Sources

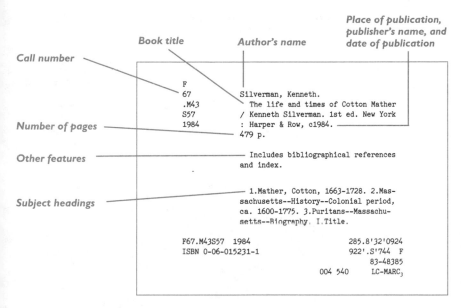

Figure 4-3   An annotated author card.

abstracts also provide summaries of the articles. Once you have found an article through a periodical index, check the library catalog to see whether or not your library has a copy of the periodical in which the article appears.

Locating Books

Once you have decided which books you want to examine, locating those books within the library is relatively easy. An online catalog usually indicates whether the book is available or has been checked out. If the book has been checked out, ask a librarian about having the book *recalled* so that you can use it. Keep in mind that when a book is recalled, the person who has the book usually has about two weeks notice before the book is due back at the library.

Stacks

If the book is available, you will want to retrieve it from the *stacks*— the shelves where the books are kept. Some libraries allow you to enter the stacks; others do not. To get books in libraries where the stacks are

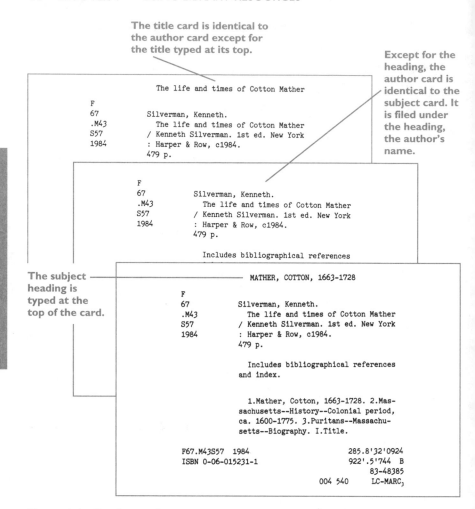

The title card is identical to the author card except for the title typed at its top.

Except for the heading, the author card is identical to the subject card. It is filed under the heading, the author's name.

```
                        The life and times of Cotton Mather
        F
        67            Silverman, Kenneth.
        .M43             The life and times of Cotton Mather
        S57            / Kenneth Silverman. 1st ed. New York
        1984           : Harper & Row, c1984.
                        479 p.
```

```
        F
        67            Silverman, Kenneth.
        .M43             The life and times of Cotton Mather
        S57            / Kenneth Silverman. 1st ed. New York
        1984           : Harper & Row, c1984.
                        479 p.

                        Includes bibliographical references
```

The subject heading is typed at the top of the card.

```
                                            MATHER, COTTON, 1663-1728
        F
        67            Silverman, Kenneth.
        .M43             The life and times of Cotton Mather
        S57            / Kenneth Silverman. 1st ed. New York
        1984           : Harper & Row, c1984.
                        479 p.

                        Includes bibliographical references
                        and index.

                        1.Mather, Cotton, 1663-1728. 2.Mas-
                        sachusetts--History--Colonial period,
                        ca. 1600-1775. 3.Puritans--Massachu-
                        setts--Biography. I.Title.

        F67.M43S57  1984                       285.8'32'0924
        ISBN 0-06-015231-1                     922'.5'744  B
                                                       83-48385
                                       004 540      LC-MARC₃
```

Figure 4-4   Catalog cards.

closed to you, you must fill out a *call slip* and give it to a library em-
ployee, who will find the book for you. On the call slip, you supply the
author, title, and call number you found in the catalog entry for the book.

Call Numbers

In the stacks, books are shelved according to the call numbers you
found with each book's name. Call numbers are in one of two major classification systems: the *Library of Congress system* and the *Dewey Decimal system*.

The Library of Congress system uses a combination of letters and
numbers to arrange books by subject area and within the subject area.

The Dewey Decimal system uses numbers to designate major subject areas, and then a combination of letters and numbers to designate subdivisions under the major classifications. You do not have to memorize the codes for the system your library uses, and you need no specialized knowledge to use it yourself. However, if you have access to the stacks, familiarizing yourself with the call numbers for your particular field will enable you not only to locate the books you have found listed in the library catalog but also to browse in appropriate sections for other books that may prove valuable. As always, your librarian is the professional to turn to if you have any problems understanding the organization and location of materials in the library.

Books on Reserve

Most college libraries have a *reserve reading room* or a *reserve shelf.* In this area, you find books that instructors have asked a librarian to pull out of the stacks and set aside for use in particular classes. However, the books remain available for anyone to use, with certain restrictions. A book placed on reserve may be checked out only for use in the library or, at best, may be taken out overnight. When a book is put on reserve, the online catalog entry usually notes that fact. Should you discover that a book you need for your research has been put on reserve, plan to read it and take notes while in the library. Try to use reserve books as early in the term as possible because you can be sure that other students will soon be competing with you for the same books.

Searching for Sources

5

Using Periodicals
and Indexes

Although many students think of library research as being limited to books, periodical articles offer several important advantages. Periodicals can be more current. A book takes many months or even years to write, and months more to be published; therefore, it may be at least partly out of date by the time it first appears, and still more so by the time you read it. Articles can be published much more quickly. Thus, in fields where information and interpretations change rapidly, such as science and technology, articles have replaced books as the primary way in which professionals exchange information and ideas. Even in fields such as history and literature, you need to check periodicals to make sure your research is up to date. And subjects in current affairs, such as *government energy policy* and *national health insurance,* will have to be heavily researched in newspapers, newsmagazines, and journals of political commentary.

Another advantage of periodical articles is their depth. They usually focus on a specific topic in more detail than books. For example, a book about the world's food supply might include a chapter on innovative proposals for increasing agricultural production, but only a paragraph or two might be about *"farming" the ocean floor.* However, you can probably find several recent periodical articles on ocean farming that cover the topic in much greater detail and depth. And, because periodical articles usually focus on relatively narrow topics, their titles often tell you exactly what that topic is and save you time in your search for relevant sources. If you were planning a paper on ocean farming, titles like these would immediately catch your eye:

- "A Proposal for Implementing Ocean Farming off the Southeastern Coast of the United States"
- "Ocean Farming: The Crop Will Not Cover the Cost"

Because periodical articles are shorter than books, they are also more likely to be available online. In fact, some scholarly journals, as well as magazines of more general interest like *Salon* and *Slate,* are now published *only* online (although you can, of course, print out the text). In addition, many other newspapers and magazines have Web sites that make available some or all of the contents of their print versions, and sometimes special online material as well. Your library's Web page may include links to several online periodicals. For information on online periodicals, ask your reference librarian or visit the WWW Virtual Library site at <http://www.comlab.ox.ac.uk/archive/publishers.html>.

Periodical Indexes

Titles of specific articles published in periodicals are listed in guides known as *periodical indexes.* These indexes appear as hardbound volumes in the reference room of your library. Each volume is labeled with the year it covers. The titles of recently published articles are cataloged in paperbound supplements. At the end of the year, the supplements are incorporated into hardbound volumes.

Most periodical indexes are also available in electronic form. Ask your librarian for help in locating these indexes, or check the library's main Web page. Most electronic periodical indexes are useful only when you are searching for recent or relatively recent sources. Before you begin a search in an electronic index, check the dates that the index covers. The dates are usually listed on the main search screen. You will probably do better to use printed indexes when researching sources for events that took place two decades ago or more, especially if you are interested in investigating sources written close to the time the events were happening.

Each periodical index has its own format, so take the time to familiarize yourself with it. Print indexes use abbreviations that are explained at the beginning of each volume. Be sure to consult these explanations before using a print index.

Most electronic indexes allow you to search by author, title, subject, or keyword—like a library catalog. Many give you other options for combining types of searches or limiting searches by date, language of publication, and so on. Each electronic index has its own set of search commands. These commands are often explained on the main search screen, and you can use the "help" command to find additional information about conducting a search.

Searching for Sources

Later in this chapter, you will have a chance to examine some typical index entries.

Accessing Computerized Sources

The following brief overview is intended to help you understand directions a librarian may give you when you first start exploring the library's electronic indexes and other computerized resources, including the text of books and periodical articles. These sources may be available in either of two modes: *CD-ROM* (compact disc—read only memory) and *online.*

Using CD-ROMs

Just as music CDs condense a great deal of music onto a small disc, so a single CD-ROM can house enormous amounts of information—the text of an entire book, or summaries of thousands of articles published in hundreds of periodicals over many years. These collections of information are referred to as *databases.* Each database offers access to a particular collection of information, such as the *Readers' Guide to Periodical Literature,* the *New York Times Index,* and other specialized indexes of magazine and journal articles. Find out which databases your library has acquired on CD-ROM and locate the ones most useful for your research.

To use a CD-ROM system, sit down at a computer terminal and insert the disc as you would a music CD into a CD player. Instructions will probably be posted at your seat or appear on the computer screen. Once you have located some useful information and examined it on the screen, you can either print it using the printer attached to the computer or copy it onto a diskette, if you bring one with you. The indexes to periodicals are kept reasonably up to date—a new disc supplementing the old one arrives every month.

Searching Databases Online

Online searches are considerably more comprehensive than CD-ROM searches in that they lead to many more databases and provide a way for you to get printouts of articles in periodicals to which most libraries do not subscribe. Many online databases are available free of charge from your library's Web page. In some libraries, however, you will be charged by the minute for online searches, so it is essential that you consult a reference librarian, who can tailor your search method to make it as fast as possible and can help ensure that your search is a success. Once you find the information you need, you can print or *download* it (move a copy of it from the source computer onto a diskette—or onto your computer if you are connected from home or your dorm room).

Locating Print Periodicals

Once you have found the title of an article that promises to be a good source and is not available in electronic form, you need to find out whether your library has a copy of the periodical in which the article appeared. Periodicals are generally listed in the online catalog, and you can search for them by title. If you do not find a periodical listed in the catalog, your librarian can tell you whether your library subscribes to it.

Most libraries have a periodical section in which you can find current issues of each magazine and newspaper that your library regularly acquires. Most of your research, however, will require that you consult back issues of certain periodicals, and these may be kept elsewhere or may have been transferred to microfilm. Again, the online catalog will tell you where periodicals are located, or you can ask your librarian how back issues are handled in your library.

Types of Periodicals

Periodicals fall into two broad categories—*popular* and *professional*—according to their intended audiences. Within each category, you may have to use several indexes. Note that the material in professional journals is likely to be very specialized, and you may find much of it hard to understand at first. Your instructor can help you as you work through such material and determine how to integrate it into your paper.

These are some of the most frequently used indexes to periodicals:

popular periodicals (magazines and newspapers)	*Readers' Guide to Periodical Literature* *New York Times Index* *Book Review Digest* InfoTrac *General Periodicals Index*
professional periodicals (often called *journals*)	*Humanities Index* *Social Sciences Index* InfoTrac *Academic Index*

In addition, many indexes have been published for periodicals in specific fields, such as art, medicine, and psychology. (A list of the most common indexes and computer databases is provided in Appendix 2.)

Searching for Sources

Indexes to Popular Periodicals

The Readers' Guide to Periodical Literature

The *Readers' Guide to Periodical Literature,* or *Readers' Guide,* is an index to articles on a wide variety of subjects published in periodicals aimed at a cross section of American readers. It is available as a multivolume set of books, on CD-ROM, and online (the online version is now called *Readers' Abstracts*). Some periodicals, such as *Newsweek, Reader's Digest,* and *National Geographic,* appeal to general interests; others, such as *Aviation Week, Business Week,* and *Art in America,* appeal to special interests. Here is a sampling of the 240 magazines indexed by *Readers' Guide* and the subjects they cover:

The American City—architecture, city planning, urban problems

Atlantic Monthly—current affairs, short fiction

Consumer Reports—evaluations of the performance of commercial products for the general consumer

Cosmopolitan—features, fashions, primarily for career women

Discover—reports of happenings and issues in science, written for a general readership

Ebony—features, fashions, of particular interest to African American readers

Foreign Affairs—political topics, for readers who are well versed in current events

HG (House and Garden)—architecture, interior decoration, landscaping

The Nation—political issues, aimed at a politically liberal audience

National Review—political issues, aimed at a politically conservative audience

New Republic—political issues, aimed at a politically conservative to moderate audience

Psychology Today—reports on recent research in all branches of psychology, designed for the general reader

Scientific American—reports of recent scientific research, written for scientifically informed readers

Sports Illustrated—sports and excellent photographs for the general public

Time—news items from the current week, written for the general public

United Nations Monthly Chronicle—issues pertaining to the work of the United Nations

Vital Speeches of the Day—transcripts for those who want to know *exactly* what was said

The print version of the *Readers' Guide* has been published since 1900 as a series, each volume covering one or more years. (The *Readers' Guide* year currently runs from March through February.) If you need material from the nineteenth century, go to *Poole's Index to Periodical Literature,* which covers 1802 to 1906. Consult the *Readers' Guide* for social science subjects—modern history, economics, political science, and sociology. It is especially valuable for topics that concern public reaction to an event at the time it was happening, such as *Franklin Roosevelt's attempt to alter the composition of the Supreme Court,* and for the latest articles on current events not yet included in books, such as *changing attitudes toward old age in the United States from 1990 to the present.*

For scientific topics, the *Readers' Guide* offers relatively few useful sources. Scientific subjects were not even included in this index until 1953. Because magazines for the general public must avoid highly technical discussions, their science writers may oversimplify and occasionally distort some of the ideas they present. If you begin your investigation of a scientific topic with a popular magazine, be sure to turn to books and scholarly journals that deal with the same topic in more depth and detail.

The *Readers' Guide* lists both authors and subjects alphabetically. Regardless of whether you are looking for a subject or an author, use this index as you would a dictionary.

For example, if you were looking for articles on witchcraft published in the last fifteen years, you would look at several volumes of the *Readers' Guide,* checking listings under "Witchcraft." In the March 1984–February 1985 volume of the *Readers' Guide,* you would find the information shown in Figure 5-1.

To find an author's work in the *Readers' Guide,* look alphabetically for the author's last name. Under it you will find all articles by the author, arranged alphabetically according to title, disregarding *A, An,* and *The.* (The word *about* above an author's name indicates that the author is the subject of an article written by someone else.)

The Magazine Index

This index covers articles from more than four hundred magazines. It is available in some libraries on CD-ROM and online (both separately and as part of InfoTrac, which is discussed later in this chapter) and in other libraries as a microform system. The microform system consists of a console with a large viewing screen and an operating knob. You need only turn the knob to move the viewer swiftly in search of subjects or authors, both indexed alphabetically. The *Magazine Index* is most useful for

The topic of interest

Related topics

Article title

Author

Illustrated with a portrait

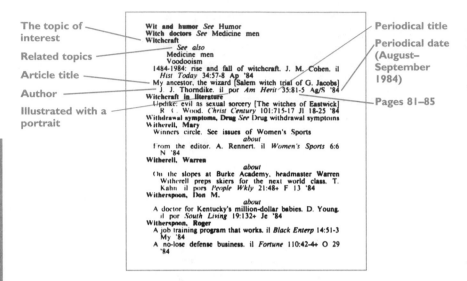

Periodical title

Periodical date (August–September 1984)

Pages 81–85

Wit **and humor** *See* Humor
Witch **doctors** *See* Medicine men
Witchcraft
　　— *See also*
　　Medicine men
　　Voodooism
1484-1984: rise and fall of witchcraft. J. M. Cohen. il *Hist Today* 34:57-8 Ap '84
— My ancestor, the wizard [Salem witch trial of G. Jacobs] J. J. Thorndike. il *por Am Herit* 35:81-5 Ag/S '84
Witchcraft **in literature**
Updike: evil as sexual sorcery [The witches of Eastwick] R. C. Wood. *Christ Century* 101:715-17 Jl 18-25 '84
Withdrawal **symptoms, Drug** *See* Drug withdrawal symptoms
Witherell, **Mary**
Winners circle. *See* issues of Women's Sports
　　　　about
From the editor. A. Rennert. il *Women's Sports* 6:6 N '84
Witherell, **Warren**
　　　　about
On the slopes at Burke Academy, headmaster Warren Witherell preps skiers for the next world class. T. Kahn il *pors People Wkly* 21:48+ F 13 '84
Witherspoon, **Don M.**
　　　　about
A doctor for Kentucky's million-dollar babies. D. Young. il *por South Living* 19:132+ Je '84
Witherspoon, **Roger**
A job training program that works. il *Black Enterp* 14:51-3 My '84
A no-lose defense business. il *Fortune* 110:42-4+ O 29 '84

Figure 5-1   From the *Readers' Guide to Periodical Literature.*

locating articles that have appeared in magazines *during the past five or six years.* However, because the index provides information from so many magazines, it includes publications that your instructor may think inappropriate for serious research. Check with your instructor or your librarian if you have any doubts about the research value of a magazine with which you are unfamiliar. Also, keep in mind that your library probably subscribes to only a small number of the four hundred magazines.

An online search of the *Magazine Index* for material relating to the keyword combination "immigration + policy + implications" turned up a single item, which is shown in Figure 5-2.

The New York Times Index

The *New York Times* is generally agreed by professionals in all fields to be the most important newspaper in the United States. In annual volumes, the *New York Times Index* lists all major news accounts and feature articles that have appeared in the *Times* since 1913, arranged alphabetically according to subject. To locate articles on a specific topic or event, choose the volumes that cover the relevant time period and then look alphabetically in the volumes for the subject. To check the *Times Index* for very recent events, use the supplements published every two weeks. At year's end, these supplements are republished as the new annual volume. The *Times Index* is also available on CD-ROM and online (both separately and as part of InfoTrac).

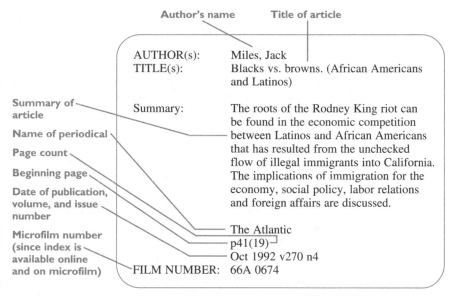

Figure 5-2   From the *Magazine Index*.

Newspaper articles are particularly useful for topics that require you to know precisely what facts and impressions were reported at the time an event occurred or to sample public opinion over a particular period of time. Here are some examples of such topics:

attitudes toward Prohibition at the time the Eighteenth Amendment was being ratified (1917–19)

reactions throughout the South to the Supreme Court decision of 1954 outlawing segregation in public schools

the extent to which the American public was misinformed about the testing of atomic bombs in Nevada after World War II

While researching public opinion preceding an event, such as an election or the ratification of a constitutional amendment, be sure to check the *Times Index* volume not only for the calendar year of the event but also for the previous year, especially if the event took place early in the year. Similarly, when investigating the reactions to an event, check the *Times Index* volumes for both the year of the event and the following year.

Every daily issue of the *New York Times* (beginning with the first issue in 1851) has been reproduced on microfilm, and many libraries have a complete set. Find the date, section, and page number of a particular news item in the *Times Index;* then request the filmstrip of the *Times* for that date and run it through a microfilm viewer.

Even if your library does not subscribe to the *Times* on microfilm, consult the *New York Times Index* for the year the event occurred; then you can find the exact days on which important events were reported. Use those dates to locate information in newspapers that your library *does* have, because most newspapers usually publish important stories at the same time.

The *Times Index* offers another convenient feature: its brief summaries of many articles may help you decide whether or not to spend time searching for and reading a particular story.

Figure 5-3 shows a sample from the *New York Times Index*. The entry "Witchcraft" in the bound volume of the *Times Index* for 1985 indicates several articles about the subject, with one referring directly to the Salem witchcraft trials.

The *New York Times Index* is most useful for social science subjects such as modern history, economics, and political science. The *Times* also reports extensively on literature and the arts.

An article dealing with the filming of a television mini-series based on the Salem witchcraft trials appeared in section II, page 29, column I of the October 28, 1985, issue of the *Times:* (M) indicates a medium-length article, (S) a short article, and (L) a long article.

WISTAR Institute. See also Cancer, Jl 12
WIT. Use Humor and Wit
WITCHCRAFT
Article on increase in fatal lightning strikes in Khureng, South Africa, during current rainy season, which has resulted in burning to death of six local people, who were charged by witch doctors with sorcery; notes that while lightning can be explained scientifically, supernatural provides natural form of elucidation; illustration; map (M), Ja 21,I,2:3
Fox Butterfield article on filming of 'Three Sovereigns for Sarah,' about witchcraft trials in Salem (Mass) in 1692; three-hour production is public-TV mini-series being filmed outside Boston and is scheduled to be shown under 'American Playhouse' banner next May; photo (M), O 28, II,29:1
Dozens of cats, dogs and chickens have been mutilated in what police in Marysville, Ohio, think may be work of satanic cult (S), D 31,I,6:6
WITCO Chemical Corp. See also Continental Carbon Co, S 11. Oil, Ja 10
Witco Chemical Corp names Denis Andreuzzi executive vice president of commercial services, Ja 23,IV,2:6
Witco Chemical Corp elects Thomas J Bickett executive vice president (S), F 7,IV,2:2
Witco Chemical Corp promotes Dr Lawrence B Nelson to group vice president, petroleum, Jl 23,IV,2:6
WITEK, Joan. See also Art, Je 15
WITHERS, William. See also NYC—Govt Employees, Ag 11
WITHERSPOON, Roger. See also Biology, S 6,15
WITHERSPOON, Tim. See also Boxing, Mr 9,10, Ag 31, S 1,2
WITHERSPOON-Jackson Development Corp. See also Housing, Jl 1
WITKIN, Isaac. See also Art, Je 15
WITKIN-Lanoil, Georgia (Dr). See also Mental Health, Ap 8
WITKOWSKI, John. See also Football, Ag 20
WITT, Arthur P. See also Lily-Tulip Inc, Jl 31
WITT, Edna Mae. See also Nursing Homes, N 10
WITT, Jon. See also Alpha Software Corp, Ja 24
WITT, Katarina. See also Ice Skating, Ja 13, Mr 22. Olympic Games (1984), F 17,18,19

Figure 5-3   From the *New York Times Index*.

The National Newspaper Index

A valuable addition to periodical guides is the *National Newspaper Index*. This index provides information on articles that have appeared in five of the nation's largest newspapers: the *Christian Science Monitor*, the *Los Angeles Times*, the *New York Times*, the *Wall Street Journal*, and the *Washington Post*. As you might gather from the titles of the newspapers included, this index can be especially useful for looking up regional news and opinion, as well as national and international news. (The *National Newspaper Index* is also available online; check your library's Web page or ask a librarian about accessing the online version.)

Newspaper Abstracts

A computerized index that also provides abstracts (summaries) of newspaper articles, *Newspaper Abstracts* covers thirty-two major national and international newspapers. Its citations go back as far as the late 1980s.

The Book Review Digest

The *Book Review Digest* publishes excerpts from book reviews that appeared within a year after a book was first published. The *Book Review Digest* does not cite every published review, but only a sample of critical responses, both favorable and unfavorable.

Each annual volume of this digest (beginning in 1905) indexes reviews of several thousand books, according to both title and author. It covers popular and scholarly works, fiction and nonfiction, and draws its material from more than eighty English-language periodicals. To use the *Book Review Digest*, you need to know the year in which a book was first published. Then you should look up the title or the author in the volumes both for that year and for the next year, because some books are not reviewed during the calendar year in which they are published. A book published in November 1991, for example, might not have been reviewed until January 1992.

The *Book Review Digest* presents the initial critical reactions to a book, helpful especially if you want to compare immediate responses with later judgments made by critics and scholars after the work had a chance to influence other writers or after public tastes changed. Examples of research assignments requiring you to use the *Book Review Digest* would be "Initial Critical Reactions to Ernest Hemingway's *The Sun Also Rises*" and "Changing Critical Evaluations of Willa Cather's *My Antonia*."

The value of the *Book Review Digest* is not limited to literary topics. For example, you might want to know how reviewers reacted to a book that presented a new view of a well-known person or event or one that unveiled a new social or scientific theory such as evolution, relativity, or psychoanalysis.

Finally, check a book you want to use as a source in the *Book Review Digest;* you can find out very easily whether or not the reviewers thought that book informative and reliable.

Indexes to Scholarly and Professional Journals

The Humanities Index *and the* Social Sciences Index

These two indexes may well provide you with all the sources you need for research papers in the social sciences and the humanities. These indexes are more specialized than those discussed so far—both of them index not general magazines but scholarly journals in a variety of fields.

Since 1974, the *Humanities Index* and the *Social Sciences Index* have appeared as separate volumes. From 1965 to 1974, the two indexes were combined in the *Social Sciences and Humanities Index,* and from 1920 to 1965, this index's title was the *International Index to Periodicals.* From 1907 through 1919, the single index was titled *Readers' Guide Supplement and International Index.* Both the *Humanities Index* and the *Social Sciences Index* are available on CD-ROM and online; the online versions are now called *Humanities Abstracts* and *Social Sciences Abstracts.*

Together, the *Humanities Index* and the *Social Sciences Index* cover articles published in more than five hundred scholarly and professional journals. (Many of these journals, however, are not available in small libraries.) The *Humanities Index,* which covers well over three hundred periodicals, lists articles according to subject in the following academic disciplines:

archeology	literary and political criticism
area studies	performing arts
classical studies	philosophy
folklore	religion
history (not included until 1974)	theology
language and literature	

The *Social Sciences Index* covers about four hundred periodicals and lists articles according to subject in the following academic disciplines:

anthropology	environmental science
area studies	law and criminology
economics	medical science
education	political sciences
psychology (not included between 1945 and 1974)	public administration
	sociology

The CD-ROM versions of both indexes are *full-text databases*—that is, they allow users to access the full text of an article electronically. Check with a librarian about whether or not your library has the full-text CD-ROMs.

Specialized Indexes

The *Humanities Index* and the *Social Sciences Index,* although highly valuable resources, cover only a small fraction of all the scholarly and professional journals published in the humanities and the social sciences. Because the number of specialized scholarly articles published each year is enormous, each field has its own annual index to specialized periodicals, many available on CD-ROM and online as well as in printed volumes. Even so, areas such as English literature cannot be contained within a single annual index, so there are still more specialized indexes.

As we noted earlier, the indexes to scholarly and professional journals will lead you to very difficult materials. Most authors of scholarly articles are writing for fellow experts and therefore assume that their readers have a strong background in the field; many articles focus on narrow topics and use highly specialized terminology. You may find much scholarly writing hard to understand, but you should become acquainted with such materials and perhaps work through an article with your instructor so you can incorporate some specialized scholarly sources into your research paper if such sources strengthen your thesis. Later in college, especially in your major, the information in scholarly journals will become increasingly accessible and valuable to you.

Appendix 2 contains a selective list of indexes to scholarly and professional journals in many major fields. If you need to find additional sources, consult the *Bibliographic Index: A Cumulative Bibliography of Bibliographies.* This work briefly describes all the periodical indexes you will probably ever need.

Abstracts

Many technical or scholarly articles are accompanied by *abstracts,* paragraph-length summaries of the article's content. Specialized indexes, including the ones listed in this chapter, often contain abstracts to help index users decide which articles are useful for their research. (See the section "Understanding Abstracts" in Chapter 16 for a discussion of how to write an abstract of your own paper.)

Searching for Sources

6

Using Other Kinds of Sources

Although you can produce a fine research paper based entirely on books and periodicals found through your school's library catalog and the major periodical indexes, other resources may give you still more information and ideas. These include other kinds of material available within your own library, the resources of other libraries and nonacademic organizations, and television and radio programs. In addition, for some topics in certain fields, you may be required to do field research in the form of interviews and surveys.

Other Materials in Your Own Library

Special Collections

Some libraries maintain separate collections of materials such as books, periodicals, personal letters, and manuscripts. A special collection sometimes relates to rather specific areas of interest: a particular author's works, the history of a particular place, or a fairly narrow field (cave exploration, Broadway musicals, or aviation engineering). Other special collections are kept separate from the main collection because their holdings are fragile, rare, or otherwise unusual. Information about special collections can usually be found on your library's Web page. Typically each special collection has its own catalog.

Microforms

In addition to books and periodicals, your library probably has a collection of *microforms*, materials available on *microfilm* (rolls of film on which printed materials are reproduced in miniature) or *microfiche* (sheets of microfilm containing images of many pages of printed material, arranged in rows). To read microforms, you need a special machine. In some libraries, an aide will help set up the microform reader; in others, you must load the reader yourself, following instructions posted nearby. Using such readers is simple, and you should be able to operate one easily after a couple of attempts. Also, most microfilm readers can print out copies of material you want to examine further, often for a small fee.

Many source materials have been preserved on microforms to save space, avoid wear and tear on delicate holdings, and increase usefulness. The most common sources available on microforms are periodicals; others include old and rare books and even facsimiles of manuscripts. Some sources, such as graduate dissertations, may be published only as microforms.

The Vertical File

Some printed sources may not be classified as books or as periodicals and so will appear in neither the library catalog nor the periodical indexes. Such materials include pamphlets, brochures, and clippings from hard-to-get periodicals on specialized topics. You can find these resources by using the *vertical file*, usually kept in file cabinets. A librarian can explain how to use a vertical file and tell you whether or not the file is indexed.

Audiovisual Materials

Many libraries now contain media sections that house films, videotapes, pictures, slides, and sound recordings. If your topic concerns the performing or visual arts, architecture, or the social or natural sciences, you will often find materials useful to your research in the audiovisual collection. You most likely will be able to search for audiovisual materials in the online catalog. In addition to materials on the arts, you can find valuable documentaries, especially in those fields having to do with human and animal behavior and society.

Other Print Sources

Interlibrary Loans

If you discover a source that you believe to be crucial to your research, and your library does not have a copy of it, you may be able to borrow the source through an interlibrary loan. Until recently, a librarian had to arrange for such a loan, and it often took weeks for the materials to arrive at the requester's library. Many libraries now have an electronic form on their computer system that enables patrons to request such loans directly. A rush loan can now be arranged within a couple of days, but you will probably have to pay a fee for such special service.

Other Libraries

Large colleges and universities may have separate specialized libraries attached to particular graduate schools or departments such as law, medicine, engineering, music, and art. Off campus, museums and professional societies often operate their own small but excellent libraries. You may have to apply formally to use such facilities; often simply verifying your school affiliation will be enough. Your local public library may also be a useful resource. Some public libraries, like New York City's, are among the greatest research facilities in the world, but even the most modest public library may have the particular periodical or book you need.

Special Printed Materials

Private businesses, nonprofit organizations, special-interest groups, and various levels of government agencies publish reports and pamphlets in great numbers. Usually these materials can be obtained free of charge by writing to the organizations. In most cases, there will be no catalog to which you can refer, so you may have to describe what you are looking for and hope the answer meets your needs. The *Monthly Catalog* of the United States Government Printing Office (GPO) lists all federal government publications that are available to the public, their prices, and the addresses from which they may be ordered. Your library should have a copy of the catalog, and you can ask your librarian where it is kept. Be warned, however, that you may wait a month or more for materials ordered; one GPO distribution center in Pueblo, Colorado, alone handles some eighty thousand requests every week.

Television and Radio Programs

The Public Broadcasting Service (PBS) regularly presents programs about the performing and graphic arts as well as the natural and social sciences. These programs are often repeated several times, so you may be able to watch broadcasts originally shown before you started your research project. Many libraries acquire tapes of programs shown on PBS, so also check your library. If your topic has to do with a current issue, be alert for interviews and documentaries scheduled on any station. Transcripts usually require four to six weeks' delivery time, and so, in most cases, you will have to make your own transcription. If possible, record the program and later transcribe word for word those portions of it you want to use, rather than trying to take notes during the program.

Interviews and Surveys

Most student research papers are written on topics that can be fully researched in a library by relying on books, periodicals, and, in rare cases, audiovisual materials as sources. Occasionally, however, you may want to engage in some firsthand investigation in order to confirm what your sources have written or to learn more about what you have read. In some courses, especially in the social sciences, you may be required to obtain some information on your own, whether by interviewing knowledgeable people or by sampling public opinion through a poll or a questionnaire.

Both interviewing and surveying call for careful planning and consultation with your teacher if they are to prove fruitful. However, do not be discouraged by the unfamiliarity of these approaches. Knowing how to ask questions effectively can be an important asset in many situations.

Interviews

You may want to set up an interview with a person whose knowledge and opinions would be useful to your research project. Perhaps a faculty member is an authority on your topic, or a local public official administers a program relevant to your research. Depending on your topic, you may well find that interviews with people who possess special knowledge or have undergone unusual experiences will yield valuable information.

If you would like to interview someone who lives too far away from you to meet in person, consider doing an interview by phone or e-mail. In fact, e-mail may be an attractive option even for a local interview because it does not require that you and the interviewee be available at the same time. The following discussion assumes a face-to-face interview, but most of the same advice applies to interviews conducted by other means.

Setting Up Interviews. When you request a personal interview, prepare the groundwork well. Here are some guidelines for doing so:

- Write, telephone, or e-mail as early as possible, explaining to the person just why you want the meeting. Specify your field of inquiry as precisely as you can, and explain why you think this interview can help you get a better grasp of the topic you are researching. Let the person know that you will limit the interview to a few pertinent questions that will not take up too much time.

• Review your questions with your instructor. Forming brief questions that will bring out the kind of information you need is an art, and you may need help the first time. You might even offer to send the questions to the interviewee in advance of the actual interview.

• Ask ahead of time whether the interviewee minds if you bring a tape recorder to the interview. If you meet objections, don't persist. Bringing the machine and asking permission just before the session starts puts the other person under unwelcome pressure to let you proceed. After all, taking notes will serve your purposes almost as well.

Conducting Interviews. The attitude you assume will be important to the success of your interview. Keep in mind that the authority is a research source and that your main concern is to find out what the person knows or believes about some aspect of your topic. At the time of an interview, you are gathering sources to test the hypothesis you have chosen to guide your research. This means that you have not yet arrived at a particular conclusion regarding your topic. Thus your job is to listen carefully to the person's responses to your questions and summarize major points in your notes. If you enter into an interview with a biased point of view, your "source" may catch the tone of your remarks and give you little, if anything, in the way of useful information or opinions.

Also keep in mind that you are asking a favor of a busy person; never let yourself think that you are generously offering an opportunity to share ideas with an intelligent listener. Here are some guidelines for conducting successful interviews:

• Do *not* arrive late. In fact, for your own comfort, try to be at least five minutes early. Most people value punctuality.

• Bring a large pad or notebook and several pens or pencils in case one of them stops functioning. Look as though this meeting is important to you.

• Come prepared with a written series of questions aimed at eventually leading to the specific information you are seeking. You may not need to stick doggedly to the list because the answers to some questions may come out quite naturally before you ask for them. But having a list prevents you from forgetting to ask all your questions, and it can help you control the flow of the interview. Furthermore, the interviewee will respect you for being so conscientious.

• If the interviewee has agreed to be taped, be sure the recorder is ready to work immediately, fresh batteries and tape already in place.

• Finally, be sure to write a note thanking the person for the interview.

You may find it helpful to read about how two students went about planning and conducting their interviews.

Example 1: Planning an Interview. Jeremy, a sociology student, decided to base his research project on a unit of the course dealing with society's reaction to antisocial behavior by young people. He narrowed his preliminary topic to *the effectiveness of curfews in reducing antisocial behavior by teenagers.*

Jeremy had become interested in curfews after seeing a TV news segment in which a group of teens were being questioned in a nearby town by police officers who wanted to know what the teens were doing out on the street during the nighttime curfew period. Jeremy's initial feelings about curfews, based on the TV segment, were that they were very difficult to enforce and, if enforced strongly, might actually make teenage antisocial behavior even worse in the long run.

After meeting with his instructor, Jeremy agreed that research derived from interviewing might provide the best information for his topic because curfews were relatively new approaches to crime prevention, especially in the area in which he lived. With further thought, he decided he would try to interview the mayor of each of three towns that had instituted curfews within the past two years. In this way, he would gather information on how the curfews were working, at least from the official and administrative point of view. Again, after talking to his instructor, Jeremy came up with the following questions for the mayors or other knowledgeable officials.

- Has your curfew succeeded in reducing crime by young people to the extent you expected it would? Are there any before-and-after statistics?

- Have police reported any major problems in enforcing the curfew? What are the penalties for those who break the law? Are parents penalized for their children's noncompliance?

- I understand that several legal challenges to your curfew are in the courts. What groups or individuals have initiated these challenges? On what grounds? Do you have any doubts that your law will withstand such challenges?

- Have any businesses or social organizations objected to the curfew? Are exemptions allowed for special events?

- Have you seen any change in the relationship between the police and young people since the advent of the curfew law?

- Would you say, overall, that the curfew law has improved the quality of life for most citizens of your town?

Searching for Sources

Example 2: Conducting an Interview. Ben, a political science student, chose the North American Free Trade Agreement (NAFTA) from a list of subjects assigned by his instructor. In his reading of magazine articles and essays from journals such as *Foreign Affairs,* Ben felt that several of his questions were not answered as clearly as he wanted. At his roommate's suggestion, he set up an interview with an economics professor, who he believed would supply him with a few answers that would confirm his hypothesis that NAFTA would turn out to be harmful to the U.S. economy. Ben felt confident that his research up to that point had given him sufficient knowledge of his topic to enter the interview without a specific questioning strategy. This attitude proved embarrassing.

After exchanging pleasantries with the professor, Ben plunged right into the questioning with "Can you tell me why anyone would want to sell us on a treaty that will cost U.S. workers so many jobs?"

After a moment's thought, the professor told Ben that he should have done more background reading before coming to see her. Saying that she did not have time to fill him in on all the details of the proposed treaty, she asked to end the interview. Ben protested that he had read numerous commentaries before reaching his opposition to NAFTA, but his defense did not satisfy the professor. Later, perplexed at his embarrassing loss of a source, Ben complained to a friend that the professor had been unreasonable.

He received a little sympathy and a good piece of advice. His friend had written several papers that involved interviews, and she pointed out that he had forgotten the fundamental purpose of the interview—to gain more information about the topic. Ben's opening question had led the economics professor to believe that Ben would not listen to her ideas because he had already made up his mind. And, because she probably supported NAFTA, judging from her accusing Ben of ignorance on the subject, she did not want to spend time arguing with him.

Ben's friend recalled some of her instructor's advice on approaching an interview: Remember that your objective is to learn something, not to show how much you know or what you think. Give any experts you consult a chance to let you know how they view the topic and what they believe are the major points to be considered. The best way to open an interview is, therefore, with a rather general approach, free of any indication that you have reached a conclusion.

In short, tempting as it may seem, do not give in to the urge to impress the expert with your own intelligence and good judgment. Throughout the session, keep opening up possibilities for the other person to impress you. After all, the other person is the expert, or else you would not have asked for an interview.

Deciding to test his friend's advice, Ben called on another economics professor, who agreed to a half-hour interview. Ben began his questioning

Searching for Sources

in this fashion: "I've been doing a fair amount of research on NAFTA, and I hoped you could help me understand some of the complex issues it raises."

The professor spoke initially about the provisions of the treaty, almost all of which Ben already knew. Ben waited patiently before asking: "How might this treaty affect American workers in industries that could employ Mexican workers, who earn much less than Americans performing the same work?"

The professor's response seemed, at first, to support Ben's opinion that U.S. workers would suffer, but the professor went on to show ways in which American labor might benefit. He finally shared with Ben his judgment as to the overall effect of the treaty, carefully detailing his argument with specific examples of both positive and negative outcomes. Ben was able to close the interview by asking for clarification of several puzzling points that had originally led him to undertake the interview.

Ben had asked both professors if they minded his taping the interviews, and both agreed. On the other hand, his roommate had interviewed a doctor in a Veterans Administration hospital about the quality of care received by Vietnam veterans, and that person refused to be recorded. Maybe the man felt uneasy because he could not be sure who might end up hearing his comments, which were in fact fairly straightforward. Some people, however, just plain feel nervous with a recorder running, and you should cheerfully respect their wishes, particularly if you want the interview to go smoothly.

Surveys

Let's assume for this discussion that the main sources for your research paper will come from a library. If, at some point, you want to make a poll or questionnaire the central feature in a research paper, you absolutely must consult your instructor to obtain far more complete guidelines than we have space for in this book. Our suggestions are intended to help you decide whether to venture into this mode of research. We surely do not want to discourage anyone, because creating one of the sources in your own paper adds an exciting personal touch to the whole project.

Someone might ask whether or not opinions gathered from the general public by a student researcher can be regarded as authoritative sources, but that is not the relevant question. A more useful way to think about polling would be to ask how sampling people's opinions can enhance the research project. Until you write a paper based primarily on field research, the opinions you gather can serve only as interesting complements to the judgments found in your other sources.

When to Do a Survey. When newspapers, magazines, or radio and television stations tell us what ordinary people are thinking about an issue, you may want to test these reports to get a firsthand sense of public opinion. You can legitimately consider doing a survey when your topic deals with an issue that directly affects the lives of some people on campus or in the surrounding community. Consider the following issues:

- AIDS
- sex education in public schools
- school vouchers
- drug use
- teenage pregnancy
- taxes
- violent crime
- police handling of sensitive situations
- women's opportunities in the workplace
- sexual harassment
- the latest war
- the quality of public education
- college admission standards
- affirmative action
- gay and lesbian rights

A check on the accuracy of media polling may seem especially necessary in certain situations. Maybe you think that the media asked questions in such a way that the answers did not truly reflect public opinion. For example, maybe they forced respondents to choose between only two alternatives and you think that many people actually prefer a compromise between the two or some other option entirely. Or maybe their sampling method was flawed. They may have selected people from one or two social or geographical groups who could be most easily approached within their reporters' deadlines.

In 1936, when polling was first becoming part of American election campaigns, a poll conduced by the *Literary Digest* magazine predicted that the Democratic presidential candidate, Franklin Roosevelt, would be defeated for reelection. On Election Day, however, he won a landslide victory. The error lay in conducting the poll by telephone. In those days, a great many American households could not afford phones, and those that could were disproportionately Republican.

Planning a Survey. If you plan to conduct a survey, you need to make several important and interrelated decisions:

- *How many questions do you need to ask?* You need to ask enough questions to get a clear sense of public opinion on the issue and to make sure that you are not oversimplifying it. But try to keep the number to a minimum so that those you survey won't feel imposed on and so you won't have too much material to analyze and work into your paper. The way you conduct the survey may also affect the number of questions you choose to ask, or vice versa.

- *How many people do you need to poll?* Again, the answer to this question is closely related to the issue of your polling method. If you need only a small sample, you may simply decide to interview all the people individually. On the other hand, if you need many responses, it may be easier and faster to do an e-mail poll. In addition, keep in mind that more responses mean more material to analyze. Ask your instructor what size sample seems appropriate for your particular objectives.

- *How should you choose the people to poll?* Do you want to survey everyone in your dorm or your online discussion group? The first twenty people who agree to take one of your questionnaires? An equal number of men and women? Students or nonstudents? Think about whether you want to focus on—or to exclude—members of a group whose opinions relate directly to your hypothesis. For example, the student writing on immigration restricted her sample population to people born in the United States whose parents were also born here so that she could avoid opinions that were influenced by a natural sympathy for immigrants. If you are not screening the respondents ahead of time, you may need to include some questions about personal background in the questionnaire to help determine whether to include particular responses in your conclusions.

- *How will you find the people you want and actually do the survey?* If you are going to hand out questionnaires at a bus stop or subway entrance, use only a few questions, and keep them brief and simple. Even so, be ready for a good many refusals and hasty responses. If you feel you need to ask quite a few questions or complex questions, plan on catching people in the cafeteria or letting them take the question sheets with them and return them to you. (*Warning:* If people take the questionnaires with them, you will need to give out two or three times as many as you hope to receive because many people will forget to return them or change their minds about participating in the survey.)

Unlike questionnaires, taking a survey by e-mail or phone enables you to ask follow-up questions that may help to clarify the answers to

Searching for Sources

your original questions. But it also makes the survey feel more personal and less anonymous—and therefore may discourage people from participating or make their responses less frank and honest. In planning the survey, you must weigh all these considerations—the number and nature of the questions, the size and composition of the sample, and the method of sampling—to decide how to proceed.

Stages of Work. Whatever you decide about how to develop and administer the survey, be sure to give yourself plenty of time to complete the job. In addition to the actual sampling itself, the work falls into several stages:

- *Selecting and formulating the questions.*   Start by going to the periodicals that have reported public opinion on your topic and using their questions as a basis for your own survey. You may want to rephrase some of the questions, especially if you suspect that the phrasing encouraged answers that did not reflect the true opinions of those polled. Because the wording of survey questions requires a good deal of sophistication about language as well as polling techniques, however, be sure to check the phrasing with your instructor.

- *Preparing the questionnaires.*   If you are distributing the questionnaires by hand, type the questions for easy readability, and leave plenty of space for comments. Reproduce more than enough question sheets. If you are doing an e-mail survey, be sure it is clear where the respondents should type their answers. For any survey method in which you do not get immediate responses, be sure to give people a deadline for responding and, for questionnaires on paper, clear instructions for where to return them.

- *Reviewing the responses and arriving at conclusions.*   In analyzing the responses and reporting them in your paper, you should throw out questions that seem to have confused or misled the respondents. In writing the paper, do not simply list all the questions and the numbers of people who responded in one way or another. You must tie all the pieces of information together into a coherent package that can be discussed in relation to the views of experts on the topic or to the results of polling by the media. Before going into detail about your findings, take time to tell readers why you conducted the survey and how you chose your sample group.

7

Using the Internet for Research

In your quest for information, you may want to venture beyond the library and explore the Internet and the World Wide Web. At this point, almost everyone seeking access to the oceans of information available on the Internet relies on the Web. So, after a brief explanation of the difference between the two, we will use the terms *Net* and *Web* interchangeably throughout the rest of the book.

Whether you are having trouble finding enough sources in the library or you simply want access to a wider variety of materials, the Internet can enhance the quality of your research. If you have not yet become an Internet user, think about what you are missing. The Net can play an important role in many aspects of your coursework, not just in the area of research paper writing. But for the writer of research papers, the Internet is most useful for:

- conducting wide-ranging searches for sources at incredible speed
- reading periodicals that are not available in your own library
- communicating directly with well-informed individuals and groups

Keep in mind, though, that in most cases Internet sources should serve as supplements to printed library sources, not as replacements for them. Just how necessary or valuable they are will depend on the nature of your particular project. Most research papers can be completed quite well without going online. If you do venture in this direction, *consult your instructor* to determine what portion of your sources can reasonably come from the Internet.

In general, the Net is most helpful for recent topics, because the databases on it usually have indexed entries from only 1995 or so. If you wanted to find sources about the Persian Gulf War (1991) that were

69

written at the time, you might not find much on the Net. If you were looking for sources about the Watergate scandal (1973–74) that were written at the time, you would definitely have to go to print sources in a library.

Using the four student papers in Chapter 21 as examples, we could say that for subjects like *Cotton Mather* and *Emily Dickinson* you would certainly need to use mostly print sources, although the papers on these subjects do each cite a source from an online periodical. For subjects such as *fire ants* and *recent immigration,* the Net is more useful. But even here, you should make it no more than a partner of the library, albeit possibly a major one.

In this chapter, we explain the basics of what the Net and the Web are and how you can go about searching for sources on them. In Chapter 8, we describe in more detail the kinds of resources available online and ways to evaluate them; the chapter ends with an extended discussion of how David Perez, the student who wrote the paper on fire ants, used the Internet in his research.

The Internet

The Internet is an *inter*national *net*work connecting millions of computers all around the world, including the central computer on your campus as well as your own computer, if you have one. Many of these computers, both large and small, are operated by persons who have set up electronic *databases,* or information sites, that can be accessed by individuals like you. These sites belong to a wide variety of "owners"— universities, libraries, government agencies, the military, nonprofit organizations, and a host of commercial enterprises.

As a matter of fact, any individual or group can set up an Internet station, or Web site, which can say whatever the owner wants about any subject. And therein lies the main problem with using the Internet for research. If you find some information on the Net that seems of value to your project, you must determine whether or not the site where it appears is operated by someone whose information or opinions can be trusted to be authoritative. Sites created by well-known periodicals like the *Atlantic Monthly* and the *New York Times,* for example, are just as reliable as the print versions of those periodicals, but unfamiliar sites need to be carefully checked for reliability.

The World Wide Web: Gateway to the Internet

The World Wide Web is far and away the most popular means of working with the Internet. Only after becoming proficient at working with the Net through the Web are you likely to want to look into other, older approaches. For the purposes of this introduction to research techniques, we shall proceed as if you are not yet expert at "surfing the Net."

The Web uses a coding process called *hypertext* as a way of connecting most of the sites (databases) on the Internet. This feature allows you to move quickly and easily within a site or from one site to another by clicking the mouse on *links*—either icons (small symbols) or "hot" text (words or phrases that are underlined or in color)—on your computer screen. Another nice advantage to the Web is that it allows you to access documents that include graphics, sound, and video. For example, you can actually see Leonardo da Vinci's painting *Mona Lisa* by connecting to the Web site for the Louvre Museum in Paris, or listen to and watch a recording of Martin Luther King Jr. delivering his "I Have a Dream" speech by accessing a collection of his speeches.

Connecting with the Internet

To do online research, you need to *access* (make connection with) the Internet, either through your college or university or on your home computer.

Almost all colleges now provide Internet access at the library or computer laboratory, and at some schools you can *log on* directly from dormitory rooms. Many public libraries also provide Internet access, sometimes for a small fee. Each college offers its own means of access, so you need to ask what is available to you. Some libraries charge fees for time spent doing research online.

If you plan to work on a home computer, you will need a *modem* to connect it with the Internet, usually via a telephone line. Once your modem has been installed, you can connect your computer with the Net in several ways:

- Use your college's connection while at home, through *dial-up access*. (Ask a librarian if this is possible at your college.)
- Subscribe to a commercial *online service,* such as America Online, CompuServe, or Microsoft Network, all of which provide easy access to the Net.
- Sign up with an *Internet service provider (ISP),* which, though cheaper than online services, may require a bit more computer expertise.

Getting onto the Web: Browsers

Access to the Web is achieved through the use of special software packages called *browsers.* The two most commonly used browsers are Netscape Navigator and Microsoft Internet Explorer. Until you become

Searching for Sources

somewhat proficient at working with the Web, there is little need to be concerned about differences between browsers. As soon as your computer is electronically connected to the Internet, through America Online, say, you merely click the mouse on the word "Internet." Immediately you will be connected to the *home page* of the browser chosen by your online service. (A *home page* is the first page you see when you connect to a Web site or browser.)

When the browser is open, you will see at the top of the computer screen a "toolbar" consisting of a row of buttons that enable you to move around between pages on the Web: "back" to the page that was on your screen previously, "forward" in the other direction, or "home" to the browser's home page. (Many Web sites made up of more than one page also include a "home" button on each page.) The remaining buttons in the toolbar serve other purposes, which you can learn about by clicking on the "help" button.

Understanding Web Addresses

To find a specific site on the Internet, you need to type in an address referred to as a *URL* (Uniform Resource Locator). Here's a typical URL, in this case, for the "Victorian Women Writers Project" site, which carries information about nineteenth-century women authors:

protocol   domain name   directory path
http://www.indiana.edu/~letrs/vwwp

As the labels indicate, a URL has three basic elements:

- The *protocol* is the kind of computer link that the URL represents. The protocol *http* stands for *hypertext transfer protocol,* which as the name implies allows the exchange of hypertext documents.
- The *domain name* is made up of two basic parts. The first part identifies the owner of the site, the person or group that has put the information on the Web. The second part identifies the general group to which the owner belongs. In this case, the suffix *.edu* indicates that the owner, Indiana University, is an educational institution. Other common suffixes include:

com	commercial
gov	government
mil	military
net	network organization
org	nonprofit organization

The prefix *www* simply indicates the name of the computer where Indiana University stores information accessible on the World Wide Web. Many URLs have no prefix before the domain name (such as *amazon.com*); other prefixes indicate different computers (such as *english* in *english.ttu.edu*).

- The third basic part of the URL, the *directory path,* may be quite long. In this example, the directory path begins with a tilde (~), which indicates that it is a *folder* of someone who has a personal computer account at Indiana University and uses the designation *letrs.* Within the *letrs* folder is a folder called *vwwp.*

Note that there is no period at the end of this address. If you accidentally typed one in, the connection might not take place. Periods are very small, but they are very important as signals to the computer. In fact, *all punctuation marks must be observed very precisely when you type in URLs.* (You will find the tilde on the far left of the top row of most keyboards.)

Finding Sources: Search Engines

Sometimes you know the address of a particular Web site you want to consult. To reach such an address, simply type it into the box provided below the toolbar and press the "Enter" key. (Each browser has its own setup, but they are all very similar.)

In the vast majority of cases, though, you are looking for any Web sites that might offer information on your research topic. To find them, you need to go to a *search engine,* a program that collects the information from a multitude of databases on the Web. (Some search engines also offer commercial advertisements or services such as news delivery and free e-mail.) When you tell a search engine what you are looking for, it conducts an almost instantaneous search and reports its results. Each search engine goes about its business in its own way, but for the kind of work you are doing, all will be more or less satisfactory.

Once you have made contact with a search engine, you usually have two choices of action:

- Work with subject directories.
- Use keyword search techniques.

However you start, try to think of searching the Web in the same way you would approach a library catalog or an index such as the *Readers' Guide,* where you need to think of basic terms that will steer you toward sources that cover your research topic. As always in this process, the ability to think of good synonyms is essential.

Subject Directories

Here you work much as you did when reducing a subject to a topic for your paper. Beginning with "history" as a discipline area, for example, you could move from a very general menu in a subject directory to ones that are more and more specific, selecting

first, "Germany"

then, "World War II"

then, "Nazi war crimes"

then maybe, if you are lucky, "art confiscation."

The menus that are offered will be those chosen by the designers of the particular search engine you are using. (That is why we said "if you are lucky" in regard to "art confiscation.") When you arrive at what seems the most specific menu the search engine provides, you can type in keywords to see exactly what the engine has indexed, as explained in the next section.

As you progress from general toward specific in a subject directory, you will come across menu options you had not anticipated, and some of these may suggest ideas for improving the search. When you see an option that seems close to the one you were expecting, try it. Sometimes you will find something useful.

Keyword Searches

You can, of course, start right out with a keyword search if you feel rather confident about your topic and hypothesis. But however you arrive at the keyword search stage, this is the point when the element of skill enters the game. You must select a few specific words for the search engine to use when scanning the Web. In making the selection, you will want to find ways to establish the range of the search. This helps you avoid finding too many possible sites to visit as well as finding the wrong ones.

Learning how to select the very best keywords requires a good deal of thought and experience. The most important basic skill is the ability to think of synonyms for the words that first come to mind, because quite often the search engine will do its job a lot better when you substitute another term for the one you had thought was just fine. This is a skill that you must learn on your own, but here are several general guidelines that can be learned quickly.

- *Use quotation marks around keywords to create a phrase*—"affirmative action"; "capital punishment"; "federal reserve bank"; "working class." The engine will search for only those situations where the words within the phrase appear together in that order. Personal and geographic names are recognized by the computer without using quotation marks, for example, George Bush, Bill Gates, Gloria Steinem, New Jersey, Central America.

- *Use AND between keywords to narrow the search.* For example,

    "U.S. Grant" AND "Lincoln" AND "Civil War" AND "strategy"

    would help you find those sources that tied Lincoln, Grant, and the war together in terms of the strategy used to win it. Each term by itself would have brought you thousands of responses. (Some search engines allow you to use the + sign or & for AND.)

- *Use OR between keywords to broaden the search.* For example,

    "African American" OR "Negro" OR "Blacks" AND "segregation"

    would help you find sources that deal with "segregation and black people," no matter what term the writers used to identify that group when discussing segregation. (Some search engines allow you to use the | sign for OR.)

- *Use NOT between keywords to narrow the search* if your search engine offers this option. For example,

    "affirmative action" AND "universities" AND "women"

    would give you sources that deal with policies promoting equal opportunity for women in universities, but

    "affirmative action" AND "universities" NOT "women"

    would seek out only those sources that deal with groups other than women who are affected by these policies. (Some search engines allow you to use the – sign for NOT.)

In doing an online keyword search, the most likely problem will be that your first probe will yield far too many possibilities. Someone investigating the topic *government funding of AIDS research*, for example, might just type in *AIDS* and hope for the best. Let's see what happened when a student new to using such a high-powered research tool did this:

1. When the student entered *AIDS*, he received a message saying that the search engine had located more than 9,000 "hits," or sites and sources that include the term. Stunned, he asked advice of a fellow student, who suggested he think of another term to help focus the search.

Searching for Sources

2. Slightly misunderstanding the advice, he typed *U.S. government* and found that the number of hits was astronomical.

3. Someone then showed him how to use AND to look for the two terms, *AIDS* and *U.S. government*, at the same time. This move resulted in a more manageable number of hits, around 600.

4. Adding *research* to the other two terms brought the number of potential sources down to 125, which seemed a manageable number because a good many of them were not available in full online or through the student's college library anyway.

When you come up with such a list, print it using whatever command the particular computer system employs. If no printer is available (or working at the time), you must write down those titles that seem most promising and come back later if they do not prove sufficient.

Whenever your search yields too few seemingly good potential sources, you can take one of two courses of action:

- *Vary your choice of keywords.* For example, instead of *AIDS*, try *acquired immune deficiency syndrome*. Instead of *research*, try *studies*.

- *Try another search engine.* Each search engine has its own peculiarities, including the range of databases it is designed to search and place in its index.

Some Leading Search Engines

AltaVista   *http://www.altavista.com*
Offers a help screen that shows you how to focus your search when you've found an unmanageable number of potential sources, but does not let you use more than one phrase—"affirmative action"—in the same search.

Infoseek   *http://infoseek.go.com*
Offers brief abstracts and quoted phrases that provide insight as to the nature of the information found at each site.

Lycos   *http://www.lycos.com*
Covers by far the greatest number of sites on the Internet and provides an abstract for each site.

Deja.com   *http://www.deja.com*
Searches over 50,000 sites of Usenet groups (see Chapter 8). Offers four modes of searching, including "power search," which helps you learn more about any authors whom you feel uncertain about as authoritative sources.

Britannica.com   *http://britannica.com*
Searches the Web and the online version of the *Encyclopædia Britannica*. Rates its findings according to the authority of the authors, among other criteria, and helps you to refine searches.

WebCrawler   *http://www.webcrawler.com*
Reputedly the fastest search engine. Does not give abstracts, but a summary of a site may be available by clicking on a button on the WebCrawler home page.

Yahoo!   *http://www.yahoo.com*
Starts with subject areas and proceeds to narrow the search one level at a time, a feature that can be helpful when you are not sure of where to go with a topic.

New search engines are continually being developed, the more recent ones tending to be directed at special fields of study, such as *http://wwwomen.com* for women's studies.

Resources for Advanced Internet Users

Before there was a World Wide Web, researchers on the Internet had to use several older protocols, such as gopher, FTP, and telnet. These protocols do not use hypertext, so instead of beginning with *http://*, URLs for the materials they provide access to start with *gopher, ftp,* or *telnet.* Most of these materials have been incorporated into the Web, but those of you who enjoy expertise with the computer and have a fair amount of patience for relatively slow retrieval methods may want to venture into these areas.

Gopher stores vast amounts of information in layers, so that you pursue your objective by moving from the very general to the more specific, one stage (menu) at a time. (Gopher got its name in part because it burrows deeper and deeper into layers of information.) If your college has a gopher system, follow the screen instructions to access the system. If an Internet search returns an address that starts with *gopher://*, once you click on that address, you will see instructions for navigating the menus.

FTP (file transfer protocol) lets you download (transfer) files from another computer into yours. *Full-service FTP* lets you transfer files between any computers for which you have passwords or access privileges. *Anonymous (restricted-access) FTP* lets you retrieve only publicly available files from archives of text, music, or art.

Many Internet sites allow you to access their files through gopher or the Web, and then to use FTP to copy or print what you find. Depending on the type of information you are seeking and your mode of access, learning FTP could be very valuable as a means of collecting documents.

Searching for Sources

Be sure to consult a librarian to learn how to use this resource because the method varies from place to place.

The *telnet (telephone network)* protocol provides access to other computer databases, where you will be working with directories and menus, from general to most specific. In effect, telnet connects your computer to another and makes it possible to use that computer as if it were your own. The procedure of telnetting differs from one computer network to the next, so you need to follow the directions posted at your location or ask for help. Today many library Web sites will switch you into telnet mode as you enter their catalogs. There is no need to worry about procedures because the libraries' home pages take you through the process step by step on the screen. One of the addresses for Princeton University's library, for example, is <telnet://libserv5.princeton.edu>.

Complete Guides to the Internet and the World Wide Web

The Internet is a huge, complex, and rapidly expanding system, and new ways of successfully mining its resources are continually being developed. These two guides will be useful if you have the time and interest to explore them:

- *Online! A Reference Guide to Using Internet Sources* by Andrew Harnack and Eugene Kleppinger (Bedford/St. Martin's, 2000) Web site: <http://www.bedfordstmartins.com/online>
- *The Research Paper and the World Wide Web* by Dawn Rodrigues and Raymond J. Rodrigues (Prentice Hall, 2000) Web site: <http://www.prenhall.com/rodrigues>

8

Planning a Strategy
for Web Research

The Internet covers all conceivable aspects of human knowledge. So before starting your research, it is wise to lay out a reasonable framework within which to operate. To avoid becoming lost in the vast amount of information that makes up the World Wide Web, plan your approach keeping specific research goals clearly in mind. Frame your strategy much the way you would if you were forced to rely solely on printed materials that can be obtained in libraries. Begin by weighing the advantages of each of the major sources of information—books, periodicals, and the Web's discussion groups, where you can readily contact other persons who share your interest in the research paper's subject.

The Web does not generally offer access to whole books, although you can read reviews and commentaries about recently published books, and these can often be helpful. Several periodicals—journals, magazines, and newspapers—appear online. In addition, many institutions, organizations, and individuals have set up reliable Web sites that provide a huge range of material that can be useful when writing a research paper. The unique contribution of the Web, however, lies in the access it provides to discussion groups, which are unavailable to researchers relying only on print sources. These are especially useful for topics of current interest, comparable to periodicals with the added dimension that you can not only "listen" to conversations about your research topic but also send requests for information to all the people who participate in the discussion group. The student who wrote on "fire ants" did just this.

Each of the three approaches—books, periodicals, and the Web—comes with a few disadvantages. The main drawback to the Web concerns the reliability of the information you come across in discussion groups and other online sites. We will describe ways to cope with this factor later in this chapter. For now, though, think of Web research in terms of a three-part strategy:

1. Go to the *Readers' Guide to Periodic Literature* and work up a list of potential sources that can be found in periodicals that appear online.

2. You may want to broaden the scope of the search beyond sources indexed in the *Readers' Guide* and yet not be ready to join discussion groups about your research topic. In that case, you need to become familiar with the use of the subject directories and keyword searches to find Web sites of individuals and organizations that could provide information relevant to your topic. (We've offered guidelines for both of these procedures in Chapter 7.)

3. You may want to become involved personally, or at least cyber-personally, with a group of people who are knowledgeable about your topic. Once you become connected to a discussion group, you can direct specific questions to other participants, some of whom will be happy to answer any intelligent questions or at least offer advice as to where you might find the answers.

Online Periodicals

For topics that call for periodical articles, your library can occasionally prove frustrating, either because it does not subscribe to a print periodical in which a potential source appears, or because the copy of a periodical you need has been stolen or vandalized by other readers. (Newspapers, such as the *New York Times,* can usually be read on microfilm viewers, but journals and magazines are generally not available on film.) When you encounter such problems, you will find that, in some cases, the items you want to read can be accessed via the Internet. As a matter of fact, working with periodical articles on the Internet rather than using their print form has several advantages:

- You can find potential sources much more quickly, either by using online indexes for individual periodicals or by doing a keyword search.

- You can print a copy of whatever you see on the screen. This saves making photocopies. You can also download a copy onto your own diskette, for later use.

- Of course, the item you need will not have been removed by another reader.

On the other hand, using the Internet for periodical research suffers from some drawbacks:

- Usually you will find only the most recent years' issues online, and some periodicals, of course, are not available at all.
- In rare cases, you will be required to pay a small fee for downloading.

When you are working with periodicals that appear both in print and online, what you see on the screen may be somewhat different from what appeared in the printed version of the periodical. Often the online version will include more information, such as links to related articles or other Web sites. Sometimes, though, the online version is just a shorter form of the print article, or even worse, an abstract. But the text on the screen should tell you this.

Journals

When working with journals online, you have two ways to proceed. If you know the name of a journal in your subject area, such as *Journal of the American Medical Association* or *Scientific American,* use the title in your keyword search. If you want to learn the names of online journals in your subject area, you can look in a subject directory or do a keyword search.

To use a subject directory, go to a search engine that provides subject areas on its home page; then click on your subject, and then on "journals." You will soon see a list of available journals, if any exist.

To conduct a keyword search, type in your subject area plus the word "journals."

If you are primarily interested in journals that are collected in libraries, use UnCover, an online database of over eight million journal articles, which permits you to do keyword searches by author, title, and subject. In addition, copies of articles can be faxed to you within a very short period of time. Unfortunately the faxing will cost you ten to fifteen dollars per article. But at least you can use this service as an index, giving you a head start on the journals located in your own library. UnCover's URL is <http://uncweb.carl.org>.

Magazines

Again, if you know the name of a magazine that seems certain to have articles on your topic, such as *Atlantic Monthly* or *Discover,* enter the title in a keyword search. An index will help you find whatever might be helpful in your research. If you want to discover potential sources wherever they may be, you can use several directories to find them in online magazines, for example:

Searching for Sources

| Electric Library | <http://www.elibrary.com> |
| NewsDirectory.com | <http://www.newsdirectory.com> |

Newspapers

Major newspapers, like the *New York Times,* the *Washington Post,* and the *Wall Street Journal,* have established their own Web sites, for example, <http://www.nytimes.com>. Although going online may be a less cumbersome way to consult newspaper articles than working with microfilm, the microfilm version gives you exact copies of each paper rather than versions modified for the Web site.

Accessing Library Catalogs

Today most major libraries have made their catalogs available online, allowing the public to search their collections of books and other resources. In Chapter 4, we discussed searching your college library catalog online. You can also search the catalogs of other libraries for items that could be borrowed, either directly or though interlibrary loans. Your college library's Web page may even include links to other university and major public libraries. In some cases, you can view the texts on screen.

The Library of Congress, which contains a copy of every book ever copyrighted in the United States, not only allows you to search its catalog by every means—word, phrase, title, author, subject—but also offers some texts in full, as well as information about its exhibitions and congressional activities. To reach this library, go to <http://www.loc.gov>.

To learn what libraries from all over the world have sites on the Web, try one of these sites:

| LIBCAT | <http://www.metronet.lib.mn.us/lc> |
| LIBWEB | <http://sunsite.berkeley.edu/libweb> |

Organizational and Topical Web Sites

Beyond information about books and full texts of articles, the Internet offers access to material made available on Web sites set up by academic institutions, corporations, government agencies, nonprofit organizations, and individuals. These Web sites can offer material ranging from information about the work these organizations and corporations do, to laws, speeches, and press releases, to texts of historical and literary documents, and to links to a multitude of other documents and related Web sites.

You can use search engines to do keyword and subject directory searches to find Web sites relevant to your topic. For example, if you were investigating trends in U.S. immigration in the twentieth century, you could go to the Ellis Island site <http://www.ellisisland.org> to learn about some immigrants' experiences in the early part of the century and to the U.S. Immigration and Naturalization Service Web site <http://www.ins.usdoj.gov> to learn about current policies and to research records of people who have become naturalized citizens. These sites provide fast and easy access to government and historical documents that your library may not have in its collections. You could also investigate advocacy groups that are working on immigration issues by visiting the Web sites of nonprofit organizations such as Human Rights Watch <http://www.hrw.org>.

Some sites can give you access to texts and pictures that you would otherwise have to travel long distances to examine in person. Such sites contain electronic texts of well-known as well as obscure literary works and digital images of famous works of art. For example, if your topic were African American slave narratives, you could read full texts of rarely found books and essays at a Web site called African American Women Writers of the 19th Century <http://digital.nypl.org/schomburg/writers_aa19>. If you were researching an art history topic, you could view more than 3,500 works of art at the Web site of the Metropolitan Museum of Art in New York <http://www.metmuseum.org>.

Discussion Groups

Discussion groups are just what the name suggests—large-scale electronic seminars or forums devoted to a particular topic, ranging anywhere from *The X-Files* to *ecology* to *computer software* to *teaching English*. When you join such a group, you will be in contact with people all over the planet who share an interest in that subject. Discussion groups fall into two main categories: *mailing lists* and *newsgroups.*

Discussion groups are likely to prove most beneficial as research tools for those who are actively engaged in a particular academic discipline. Much of the value comes from listening in on the conversations of other people who are thinking out loud about questions in their chosen fields. Of course, when you have joined a newsgroup or mailing list, you will eventually want to add your own two cents to the dialogue. And, when working on a research paper, you can ask questions, knowing that someone out there will give you an interesting and possibly valuable response.

In addition, discussion groups can be useful for:

- getting leads about additional sources for your topic
- doing field research, such as sampling public opinion

Mailing Lists

Mailing lists, also known as *listservs,* give you the chance to communicate via e-mail with a group of people who share your interests in a topic. Messages (comments, questions, answers) go to a central computer called a *list server,* which then relays the messages to everyone who has subscribed to the list. You can, however, choose to respond either to the individual sender of a message or to everyone.

Once you know the name of a list you want to join, send an e-mail to the host to find out how to subscribe to it. The procedure may be as simple as stating "subscribe (list's name) (your name)." (There's no reason to mention your e-mail address because it automatically accompanies any e-mail you write.) If you first need to see what lists are available on your topic, you can write to a list server.

One of our students, Mary Kim, was researching the possible connection between breast cancer and diet. To find discussion groups relating to cancer, she sent this message:

> To: listserv@listserv.net
> Subject: send list
> Message: list global/cancer

When she received by return e-mail the names of six cancer-related discussion groups, she chose the one dealing with breast cancer, of course. This was her next message:

> To: listserv@listserv.net
> Subject: (leave blank)
> Message: subscribe breast-cancer Mary Kim

In a few minutes, she received an e-mail response stating, "Your subscription to BREAST-CANCER list (breast-cancer discussion list) has been accepted." She also received a description of the group's purpose and guidelines for participating in the discussion. Instructions for canceling the subscription were also included. Mary saved these to use when her research was ended.

Newsgroups

For those just beginning to wrestle with research papers, newsgroups are more likely to yield results. David Perez, writing on "fire ants," contacted two such groups, as you can see at the close of this chapter.

Newsgroups operate slightly differently from mailing lists. Here all the messages go to a "bulletin board," and you have to go to it every time you want to see what has been posted. With a mailing list, the messages go to your PC and are kept on file there, just like all your other e-mail.

This might seem quite convenient, but if a huge backlog of these messages starts to accumulate, you may wish you were using a newsgroup so that you could thumb through the postings without having to erase them as you move along. On the other hand, in a newsgroup, the server removes "old" messages every so often, forcing you to keep an eye on changes. Be sure to copy anything that seems useful before it is erased.

For a schedule of newsgroup lists, you can visit the Deja.com Web site at <http://www.deja.com>.

Warning: Some browsers are not set up for accessing newsgroups. If your browser lacks this service, you can access the newsgroups directly from the Web via <http://metalab.unc.edu/usenet-i/>, which also gives you the opportunity to browse the Usenet groups or to search for a particular Usenet group. ("Usenet" is an old term covering all newsgroups as a systemic activity.)

A Few Words of Caution

- *Be sure to frame any questions you ask a discussion group fairly specifically.* David Perez would not have gotten very far if he had merely asked, "Can anyone tell me about fire ants?"

- *Be careful not to ask an obvious question.* Such a question would be one that the group members assume everyone in the group already knows the answer to. To avoid being "flamed" by an angry participant for asking such a question, look at the group's home page and find the FAQ link. Click on it and read the most Frequently Asked Questions and their answers so that you won't look foolish.

- *Remember that discussion groups are not always reliable sources of information.* The information is usually not reviewed by editors before publication, the way information in books, scholarly journals, and magazines is. Although some groups edit postings, mainly to exclude offensive or inappropriate material, generally anyone can write almost anything to these groups.

Evaluating Online Sources

Our warning about the possible unreliability of information obtained from discussion groups applies to many other kinds of online sources as well. The main difference between online sources and those found in print lies in the publisher. When a source has been published as a book or periodical, editors have usually checked the authors' credentials and tried to determine the reliability of their work. To be sure, some people who write books and articles are concerned more about their writing's public appeal than about its accuracy. But these works can be validated in two ways: by the author's reputation in the field, and by the reputation of the periodical or publisher. The *Newark Star-Ledger* is clearly far more reputable than some scandal "newspaper" you see at the checkout counter in a supermarket. With magazines such as *People* and *Discover*, the first falls into the "popular" category, whereas the latter is a most authoritative publication. Appearances usually signal the reliability or lack of it; a magazine *can* be judged by its cover. A librarian or your teacher can settle any questions you may have.

With the Internet, making such judgments is not so easy. Any member of a discussion group and any person or group who has taken the trouble to establish a Web site can make statements that reflect uninformed opinions and organizational agendas rather than expert judgment and established knowledge.

Of course, the general guidelines we outline in Chapter 10 that apply to all sources of information—coverage, currency, bias, and so on—are equally important for Internet sources. In addition, here are some specific guidelines to consider when deciding whether or not an online source can be trusted:

- If a Web site domain includes .edu or .gov, you can feel somewhat safe (unless, like Fox Mulder, you suspect anything with a .gov label). You need to watch out for .edu addresses that contain the tilde (~) in the middle, however, because that symbol signifies a personal account within the university and could be one assigned to anyone connected with the institution, not just the faculty. The .com domain might seem dubious because "commercial" makes you think you are being sold a product or service. But most periodicals are commercial, and many are among the most reliable sources. So, you need to keep on your toes, asking your teacher any time you are in doubt about a source.
- The search engines Yahoo! and Magellan <http://mckinley.netcom.com> mark their "strongest" sites with asterisks (*), and Britannica.com uses a star system to the same effect.
- If there is a "last modified" date at the end of the source, note how recent it is.
- Check the background of the source:
  - Has the writer been published in print? Was that publication authoritative?
  - Is the name one you have seen mentioned in sources known to be reliable?
  - Is there a link to the writer's home page? If so, make the detour and look for the writer's credentials and what else the writer has published. *You may also find other useful sources there.*
  - Check out any other links you find connected to the source.

- You can always try to corroborate information by going to reliable online or print sources.

A Student Uses the Internet in His Research

David Perez enrolled in a course called Current Issues in Ecology, which required him to write a paper on one of three subjects. He selected *the disruptive effects of a transplanted species on its new environment.* Of course, this could not become a topic until he thought of a particular species to investigate. From the course readings, David remembered being interested in the way some ants, such as army ants, invade territories, often wreaking havoc on their neighbors. In discussing this possibility with his instructor, David learned that army ants cannot be considered "transplanted" when they march across the landscape. But the instructor did say that ants would be a good choice. David needed to find a species that had severely affected an ecosystem after having been transplanted by some human agent from one part of the world to another.

David began his research by consulting his college library's encyclopedia, which had recently become available on CD-ROM. His reading about ants in general was not immediately fruitful, but the encyclopedia's index listed entries for specific kinds of ants as well, including one for *fire ants.* In reading this entry, David learned that the red fire ant (*Solenopsis invicta* in Latin), a native of South America, had accidentally been carried, probably on a freighter, to a port in the southeastern United States. Over the years it had spread out across that part of the country, creating a number of problems in its new ecosystem. The article included a bibliography referring to *The Ants,* a book by B. Holldobler and E. O. Wilson. David was able to find this book in the library.

While reading the book, David had to struggle through a fair amount of highly technical information about fire ants in general before he found several comments about *S. invicta,* his target species, that would definitely fit into his paper. However, other books on ants had nothing on *S. invicta,* so David's next step was to look for periodical articles.

Soon, however, David realized that because the fire ant had been causing trouble for the last twenty years, he might have to search through a great many volumes of the *Readers' Guide to Periodical Literature* before finding all the information he needed. He turned for help to a librarian, who suggested that David do three things: (1) use the computer terminal to access databases for his periodical search, (2) browse the World Wide Web to see if any relevant information appeared there, and (3) join an Internet discussion group to see if he could contact some ant experts.

David went over to the student computer center, where he was assigned a free account that allowed him access to the Internet. In addition, he got some advice from a student technician about which newsgroups might meet his needs. Two groups—*alt.sci.misc* and *alt.sci.ecology*—seemed likely candidates, so he joined both groups. Looking over the various postings for each group, he thought that the second one might yield better results. As it turned out, he was right.

After posting his question to the *alt.sci.ecology* group, David knew he could not expect answers for at least a day or two. While waiting, he followed the librarian's advice and did some research in the library's online resources. David began by choosing a database for periodicals. The search process involved thinking of several keywords that, when combined into a single typed entry, would find what he wanted as fast as possible. The words he selected were *fire ant* and *ecology*. So, following the procedure for the particular database he was using, he typed the command K="fire ant" and "ecology."

Almost immediately he found a reference to an article in *Science*, a major scientific journal. After reading the abstract that appeared on the computer screen, David decided he needed to read the entire article. Fortunately his library subscribed to this journal, which was available on microfilm. A microform reader allowed David to photocopy the article for a small charge.

Another database took David into all the newspapers in the library system. (Newspapers are periodicals, to be sure, but this system separated newspapers from journals and magazines.) Using the same three keywords, he was rewarded with two articles on *S. invicta*. The first dealt with a town in Brazil that had had to be evacuated due to a red fire ant infestation; the second told of an escaped convict who had happily returned to jail after spending forty-eight hours in the woods being stung by these ants.

Although David was amused by the convict's story, he decided it did not belong in a scientific paper focusing on the ant's disruption of an ecosystem. The first article did not apply to the fire ant's activities in the United States, the ecosystem to which it had been transplanted. However, if the creature could cause great distress in a human community, clearly it could do much worse harm to less advanced creatures in its ecosystem. So David knew he was on the right track.

Two days after posting his questions to the Internet groups, David received several e-mail responses. One of these messages proved to be very useful. Nadine Cavender, associate director of the Ecological Society of America, could not offer firsthand information, but she forwarded a press release issued by the Department of Agricultural Journalism at the University of Wisconsin–Madison. The press release reported in detail a study done in Texas that showed how the red fire ant had drastically reduced the numbers of northern bobwhite quail living in its neighborhood. David had struck gold—a very recent scientific article describing the devastating effects of *S. invicta* on an indigenous species.

David now decided to find out whether the World Wide Web had any sites relating to this topic. He accessed the Web through Netscape Navigator, a Web browser (see Figure 8-1). To browse the Web, David would have to use one or more search engines. He decided he would begin by typing "fire ants." If that term turned out to be too specific and did not lead to any information, he might try related keywords such as *insects, environment,* and *ecology.*

David chose Lycos as his search engine. In a box in the upper part of the screen (not visible in Figure 8-1), he typed Lycos's URL:

http://www.lycos.com

Soon the Lycos logo materialized on screen, and the words "Search for:" invited him to type in the keyword or keywords he wanted to use in his search (see Figure 8-2). David typed in "fire ants" and pressed the

Figure 8-1   A section of the Netscape Navigator home page.

enter key. In a minute or two, a list of documents appeared on the screen (see Figure 8-3). These were the first four of the many documents linked to Lycos that contain the words "fire ants."

Surveying the list, David discovered that some of the documents seemed likely sources of information for his paper, whereas others were related to his topic only distantly or not at all. For example, one item was a link to a comic strip involving ants! Knowing his time was limited, David decided to concentrate on his topic and double-clicked on the first item on the list.

David now realized that this article was part of an online journal called *EcoLink*. Although the article was rather specialized for his purposes, he used the Print command to print out its text. He then selected the Go menu at the top of his computer screen and clicked on the Back command until he had returned to the list of Lycos documents. Two of the documents (including item 4 in Figure 8-3) appear as sources in his paper.

David could have used other search engines to come up with still other materials. (He would also have found that some of the search en-

Figure 8-2   A section of the Lycos home page. Lycos allows users to search the Web by subject category or by keyword.

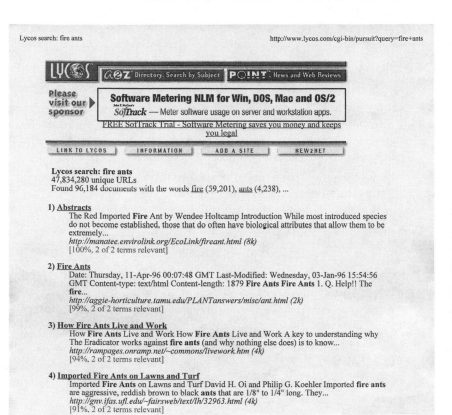

Figure 8-3   A partial listing of the documents located by a Lycos keyword search. Each item gives information about the document's contents as well as the URL at which it can be found.

gines led to the documents he had already read via Lycos.) However, he decided that he now had enough material for his paper.

Thus we see how a student was able to use the Internet to supplement a standard library search. We advise you to become familiar with the Internet because it can be a powerful tool in the writing of research papers.

Reviewing Part Two

Questions

1. Suppose you are looking for a particular biography of Queen Elizabeth I of England, *Elizabeth the First* by Paul Johnson. How can you find this book in the library catalog? How can the catalog help you locate other books about Queen Elizabeth?

2. How is each of these pieces of information, found in entries in the library catalog, useful to researchers?

   author   date of publication

   title   number of pages

   subject   notation about a bibliography

   call number

3. What kinds of materials are listed in periodical indexes? Why might a researcher need to use several different indexes?

4. For each of the following topics, what additional resources (besides library books and periodical articles from indexes) might you look for?

   • the latest government recommendations about energy conservation

   • a seventeenth-century book (all known copies are owned by British libraries)

   • the inaugural address of President John F. Kennedy

   • the kinds of jobs accepted by recent graduates of your school

   • the history of the town in which your college is located

   • your city's model program for pest control

   • the major works of a particular artist

   • the position on a controversial issue taken last week by the governor

5. Which three features of the Internet seem most likely to be useful in a research project such as the one you are planning to conduct?

6. What is a URL? If you have a topic but not a URL related to that topic, what can you do to find information on that topic via the Internet?

7. Why is it highly unlikely that you could effectively search the Internet without talking with librarians? In consulting these people, what questions would you be likely to ask?

8. What might be the greatest problem with relying on sources from discussion groups? What steps can be taken to address the problem?

Exercises

1. Use the library catalog to look up a fairly recent work of fiction by a well-known author. Consult the library's classification guide to find the shelf where the book should be located. Use the *Book Review Digest* to find out if the book was reviewed during the year it was published or the following year. Report your findings.

2. Using microfilms of the *New York Times*, find the most important story reported on the day and year you were born. (The "lead" story is usually in the upper right corner of the front page.) Then, in the *New York Times Index*, find a listing for this article and the next *Times* article on the same subject. Copy both listings, converting all abbreviations to the full forms of the words that they represent.

3. Use the *Readers' Guide to Periodical Literature* to locate an article published during the past year, offering an opinion or commentary about your favorite hobby, pastime, or field of interest. Check your library's catalog to find the periodical that contains the article. Read the article, determine the author's topic and thesis, and explain briefly why you agree or disagree with this thesis.

4. Choose one of the topics listed under Question 2 in Reviewing Part One questions. Do a subject search in the library catalog to find the titles of three books related to the topic. Write out these titles and their call numbers, and describe briefly where in the library each is located.

5. Think of a fairly specific topic in psychology or medical science that interests you. Use the *Social Science Index* to discover how many articles have been written on that topic during the past three years. Record appropriate article and journal titles and any other information provided in the index description. Convert all abbreviations to the full forms of the words they represent.

6. Look up one of the listed topics in a subject directory on the Internet (using the information in Chapter 7 as a guideline) and write a one-page summary of what you find out about the topic. Do not merely list each subheading displayed on the menu. Describe how the menu is organized and what areas the topic is divided into, giving examples of the more minor features. Include in the summary a one-paragraph description of what you found in a particularly interesting subheading (file).

    *   the Holocaust
    *   *The X-Files*
    *   the NFL, LPGA, or WNBA, or major league baseball
    *   tennis, golf, bowling, or bridge

- diets
- addictions
- Italian cooking, Chinese cooking, or the like
- gay and lesbian issues
- Native American issues
- AIDS
- Sweden
- cats, dogs, horses, or tropical fish
- hunting or fishing
- Israel
- terrorism
- men's or women's fashion
- UFOs
- silicone implants
- senior citizens' issues
- JFK
- Nixon
- Vietnam
- ants, bees, or spiders
- snakes or sharks
- group therapies

7. Use the Internet to find five sources for one or more of the following topics:
   - the effect of corporate downsizing on blue-collar workers
   - groups that deny the reality of the Nazi Holocaust
   - the authenticity of scientific concepts appearing on *The X-Files*
   - the effect of the anti-terrorism bill of 1996 on legal immigrants and naturalized citizens
   - the effect of the government's farm subsidy bills on small farmers during the last fifty years

8. Set up your own e-mail account and use it to ask your teacher for advice at least once while writing your research paper.

9. Join an interesting mailing list or newsgroup and report (in a couple of pages) on what issues seem to concern the group's members most.

10. Think ahead to possible uses of the Internet in your research project. Draw up a step-by-step plan of action for using the Internet as a resource for your research paper.

Part Three

Working with Sources

Working with Sources

9

Developing a Working Bibliography

Now that you have a good idea of the research aids available in your library, you can begin the process of searching for sources by developing a *working bibliography*—a fairly long list of possible sources for your paper. These titles may have come from the *Readers' Guide to Periodical Literature*, from the library catalog, from the Internet, or from bibliographies you saw in your background reading. Ultimately, you will use some of the information you find in these sources to support the thesis of your paper. Those sources that provide specific ideas and information for the paper will be listed in your *final bibliography*, which will be called Works Cited or References.

Setting Up the Working Bibliography

To begin putting together a working bibliography, decide on a format for recording information about possible sources. You could use three- by five-inch note cards for *bibliography cards*, or you might want to set up a computer file or note-taking software. Then, whenever you come across the title of a book or article that seems worth checking into, make a bibliography entry for it.

If you use cards, create a separate card for each item, and keep the cards in alphabetical order. Cards are handier for this purpose than a simple list because they can more easily be kept in order as you add and drop items from your working bibliography. If you are working with a word processor, you can keep these bibliographical notes in a special file, which you will constantly be updating. Some commercial note-taking software programs allow you to create separate entries for each source you consult, which you can search and sort by various keywords. The file you generate will, after you have pruned its contents, produce the Works Cited section of the final paper.

If your library catalog allows you to print entries as you search, you can save time in gathering your working bibliography. Similarly, you might be able to print results from electronic database searches. You can print out and organize lists of sources produced by a particular keyword, or separate each entry and sort, drop, and add entries alphabetically as you would cards. Be careful, though, not to find yourself collecting just any source you come across because of the convenience of printing.

Some libraries allow you to send an e-mail to yourself or to download to a diskette results from catalog and database searches. You can then easily add the results to your computer file or print out the entries and file them like cards. Before you rely on downloading or e-mailing search results, be sure the computer entries contain all the information you will need to locate the book or article. You ought to test the system before you do an extensive search to be sure you can successfully retrieve downloaded and e-mailed entries.

For a working bibliography entry to be useful, it must contain all the information you will need when you prepare the footnotes or endnotes and the Works Cited or References list for your paper. In addition, the entry should give you whatever information is needed to find the book or article in the library.

Books

To make an entry for a *book,* record the following information (see Figure 9-1):

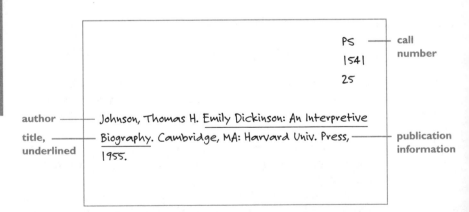

Figure 9-1   Bibliography card for a book.

- name of the author and/or the editor, last name first
- title and subtitle of the book, underlined
- place of publication
- publisher's name
- date of publication
- library call number (in upper right corner)

Periodicals

For a *periodical article,* follow this guide (see Figure 9-2):

- name of the author
- title of the article (in quotation marks)
- title of the periodical (underlined)
- volume number and date of publication
- numbers of the pages on which the article appears
- location in a library

If you are using cards, be sure to place in the upper right corner of every bibliography card the library call number or other "locator" information from the library catalog. If you are using computer files, place the locator information at the top of the entry. Whatever method you use, take extra care to copy all bibliographical information accurately. Misspellings, incorrect punctuation, careless omissions, and other mistakes in copying can waste time in return trips to the library.

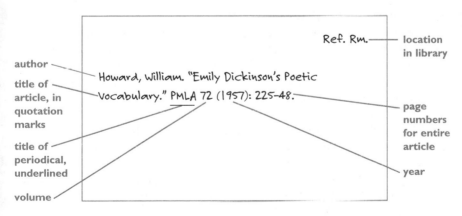

Figure 9-2   Bibliography card for a periodical article.

Gathering Potential Sources

You will almost always collect more titles for your working bibliography than will appear in your final list of Works Cited or References because many potential sources will, on closer reading, prove to be no help in the investigation of your hypothesis. The problem is that when you are looking through the library catalog or a periodical index, you must try to judge the value of a book or an article by its title alone or by the heading under which you found it. Because you do not want to miss a potentially useful source, you must add to your working bibliography every title that sounds even slightly promising.

Of course, quite a few of these potential sources will turn out to be worthless for your purposes, so your working bibliography will shrink accordingly. However, while you are dropping disappointing items from your list, you may be adding titles that are mentioned in the useful sources. You should, therefore, expect to be adding and dropping potential sources from your working bibliography throughout your research.

Four Students Gather Their Sources

Fred Hutchins began assembling a working bibliography while reading background sources about Cotton Mather. First, he came across several potentially useful titles at the end of the encyclopedia article on Cotton Mather. He then went to the library catalog to learn whether those titles were available in his library. Three books were available, two of which yielded information that helped support his eventual thesis. Furthermore, all three books contained bibliographies that led to other useful sources. From these sources, Fred was able to acquire a sizable working bibliography before he began a methodical search through the library catalog and periodical indexes.

Once he had followed up these early leads, Fred went back to the catalog. He did keyword searches using the subject headings that were related to his topic, such as "Mather, Cotton," and "Puritans and Massachusetts." Then, following up on clues from the background reading he had done, Fred did a keyword search for sources on "witchcraft" and then "witchcraft and New England."

Fred rejected a number of items, such as Christina Larner's *Enemies of God: The Witch-hunt in Scotland,* because their titles indicated nothing that applied to the Salem witch trials. However, he made out bibliography entries for any title that seemed likely to prove useful. Later, when he examined each of these books closely, he eliminated most of them from his working bibliography because they turned out to be general overviews or surveys, much like those in textbooks, which repeated the same basic facts about Mather and his relationship to the Salem witch trials.

Finally, Fred searched through several periodical indexes, looking under "Mather, Cotton," and other relevant headings. Some titles clearly indicated little or no relationship to the witch trials, so Fred left them off his working bibliography. Others sounded vaguely useful, but these, too, Fred later rejected—either because they did not relate directly to his topic or because the information they provided had already been recorded in his notes. In the end, Fred used two periodical articles as sources. One was extremely valuable for its brief discussions and analyses of several theories attempting to explain the Salem witchcraft outbreak; the other provided information about an important subtopic in Fred's final paper.

Do not be misled by Fred's using just two periodical articles in his paper. His case is fairly unusual. Many papers, especially those dealing with topics in the sciences and the social sciences, list more articles than books as sources. (For example, see David Perez's paper on fire ants in Chapter 21.)

The student who researched the economic and social impact of new immigrants on the United States used the same basic strategies for gathering sources but with somewhat different results. Shirley's Works Cited list contains five essays from two books of collected essays, five books that discuss immigration from particular viewpoints, one periodical article, and one personal interview. Along the way, Shirley interviewed more than twenty other people and sampled a number of books that told of the experiences of individual immigrants, past and present, in their struggles to find security and success in America. She found most of these interesting and some of them quite moving. In the end, however, she decided that they were too personal and too subjective for the kind of general paper she had in mind.

The student who researched Emily Dickinson used the same basic strategies for gathering sources but again with somewhat different results. Susanna's final list of Works Cited contains several books about Dickinson's life and works, two periodical articles (one of which she found online), an essay from a collection of literary criticism, two collections of the poet's works, and a collection of the poet's letters. Along the way, she skimmed numerous other books and articles, but most of these contained analyses of Dickinson's poems, with no useful references to the poet's life.

David Perez's experience was far less extensive because the scope of his assignment was restricted to a "report" rather than an open-ended research paper.

The search for sources is a journey into the unknown that tests your imagination, perseverance, and ability to plan. Sometimes this search can be frustrating because many clues lead nowhere and seem to waste your time. But do not try to save time by hastily rejecting items whose titles do

Working with Sources

not indicate a clear and immediate relation to your topic. Always follow up on ambiguous clues. *The possible source that is discarded unseen may be the one that could have helped you the most.*

Reassessing Your Topic

While searching for sources, you may reach a point where you doubt the topic is workable, either because you are finding far too many potential sources or because you have found too few. If, after several hours of intensive searching through various indexes as well as the library catalog and the Internet, you have discovered only two or three *possible* sources, your topic needs to be broadened. On the other hand, if you quickly find dozens of potential sources, you need to reduce the scope of the topic and/or sharpen the focus of your hypothesis. If when searching the library catalog you discover that many potential sources have been checked out or are in periodicals to which your library does not subscribe, you might want to consider refocusing your topic.

We hesitate to talk in terms of specific numbers because the number of sources does not directly indicate how much information you have collected. You might take a couple of pieces of information from just one or two paragraphs in one source, and then take more than a dozen lengthy notes from an entire chapter in another source. The crucial question is whether you have enough sources. Your research cannot be considered complete unless you provide a full range of points of view.

Narrowing a Topic That Is Too Broad

We saw how one student limited his subject—*Cotton Mather*—to a reasonable topic—*Mather's complicated role in the witch trials*—after a conference with his instructor and a background reading session in the library. Fred had some familiarity with his subject, which made it easy for him to take full advantage of the advice he received. However, another student, who knew relatively little about her subject—*abnormal psychology*—ran into trouble with her topic at a somewhat later step in the research.

Being curious about the many strange paths human behavior often takes, this student decided to concentrate on just one disorder, schizophrenia. It seemed reasonable to plan to discuss its cause and some of the therapies presently practiced in the effort to conquer this puzzling, distressing problem. During her preliminary research, she formed this hypothesis: "Since the exact cause of schizophrenia is not yet known, treatment is often difficult."

Her psychology textbook contained fewer than three pages on the topic, and an encyclopedia covered it in just one column. So the topic did not seem too broad. Only after the student had gotten fairly well into her search for sources did she realize that there were far more books and articles on schizophrenia than she could hope to read. The college library held more than a dozen books and hundreds of articles dealing directly with the causes and treatment of schizophrenia. What she believed to be a topic was actually a subject area, and a broad one at that. What should she do? Go back to the background sources, which had not clearly indicated the trouble she ran into? She checked with her instructor, who recommended that she look through her working bibliography to see if the titles might suggest some direction in which she could reasonably move. After all, why waste the time that had gone into the search for those sources?

The student noticed that several of the titles mentioned the *nature* of schizophrenia, others its *causes*, others its *effect on those living with schizophrenics*, and still others its *treatment*. She remembered from her background reading that doctors use several different methods of treatment because of the uncertainty regarding the causes of the disorder. Although she was interested in the treatment of schizophrenia, she realized from looking at her working bibliography that this, too, was likely to prove too broad for her paper. So she reviewed her background reading notes and class lecture notes once more and decided to narrow her topic still further, to one kind of treatment. Her new topic became *treatment of schizophrenia in a community setting*. She also needed to form a new hypothesis and decided on "Treating schizophrenia in a community setting is a new idea that works."

In assembling a new working bibliography, the student began with titles from the old one. But something seemed wrong. She could not eliminate many of the thirty titles in her working bibliography because any book on schizophrenia might refer to the type of treatment she was investigating. Clearly, her hypothesis needed to be revised again, this time to give it sharper focus. Reviewing those background notes that mentioned the new method of treatment, she realized that it was applied only to severe cases. And its proponents did not claim success in all cases; they merely claimed that their method produced better results than treatment in institutions. This led the student to recast her hypothesis again: "Treating severe schizophrenia in a community setting has in some cases proven more successful than treatment in traditional institutions."

The sharper focus provided by the revised hypothesis saved the student from reading and taking notes on matters that were not directly related to her purposes, such as treatment occurring outside of mental institutions (but not in community settings), the history of treating schizophrenia, or the treatment of mild forms of schizophrenia.

Let's compare the way in which the two hypotheses are worded. The first contains only two terms, other than *community setting*, that give any

Working with Sources

focus to the topic—*new idea* and *works. New idea* refers to a minor point that can be made simply by giving the date of the first use of this method. *Works* gives some focus, but it is rather vague, lacking the sense of scientific validity carried by *has proven more successful.* In contrast, the second hypothesis has four key terms—*severe, proven, successful,* and *traditional institutions*—that helped the student search for sources and read them far more efficiently. The word *severe* warned her to skip over passages about milder forms of the disorder that do not force sufferers to be committed to mental hospitals. *Proven* kept her attention focused on the need to find specific evidence for or against her hypothesis. The term *successful* made her think about finding a valid basis for judging success—a difficult problem in this situation because schizophrenia is rarely, if ever, cured; the sufferer's symptoms only become less distressing. The student had to look closely to find the criteria used by her various sources in order to determine how much improvement could reasonably be considered "success." *Traditional institutions* reminded her that if she wanted to show that this method was successful, she had to compare it with well-established treatments rather than with other experimental approaches.

Revising a Topic That Is Too Narrow

You may never find yourself with a topic that is too limited to research; most newcomers to research tend to come up with topics that are too broad. And, if you remember the warning about topics that can be completely researched by reading just one source—*how bees communicate,* for example—then you are even less likely to err in the direction of "too narrow."

A student who had read an article on lions in *Natural History* found himself with no sources beyond that article except for two brief summaries of that article, one in the magazine *Newsweek* and another in the *New York Times.* His topic was *the effect of the severe drought of 1973 on the rearing of lion cubs in the Serengeti Plains of East Africa.* The *Natural History* article provided all the necessary information; *Newsweek* and the *Times* merely reported the story by summarizing the original article, so they could *not* be considered "different" sources because they did not present any new information or a different point of view.

Stuck after a long but futile search, the student went back to the step he had previously cut short—background reading. He had done nothing more than read about lions in an encyclopedia article on African wildlife.

As the student read additional background studies, he thought about ways to expand his topic. These ideas passed through his mind: "The lions had trouble due to a drought; are there other more common problems they face as parents? Is there a *mild* drought every year? (The article had dealt with a particularly severe one.) Do they normally have trouble feeding themselves as well as their cubs? Who gets fed first, the parents or the cubs?" His new readings revealed that lions face famine every year in the Serengeti Plains because they do not follow the herds of antelope that migrate each winter to greener pastures.

The student now realized that he should broaden the problem from *the drought of 1973* to the *regular shortages of food* due to droughts and the disappearance of the antelopes. He also broadened his focus to include the adult lions as well as the cubs. Thus he arrived at the topic *the ways in which lions manage to survive periodic food shortages.* At this point, the writer still could not see how to frame a hypothesis, so he deferred that step until he had gathered some sources. He was hoping to find some difference of opinion or at least different sets of data in the sources, or else he would once more be left with a topic that could be handled entirely through one source.

After collecting more than a dozen titles of potential sources, this time looking in a few scholarly periodical databases as well as popular indexes, he skimmed through them to see what they had to offer. (The next chapter explains how to go about this important step.) Sure enough, other observers of lions clearly had not seen the same thing or had drawn different conclusions about what they saw, especially about the roles played in the hunt by males and females. A quick glance at the sources enabled the student to form a reasonable hypothesis: "In her effort to survive under sometimes difficult circumstances, the female lion plays a more aggressive and critical role than the so-called king of beasts."

Working with Sources

10

Evaluating Potential Sources

Once you have compiled what seems to be an adequate working bibliography, you are almost ready to begin reading the sources and taking notes. Before you undertake this challenging work, however, check to see if the sources provide enough ideas and information to allow you to do a thorough job of research. This is best done by skimming each source to gain a rough idea of what it says about your topic.

The purpose of skimming is to find out quickly whether or not a source is useful and, if it is, how much relevant information it contains. Skimming not only allows you to avoid a close reading of unhelpful sources but also gives you a chance to evaluate your hypothesis. A skimming of his sources told Fred Hutchins that his initial hypothesis needed expansion to include an account of Mather's complicated personality.

Quite often, you will find that a possible source's title was misleading and that the source contains nothing pertinent to your specific topic. For example, if your topic dealt with *the role parents play in adolescent alcoholism,* you would probably have included an article entitled "Teen Drinking Habits—Tragic Facts of Life" on your list of potential sources. Let's say you skim the article and find no reference to parental influence. Indeed, the article turns out to be a sermon, presenting several case histories involving teenagers who were injured as a result of drinking and concluding with a warning to adolescents not to drink. There are no documented facts or figures here—just a frightening picture of the perils of alcohol. You can safely drop this item from your list of sources.

If skimming leads you to reduce your list of potential sources to fewer than five, go back and look for more sources. If you cannot find any, check with your instructor to see whether you should try to broaden your topic or continue with what you have. Your instructor's advice will depend largely on how much information the remaining sources offer and how adequately they cover the variety of views that experts have expressed on your topic.

If skimming leaves you with a great many substantial sources, you may want to limit the topic or sharpen the focus of the hypothesis. Of course, several sources may offer much the same information and arrive at the same general judgment; in that case, you need read and take notes on only one of them, thereby reducing the overload of sources. It is not easy, especially when first undertaking research, to judge whether two or more sources duplicate one another. The main points to keep in mind are that you cannot afford to miss any valuable information, and that you must not leave out any of the various viewpoints on your topic.

Skimming Books

Skimming a book to determine its general content and organization can save you time when selecting sources for your working bibliography. Here are some skimming techniques you might find useful in evaluating books as possible sources:

- Read over the table of contents to get a general outline of the whole book.
- Look for a chapter title that might have relevance to your research project.
- Turn to that chapter and read the headings that mark the subdivisions of the chapter. If the headings indicate that the chapter is devoted to a continuous discussion of ideas and details relevant to your topic, you have probably found a useful source.
- Read the first and last paragraphs of the chapter if you need further evidence of the chapter's content and its importance to your topic. Together, these paragraphs might provide a quick summary of the author's major points.
- Read the first sentence of each paragraph. By so doing, you are likely to take in a number of the author's main ideas, thereby providing yourself with more information on which to base your decision about the relevance of the book to your research needs.
- Take note of any pictures, maps, or illustrated data appearing in the section you are skimming. Read the captions associated with the illustrations to get some sense of how the visuals relate to the content. Graphs and tables can be especially useful in helping you grasp the thrust of social science content.

After skimming the subheadings of a chapter with a promising title, you might find that only one or two subdivisions seem likely to refer to your particular topic. If so, you can skim these subdivisions using the same techniques you would use for a whole chapter.

Using Indexes

Many books, especially scholarly works, provide indexes so readers can find particular ideas and details referred to in different sections of the text. Indexes can facilitate your skimming because they provide page numbers for all topics mentioned in the book at hand, allowing you to find out quickly if the work has much to say about a particular aspect of your research topic.

When you are using an index, take the time to check all the headings that might be relevant to your topic, not just the obvious ones. For example, if your topic were *reading problems of grade-school boys as opposed to those of grade-school girls* (in this age group, boys with reading trouble outnumbered girls by a ratio of four to one), you would naturally look in a book's index under *reading, grade-school,* and *boys.* Some references would probably be listed under *reading,* but the other two terms might not appear in the index. In that case, you could look under synonyms such as *elementary school* and *male.* Do not stop at synonyms, however. Think of different ways to approach the topic that might lead you to other, possibly more fruitful headings, such as *learning disabilities,* or *disabilities, learning,* or *gender as a factor in learning.*

If you have reason to believe a particular book holds value for your research but offers few aids for skimming, such as nicely titled chapters and helpful illustrations, do not give up. The book is likely to have an introduction or a preface in which the author explains his or her approach to the subject. In this explanation, key words and emphasized ideas will certainly catch your eye. Using these words and ideas in conjunction with the index, you should be able to locate passages to which you can apply skimming techniques.

Skimming Periodical Articles

Articles rarely come with outlines that might serve as tables of contents, but some of them include *abstracts* that summarize their theses and major supporting points. As we mentioned in Chapter 5, some periodical indexes may include abstracts, which can help you decide whether or not you should take the time to locate the article. If a summary indicates that an article may be worth a close reading, you do not need to skim it. If, on the other hand, the summary does not mention material that is likely to help you, do not discard the source; skim it by reading the first line of every paragraph to pick up the main ideas.

You should not abandon the source unless skimming uncovers nothing useful. Even then, do not discard the bibliography entry because the source might become useful if you have to revise your topic.

Taking Notes While Skimming

When skimming a potential source, take brief notes that tell you how the source might prove useful, or why it is not useful. Write these notes on the backs of the bibliography cards or, if you are working on a computer, following the source entry.

To determine how useful a source may be, keep these questions in mind:

- Is this information relevant to my topic?
- How much useful information does it seem to offer?
- Does this source support or contradict my hypothesis?

You do not have to take detailed notes at this time. Simply indicate the possible value of the source. (You may want to record the page numbers for the material related to your topic so that it will be easier to find later.)

Keep all the bibliography entries. Do not discard them even if the sources look unpromising. If you are later forced to change your topic slightly, these items may become quite valuable. You will not want to waste time looking up a source you had previously skimmed. (If you are working with cards, you can simply save the cards; if you are working on a computer, you can save in a separate file any sources that you don't expect to need to look at in depth.)

Judging the Usefulness of Sources

As you skim through potential sources, try to evaluate each one in terms of its possible usefulness to your research. This section discusses some important points to keep in mind.

Depth of Coverage

Not every book or article that deals with your topic will contribute to your investigation. In general, any source that treats your topic in depth will be more valuable than one that treats it superficially. You are looking for sources that give you a clearer, fuller understanding of some aspect of your topic and thereby provide grounds for accepting, rejecting, or in some way modifying your hypothesis.

When Fred Hutchins started skimming books on New England history, he found that all of them mentioned Cotton Mather and most summarized his involvement in the Salem witch trials. The information and conclusions presented in these books had probably been boiled down from other historical works that had investigated the situation in far greater detail. (Ideally, it was these original sources that Fred thought he should read firsthand.) One of the general history books summarized Mather by saying he "was not a cruel, bloodthirsty persecutor of suspected witches; rather, his attitude toward the Salem witchcraft outbreak must be studied in the context of the times in which he lived, the traditions of his religion, and the erratic nature of his personality." Such a sweeping generalization is not necessarily wrong. In writing a research paper, however, you are expected to go beyond mere generalization to find specific evidence, in this case, primary accounts and well-founded interpretations of what the Salem "witches" meant to Cotton Mather. Otherwise, neither you nor your readers will have a sound basis for deciding whether or not your judgment is well supported.

Currency

Another important factor to keep in mind when evaluating sources is that some may be out of date. Especially in the natural and social sciences, knowledge is expanding so rapidly that theories, and even facts, are often revised or discarded within a year or two. Even history may be rewritten when new evidence comes to light or when a historian examines an old event from a new angle.

Therefore, if you investigate topics that involve current issues or the developments in a scientific field, you *absolutely must* find the latest possible sources. A book on astronomy, for instance, is partly out of date even before it is published. This does not mean that most of what it says is inaccurate, but some of the facts and theories concern phenomena about which new, more powerful telescopes are yielding fresh information daily. Current social problems such as *child abuse* and issues such as *toxic-waste disposal* also demand that you work with the most recently published sources. Because the information in books can never be totally up to date, you need to rely heavily on periodical articles when researching these kinds of topics.

Bias

Writing is done by people, and each person has a unique point of view. This means that almost no piece of writing can be entirely neutral or objective. News reports and even scientific reports have a *bias,* or *viewpoint,* just as do memoirs and letters to the editor. Given that each of your sources is written from a particular point of view, your task is not to discard all the sources because they are not "pure" or "objective," but to be aware of the nature of their biases and how these biases may affect *what kind of* information is presented and *how* it is presented.

Sometimes a source's viewpoint is apparent at first glance. For example, a book titled *Collegiate Sports: Opportunities to Excel* is likely to have a very different perspective on its topic from an article called "How 'Special Treatment' for College Athletes Has Undermined Educational Standards." At other times you will be able to determine a writer's biases only by examining closely *which aspects* of a topic are being emphasized and *how* they are being discussed.

Be especially careful in evaluating sources you find on the Internet. When you visit a Web site offering information or opinions on a topic, try to find out who the author is. Most reputable sites give such information. Notice whether the Web site is a commercial (.com), educational (.edu), or government (.gov) site and if it gives other clues as to its sponsors. Sites ending in .org are normally operated by special interest groups concerned with environmental issues or social causes. Commercial sites (.com) include not just businesses interested in sales, but periodicals like the *New York Times* and *Atlantic Monthly*. Are there advertisements on the site? Has it been updated recently? These questions can help you determine whether the site is a reliable one for your project. For more detailed advice about evaluating Internet sources, see Chapter 8.

You might be able to get a jump on evaluating a written source by learning something about the person who wrote it. If a thumbnail biography of the author appears in the text, read this material for such information as the author's academic or professional background, area of expertise, and political or philosophical leanings. You can also search your college catalog for additional works by the author and see if he or she has written other books on the same subject as the text you have at hand. In short, with a little effort, you might accumulate some useful impressions and expectations about the author's views and the possible value of the work you are considering as a source for your paper.

Variety of Viewpoints

While putting together your working bibliography, remember to look for works that express various points of view. A paper that depends mainly on the opinions and interpretations of one writer might well be criticized for being one-sided. For example, look at the following list of books dealing with the strategies of the two major military commanders who faced each other during the American Civil War. The topic of the paper is *Lee and Grant: the old vs. the new style of warfare*.

Working with Sources

Hypothesis: "The South's initial military success was due in large part to Robert E. Lee's mastery of the traditional theories of warfare, but the tide of battle turned when Lee was unable to cope with Ulysses S. Grant's new strategy of Total War."

Sources:
1. *Glory Road,* Bruce Catton
2. *Grant Moves South,* Bruce Catton
3. *Grant Takes Command,* Bruce Catton
4. *Mr. Lincoln's Army,* Bruce Catton
5. *The Civil War,* Bruce Catton
6. *Robert E. Lee,* Douglas Freeman
7. *Lincoln Finds a General,* K. P. Williams

This list of sources is so heavily weighted with Catton's works that his views are almost certain to dominate the paper. An experienced researcher would notice this imbalance and take steps to remedy the situation. Maybe some of Catton's books could be dropped if they largely repeated one another in regard to this topic. In any event, other historians' ideas must be added to the Works Cited so that readers will be presented with a variety of historical judgments regarding these two military geniuses.

One further question about "balance" comes to mind when looking over this list of titles. Isn't something wrong when four of the titles focus on Grant while just one deals with Lee? After all, the topic suggests equal treatment of the two men.

Primary versus Secondary Sources

Another kind of topic may send you back in time for many of your sources. For example, if you picked a topic involving the constitutional amendment that granted women the right to vote, you would probably want to find out what the general public as well as the leading social commentators thought about the issue in the years immediately before its passage in 1920. A recently written historical account of those years would get you started, but you might wonder whether the account missed something or even slightly distorted the picture of that historic crusade. Fortunately, you could check for yourself by reading some newspaper and periodical articles of that era that have been preserved in libraries, usually on microfilm.

The two sources we just mentioned are referred to as primary and secondary sources. *Primary sources* are those that *secondary sources* write about. In historical research, newspapers and magazines published at the time of the event (as well as diaries and correspondence by people who observed the event) are the sources used by later historians, whose writings then become secondary sources for your research. In literature, the

Working with Sources

term *primary* refers to the literary works themselves, whereas *secondary* refers to biographies and critical studies of the author's work.

If this kind of research sounds interesting, you should be aware that some good topics focus on the way the literary works of now-famous authors were received when they were first published. For such research, you would use the *Book Review Digest* and a newspaper index. See the section on the *Book Review Digest* in Chapter 5.

Journals versus Newspapers and Magazines

In Chapter 5, you learned that periodicals fall into two main categories: magazines and newspapers, which are designed to be read by the general public; and professional journals, which are written for experts. Each category poses distinct problems for research paper writers.

The journals, because they are written for experts, are often difficult to read unless you are familiar with the technical terminology and the specialized topics under discussion. However, journals are important because they usually contain the most up-to-date findings about the topics they cover. Magazines and newspapers, because they are written for people with a general educational background, usually avoid using a great many specialized terms and do not assume that readers possess an expert knowledge of the subject. The problem with magazines and newspapers grows out of their effort to make complex ideas understandable. Simplifying sophisticated subjects often leads to some degree of distortion. Also, magazines and newspapers tend to leave out what could be important details from your point of view—complex examples and sophisticated theoretical explanations and descriptions.

You need to learn how to make the best use of both categories of periodicals if you hope to write good research papers. Here are some guidelines that can help you handle the problems we just described.

If you are writing a paper for a science course, you will probably have to struggle with several journal articles. In that case, start your search for sources by looking through the *Readers' Guide* and a newspaper index. Magazine and newspaper accounts, which are usually very readable, will give you the general idea behind whatever recent discovery or theory your topic deals with. Then, when you move ahead to reading a journal article, you will be in a stronger position to understand the technical vocabulary, and you will have become somewhat familiar with the subject.

If, however, your topic focuses on a current social problem, you may not have to resort to an academic journal. Social issues appeal to readers of varied interests, not just to experts in one field. For this reason, you can often find full discussions of an issue in newsstand magazines that are written for an educated but otherwise general audience.

For example, one can understand the controversy over the use of nuclear energy without expert knowledge of how a nuclear plant is constructed or how a nuclear reaction takes place. Research into this topic would focus on sources that consider such matters as the efficiency of nuclear power plants and the possible outcomes—social, environmental, and political—of their use. You don't have to be a nuclear physicist to understand the debate, so you might very well limit your search for periodicals to the *Readers' Guide* and a newspaper index. In any case, it is a good idea to ask your instructor what kinds of sources you will be expected to use, given your particular topic.

Reviewing Your Hypothesis

After skimming and evaluating the sources, review your notes to check the direction your hypothesis is taking. If you see that the sources do not fully support the hypothesis, make whatever modifications are needed to bring it into conformity with the sources. Do not plow straight ahead. Stop and consider what you have just learned through skimming. Revising the hypothesis will bring it into sharper focus, and this will make the next step—reading the sources in depth—much easier.

Taking Effective Notes

Taking good notes is not simply a matter of copying down as much information as you can, as fast as you can. You must be selective. Although you will surely end up with more information in your notes than will ultimately appear in your paper, you don't want to go too far in that direction. Yet you also want to be sure to record everything you will need in order to support your thesis. For notes to be effective, then, it is essential to keep your hypothesis firmly in mind at all times.

Using a Preliminary Outline as a Guide

Eventually, after you complete your research and settle down to writing the paper, you will need to construct an outline in which you organize all the information you have collected. Looking at the outline, you will be able to fit each group of notes into its appropriate place in the overall framework.

Now, wouldn't it be nice to have that outline in place *before* you begin taking notes? Then you would have a good idea of where each note fits into the paper. Furthermore, such an outline would make it easier to judge whether a particular piece of information is truly relevant and therefore worth recording in a note.

Using your background reading and hypothesis, you should be able to construct a *preliminary* outline consisting of key questions (subtopics) that you hope to resolve through the research. Once you have the outline, you can assign each note to one of the subtopics by writing the subtopic at the top of the note card. This preliminary outline is called an *ongoing outline* because, as you get well into the note-taking, you are likely to see reasons to add to or modify the subtopics that make up this outline. When it is time to construct the final, rather detailed outline before writing the paper, this ongoing outline will prove quite helpful.

Here are two sample preliminary outlines, one for Fred Hutchins's research on Cotton Mather, the other for Susanna Andrews's research on Emily Dickinson.

Cotton Mather

1. CM's position in the Salem community
2. CM's role in the trials
3. CM's character and personality
4. CM's writing about witchcraft
5. CM's religious beliefs
6. The witchcraft trials: data, evidence, punishment
7. Definition of "witch"

Emily Dickinson

1. ED's character and personality
2. ED's ideas about poetry
3. ED's published poems; others' reactions to them
4. ED's family tree

Using a Statement of Purpose as a Guide

Instead of an outline, or along with an outline, you may find it helpful to write a *statement of purpose* once you have a plan for carrying out your research project. Some instructors may even require you to present a statement of purpose for their approval before you get very far into the project.

Writing a statement of purpose is a good way to bring together your ideas and make some decisions about the kinds of sources you will need to find. In addition, having this statement at hand while taking notes will help you avoid wasting time pursuing ideas that, although interesting in themselves, are not directly relevant to your research project.

Here is the statement of purpose written by the student who did his research on fire ants. After examining this statement, read his paper in Chapter 21 to see whether he carried out the assignment in line with the ideas presented here.

Statement of Purpose

By using Solenopsis invicta, a South American fire ant, as an example, I will support the concept that an ecosystem can suffer great damage from invasion by an aggressive alien species. What I have already read about S. invicta shows why ecologists consider this ant a threat to biodiversity. To demonstrate the extent of the threat, I will try to find scientific sources that deal specifically with S. invicta's destructive capacity. These sources must be as up to date as possible because scientists are undoubtedly learning more about this troublesome ant every day. I also want to instill in my readers a greater appreciation of the work being done by ecologists to preserve native species and their habitats. Finally, I will explain what scientists are doing, or hope to do, to control this particularly destructive creature.

Practical Aspects of Note-Taking

When taking notes, you cannot know just how each piece of information will finally be used in the paper. One thing is certain, however: you will present your information in a different order from that in which you recorded it. Therefore, you will want a flexible method of note-taking that makes it easy to find the best possible arrangement of your information. You can use note cards, a notebook, or a computer file; each method has its advantages.

Using Note Cards

Use four- by six-inch cards, and record just one idea, or a small group of closely related facts, on each card. Write notes on only one side of each card. (If you need to photocopy your notes, you will be glad the backs are blank.)

The main advantage of note cards is that you can spread the cards out on a table and arrange them into groups representing the subtopics of the paper. These groups (subtopics) will become the major sections of your paper. Because you may decide to shift a note from one subtopic to another, having your notes on cards gives you flexibility while you are rethinking the organization of the paper. Another advantage of using cards rather than a loose-leaf notebook or a computer file is that this space restriction will help you avoid the time-wasting tendency to use too many words and record more information than necessary.

Using a Notebook

If you feel more comfortable using a notebook, perhaps because you are worried that cards are easy to lose, write on just one side of each page and leave a fair amount of space between notes. This will allow you to cut each page into separate notes that can be grouped under subtopics when you are ready to organize the paper.

Working with Sources

Whatever you use, cards or a notebook, be a big spender. Do not try to squeeze as many notes as possible into the space available. The satisfaction gained from being thrifty cannot compensate for the frustration of trying to untangle a tightly bunched, loosely connected set of facts and ideas. Each card should focus on just one idea. If you include two ideas or sets of facts in the same note, you may want to separate them later, and this will not be possible unless you leave enough space between them as you take the notes.

Using a Word Processor

If you are preparing your paper on a word processor, you can create a separate file for your notes, using subtopic headings to organize them. Your notes can include your own ideas as well as material from your reading. If your subtopics change, you can move notes around accordingly. Periodically you can print out the notes to get an overview of the information you have collected so far. When you start drafting your paper, you can move notes from the notes file into the file that contains your rough draft.

Make a backup copy of any computer files at least twice per hour. Then, even if you accidentally delete or otherwise lose a file or part of a file, the bulk of your painstakingly gathered research materials will be safe.

Note: If you paste direct quotations or paraphrases from your computer notes into your paper, do not forget to include the source information.

Entering Information onto Cards

We think it is important to develop a single format for putting information on cards and then to follow it consistently. Later you may want to thumb through the stack of cards to look for a particular piece of information or simply to find any piece of information that might strengthen a particular section of the paper. In either case, you want to know at a glance if a card has what you want. Using a consistent format makes this easy.

Follow these guidelines when preparing your cards:

- *Use a consistent format.* In the upper right corner of each card, identify the author and title of the source, and be sure to add the numbers of the page or pages from which you are taking the information. We need to stress this seemingly minor point. *If you forget to take down this identifying data, you could lose hours retracing your steps when the time comes to insert notes in your research paper to show exactly where you found your information.*

- *Record complete information about the source—author(s), title, page numbers.* Use only the front of the card when recording information. Don't be tempted to save a penny by finishing up on the back because you may miss that piece of information when reviewing your notes. If you run out of space on the front, continue the note on a new card and clip the two cards together.

- *Highlight key words and ideas.* Leave lots of white space to make it easier to review your notes. Main points should easily catch your eye. Underline *major ideas*. Capitalize KEY WORDS. Minor points should be clearly subordinate to the major ideas they support, so use numbers or letters to indicate subordination or sequence. (See Figure 11-1 below and on page 120.)

- *Indicate the subtopic under which the information falls.* Write the appropriate subtopic, taken from your ongoing outline, at the top of each card, using more than one subtopic if a note seems to refer to more than one. Quite often, you will discover new subtopics while reading the sources. When Susanna kept reading references to a man who had published a few of Emily Dickinson's early poems, that man became worthy of a subtopic all to himself. As soon as you see

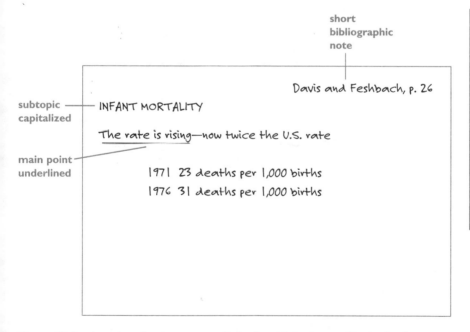

Figure 11-1   A series of notes on an article about infant mortality in the former Soviet Union in the 1970s. (The second and third cards, on page 120, show how a long note is continued from one card to another.)

subtopic

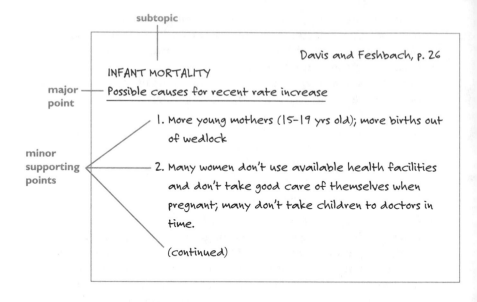

subtopic

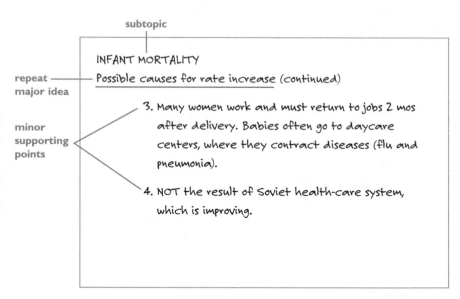

Figure 11-1   *(Continued)*

Working with Sources

a new subtopic emerging, add it to the ongoing outline. When taking a break from reading, go over the previous note cards and add the new subtopic where it fits. Reviewing earlier notes from time to time helps keep the scope of your project clearly in mind.

- *Be accurate.* When taking a note on a passage that contains numerical data and statistics, be extremely careful to copy the information with absolute accuracy. If you are taking handwritten notes, write all figures with care; for example, a hastily written 9 can later look like a 7. And don't misread zeros in large numbers, writing "2 million" for "200,000."

In the preceding discussion of creating a format for note entries, we focused on working with note cards. The same principles apply when using a notebook or a word processor, even though the mechanics will be a bit different. Your notes will be easy to read and easy to incorporate into your paper if you follow the suggested guidelines above.

Working with Sources

12

Quoting, Paraphrasing, and Summarizing

As we have said, effective note-taking consists of more than copying relevant passages out of your sources. In fact, the more direct copying you do, the less useful your notes are likely to be. This section explains why.

Note-taking for a research paper has three fundamental objectives:

- to record the general ideas that will form the skeleton of your research paper
- to record specific pieces of information that flesh out these general ideas
- to preserve the exact wording of some statements so that you can quote them directly in the paper

Many students waste time copying down long passages, word for word, because they have been misinformed, that research papers should contain a large number of quotations. This is just not so. In fact, the opposite is true.

For most research assignments, you should restrict the use of direct quotation to, at most, 20 percent of the paper. (This limit does not apply to literature topics for which you must quote from the literary works you are discussing — primary sources — as well as from secondary sources.) For some topics, especially in the physical sciences, excellent papers can be produced without using any direct quotations at all.

One important reason for limiting the amount of quotation is that by restating in your own words most of the ideas that appear in the sources, you show that you understand what you are talking about. Furthermore, you will be reading a wide variety of sources, each written in a distinctive style.

So, if you were to string together a good many quotations from these sources, the paper would end up with a very uneven style.

Finally, producing a convincing paper from a collection of quotations is almost impossible. Even though it might seem easier to quote than to paraphrase and summarize, the resulting "paper" would amount to a confusing, loosely related set of statements. Actually it is easier to express most of the ideas and information in your own words than it is to try to piece together dozens of quotations into a smoothly flowing, coherent essay.

Paraphrasing

To paraphrase is to express another person's idea in your own words. The value of paraphrasing goes far beyond meeting the requirement to express what you have read in your own words. For one thing, a good paraphrase usually takes fewer words than the original to convey the essential meaning. Even more important is the increased understanding that comes from trying to paraphrase what you are reading. Psychological experiments have shown that putting a difficult idea into your own words makes a stronger impression on your memory than merely copying the idea word for word. In fact, if you have trouble restating the idea, you probably do not thoroughly understand it.

In general, therefore, paraphrase any ideas that go into your notes unless there is a good reason for quoting the exact words in the source. (Several common situations that call for quotation are discussed later in this chapter.)

The following examples reveal two benefits to be gained from paraphrasing: brevity and clarity.

original	Will reputable scientists ever accept the claim that extrasensory perception and other paranormal powers really exist? It appears that many of them have.
paraphrase	Many scientists today believe in the reality of ESP and other paranormal powers.

The idea of "reputable" is not needed in your note; you know that you are looking only for real scientists — not those who simply call themselves scientists, as do some people who work with ESP.

original	Contrary to popular belief, exercise has never been shown conclusively to prolong life.
poor paraphrase; so close to the original as to be plagiarism	Contrary to popular thinking, exercise has never been conclusively demonstrated to lengthen life.

good paraphrase	No one has ever proved that exercise lengthens life.

There's no need to record "contrary to popular belief" if that is not the point you are interested in. Being careful to exclude unnecessary information from your paraphrase will help avoid the sort of "partial paraphrase" that can slip into *plagiarism,* a serious problem discussed at length on pages 145–149.

original	Olfactory receptors for communication between different creatures are crucial for establishment of symbiotic relationships.
two reasonable paraphrases	The sense of smell is essential to cooperation among different animal species.
	Cooperation between different animal species is made possible by their sense of smell.

The original, which comes from a biology journal, shows how difficult highly technical periodicals can be. Obviously the notetaker had already learned some of the specialized vocabulary of the field or had looked up the meanings of the technical terms. Notice that either paraphrase would be much easier to understand than the original when reviewing notes and organizing information into an essay.

Summarizing

A summary greatly reduces the length of what you have read, which might be anything from a long paragraph to an entire periodical article. Writing effective summaries requires good judgment because you must decide what can safely be left out of the notes without losing or distorting the basic idea.

The essential consideration when writing a summary is: What is my purpose in using this material? Sometimes the entire passage contains valuable information. At other times, only part of the passage seems useful. So some summaries will be quite a bit shorter than others. Just remember not to make a summary so short that it leaves out something that seems relevant to the hypothesis.

When working on a single paragraph, you may find that it contains a clearly stated topic sentence aptly supported by several details. In that case, you can simply paraphrase the main idea and then decide whether you need to note briefly any of the details, either for use in your paper or to reinforce your understanding of the main idea. In the following example, as in much professional writing, the main idea is stated in the first sentence.

original

Zoologists define *species* as a category of animals whose members are capable of mating and producing offspring which are also able to reproduce. Thus, dogs constitute a species because even males and females of the most dissimilar breeds can produce mongrels that can, in turn, reproduce. However, the mating of a horse and a donkey, although the two are more similar in appearance than, let us say, a poodle and a boxer, yields a mule, which is always sterile. Thus, they are placed in separate species. A lion and a tiger, although of different species, can produce a "liger" or a "tiglon," which in very rare cases may be fertile. This exception betrays a slight weakness in our definition of the term *species*.

Whether you should include certain details in your note depends on your hypothesis. If your use for this source goes no further than the definition of *species*, you probably do not need the specific examples. If, however, you intend to develop the concept of *species* in your paper, you may need them (see Figure 12-1). The example of the "liger" and the "tiglon" would be needed only if you planned to discuss the fact that a scientific term can be less precise than most of us tend to believe.

SPECIES

Definition of species—mating

Two animals are said to belong to the same species if they can produce <u>fertile</u> offspring.

Ex: poodle + boxer but <u>not</u> horse + donkey (mule is
   sterile)

Figure 12-1   Summary note card.

Working with Sources

Often your summary of a paragraph will consist of a general idea derived from just a few details that directly relate to your hypothesis. Assume when reading the next example that you are working with the hypothesis "Most scientists believe that some form of life probably exists on planets circling other stars in the universe."

original

Our solar system consists of nine, maybe ten, planets, which are circled by more than sixty moons, plus around 5,000 fairly large rocks, called asteroids. In addition, the Sun's neighborhood is home to an untold number of comets, fifty of which appear in our skies periodically, and many megatons of cosmic dust. Ever since Galileo's discovery of Jupiter's four largest moons in 1610, Earthlings have wondered about the possibility of extraterrestrial life. Only in the last five years, however, have astronomers been able to do much more than speculate about the existence of other solar systems, for Earthbound observers were hindered by our atmosphere, which blurs even the best images gathered by their strongest telescopes. In 1990 a breakthrough occurred when the Hubble telescope was placed in orbit high above that atmosphere. Recently our Eye in the Sky has been transmitting pictures of actual Jupiter-sized planets hurtling around distant stars. Those seen so far are thought to be too close to their stars to sustain life as we know it. But new discoveries are emanating from Hubble at an amazing clip!

summary

The Hubble orbiting telescope has recently revealed the existence of planets circling stars, but none so far seems at the right distance from its star to support life like that on Earth.

The background information about the numbers of objects in the solar system, and about Galileo's discoveries, has been left out of the summary because you do not need it to understand the main idea — that although we now know that some other stars have planets, none as yet could sustain our kind of life. This illustrates the value of trying to keep notes brief. If some of the background information had been new to you, you might have been tempted to add it to your notes just because it was unfamiliar. But doing so would not have helped you when it was time to write the paper. Always rely on your hypothesis to guide you in deciding whether information is truly relevant to your purposes.

Quoting

Once you accept the principle that you should paraphrase or summarize most of the ideas that go into your notes, you will be better able to judge when quotation can be both appropriate and effective. There are four common reasons for quoting from your sources — *conciseness, accuracy, memorable language,* and *authority.*

Sometimes your best efforts at paraphrasing will produce a version that is either longer and clumsier than the original or somewhat inaccurate. In either case, you should quote all or part of the original statement. On other occasions, a source may express an idea so brilliantly that you want to preserve its beauty and power. Finally, you may want to support an idea or one of your conclusions by quoting a key statement or two from an established authority on the subject. None of these reasons for quoting is, however, an excuse for avoiding the effort necessary to create a successful paraphrase. You must learn to recognize those special times when these reasons are likely to be valid.

Examples of four situations in which direct quotation is desirable are presented here, along with some further advice on when to quote rather than paraphrase or summarize.

Conciseness

You find that you cannot paraphrase an idea without using many more words than the source.

A common instance of this occurs when you decide to introduce a specialized term into your paper. You think it should be defined, but your attempts to paraphrase a definition are long and awkward. In that case, you should quote at least part of the definition from the source.

excerpt from paper   Noam Chomsky can be considered a reductionist —
someone who believes that "all complex phenomena
are ultimately explained and understood by analyzing
them into increasingly simple and supposedly more
elementary components" (Pronko 497).

Works Cited entry   Pronko, N. H. *Panorama of Psychology.* Belmont, CA:
Wadsworth, 1969.

(The note refers to the source of the definition, a textbook that the student used solely for the definition and not for any information related

Working with Sources

to Noam Chomsky. That textbook must, however, be included in the list of Works Cited for the research paper, and the student therefore made out a bibliography card for the source as well as a note card for the quotation.)

Note: This source is not out of date even though it was published in 1969 because the definition of a term such as *reductionism* does not change with time.

Accuracy

You find that you cannot effectively paraphrase an idea without distorting the author's meaning.

If, for example, a writer said that "virtually all women have experienced fantasies in which they were born as men," any paraphrase is likely to be more or less inaccurate.

questionable paraphrases	Most women wish they were men.
	The majority of women have dreamed that they were men.
	Almost every woman has a dream or daydream in which she has been born a male.

The first paraphrase grossly distorts the meaning; the second comes closer, but is not entirely accurate; the third is accurate but longer than the original. In such cases, you would do much better to quote the source and let your readers draw their own conclusions. Then they can compare their interpretations with those you put forth in your paper.

Memorable Language

You believe that the words or ideas expressed by your source are so vivid or powerful that the meaning cannot be captured in a paraphrase.

Restrain yourself in this matter; beware of quoting someone merely because you feel you cannot say the same thing as well in your own words. On the other hand, an example of brilliant language that cries out for quotation comes from a speech by British Prime Minister Winston Churchill, in which he referred to the behavior of Russia as "a riddle wrapped in a mystery inside an enigma."

In the same vein, you should quote famous remarks whether or not the word choice is brilliant or difficult to paraphrase. President Harry Truman once advised timid politicians, "If you can't stand the heat, get out of the kitchen."

Finally, you may come across a remark that is so startling that your readers deserve to see the original. The brilliant biologist J. H. S. Haldane described Albert Einstein as "the greatest Jew since Jesus." Such a striking comment would surely lose a great deal if paraphrased.

Authority

You want to support a conclusion you have reached in your research by quoting the words of an expert on the subject.

The authors of many of your sources are probably experts on their subjects, at least in the sense that their ideas have been thought authoritative enough to be published. Still, you need to be selective in this regard. Choose writers whose credentials are known. Reporters for *Newsweek* or the *Washington Post* are experts only on journalism, although they may be fairly well informed on the topic at hand. An author referred to in an earlier source (or in a biographical sketch accompanying her article in *Scientific American*) as "a leading gerontologist" can be treated as an expert in the study of aging.

At any rate, remember that you cannot rely entirely on expert opinion, whether quoted or paraphrased. You must also work to support your conclusions with hard facts and clear reasoning.

Quoting Out of Context

Because you are always quoting just a small part of any source, you must take great care to see that *everything that you did not quote agrees with the idea that you did quote.* This principle applies to paraphrasing as well. The next example shows how someone could read a passage hastily and then produce a serious misrepresentation of its author's meaning.

student's source   It is currently very fashionable among popular social critics to blame television for the recent widespread increase in juvenile crime statistics. The argument usually pursues this line of reasoning: Many parents today neglect their children by allowing them complete freedom in watching TV. The shows these children choose to watch often present violence in an attractive form, and some have even gone so far as to depict clever ways of committing crimes. Many of these children later re-enact the violent acts they have witnessed on TV in order to recapture the thrills.

> I contend, however, that this widely accepted expla-
> nation of a serious social problem is too simplistic.

Anyone who read that passage and then produced the following quotation would be grossly distorting the author's meaning.

quotation out of context

> Sociologist Jane Doe joins those people who
> denounce violence on television as the primary
> cause of the sharp increase in the number of crimes
> committed by young people: "Many children later
> reenact the violent acts they have witnessed on TV
> in order to recapture the thrills" (41).

Apparently the student missed the two signals that tell the reader that Jane Doe disagrees with the points listed. First, the words "It is currently very fashionable among popular social critics..." carry a mocking tone. Second, the student completely ignored the clear-cut assertion that opens the next paragraph: "I contend, however, that this...is too simplistic."

Blending Quotation with Paraphrase

The most effective way to avoid quoting too many words is to combine quotation with paraphrase. A good guideline is to quote only the part of a passage that relates directly to your hypothesis. Below, you can read the context surrounding Winston Churchill's famous remark about Russia, and you will see the advantage of quoting just the most pertinent part of a source. In 1939, Churchill was attempting to alleviate British fears that Russia might not enter the war against Nazi Germany. Part of that speech is presented here, along with a note card showing how quotation can be blended with paraphrase or summary. (The student's hypothesis was "Before and during World War II, Churchill demonstrated a clear understanding of other nations and the ways their leaders thought.")

original speech by Churchill

> I cannot forecast to you the action of Russia. It is a riddle wrapped in a mystery inside an enigma; but perhaps there is a key. That key is Russian national interest. It cannot be in accordance with the interest or safety of Russia that Germany should plant itself upon the shores of the Black Sea, or that it should overrun the Balkan states and subjugate the Slavonic peoples of Southeastern Europe. That would be contrary to the historic life interests of Russia.

Working with Sources

The note in Figure 12-2 supplies a connection between Churchill's words and the student's hypothesis—that when others were confused (in this case, about Russia), Churchill's intuition or plain old political savvy led him to the truth. The note shows this point better than a lengthy quotation from the speech.

Entering Quotations onto Note Cards

When writing a note, you must be extremely precise in placing the quotation marks and absolutely accurate in recording the author's words. This need for accuracy when quoting can be better understood if we examine some problems that can occur when you are reviewing notes in preparation for writing the paper.

Problem 1:   Because quotation marks are small, they can be overlooked when you are transferring information from your notes to your paper. To avoid missing a quotation mark or two, use very heavy strokes or even the marks « and » (guillemets). This will ensure that you do not confuse quotations with paraphrases. (See Figure 12-3.)

Problem 2:   If a note summarizing several pages of a source includes a quotation, you must record the page number where the quotation appeared, as well as the page numbers of the full passage being summarized. Be sure to record the page number of each direct quotation. (See Figure 12-3.)

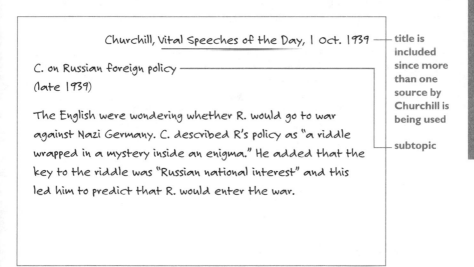

Figure 12-2   An example of blending quotations with paraphrase.

Working with Sources

Herman Arthur, "To Err Is Huperson; to Forgive, Divine," Amer. Education, Winter 1980, pp. 30–32

SEXISM

Correcting sexism in language

In getting rid of sexism, teachers must avoid awkward and ugly constructions such as he/she. «Like badly tattered fig leaves, they call attention to what they are trying to conceal.» (30)

Three suggestions: (1) Do away with most feminine suffixes, such as -ess and -ette; (2) provide substitutes for man and woman suffixes, ex: mail deliverer instead of mailman; (3) avoid he/she and him/her constructions by using it when sex is not specified.

page numbers of section being summarized

summary with direct quotation clearly marked

page number of quotation

Figure 12-3 An example of a carefully recorded quotation.

Problem 3: Sometimes you will want to leave words out of the middle of a quotation because they are not relevant to your purpose. A reader is entitled to know about such an omission, so you must use an *ellipsis,* which consists of three dots in place of the omitted words. The following example shows how a quotation can be shortened by an ellipsis. (The passage also demonstrates a smooth blend of quotation and paraphrase.)

student's source

Muldrow is by temperament a primitive whose profoundest ambition is to shuck what traces of civilization persist in him.

To criticize Muldrow for being unlikable would be accurate but off the point, given Dickey's unstinting pains to have him so. I suspect that in each successive draft of the novel (which was long in gestation: it arrives six years after Dickey's second novel, *Alnilam,* and twenty-three after his best-selling first, *Deliverance*) he strove to make his hero hardier, terser, chillier; Muldrow is, like the knife with which he dispatches so many victims, a thing of patiently honed steel.

omitted words

Works Cited entry

Leithauser, Brad. "Haunted by the Good War." Rev. of To the White Sea, by James Dickey. New Yorker 27 Sept. 1993.

excerpt from
student's paper
As for the relentless brutality of Dickey's heroes, critic Brad Leithauser observed about Sgt. Muldrow in To the White Sea:

> Muldrow is by temperament a primitive whose profoundest ambition is to shuck what traces of civilization persist in him. To criticize Muldrow for being unlikable would be accurate but off the point, given Dickey's unstinting pains to have him so. I suspect that in each successive draft of the novel [. . .] he strove to make his hero hardier, terser, chillier; Muldrow is, like the knife with which he dispatches so many victims, a thing of patiently honed steel.

The ellipsis lets readers know that something was omitted. They must then trust that the omitted words were not essential to the point being made in the paper. In this case, the dates of the earlier novels interrupt the student's comment and would distract the reader's attention.

You might ask why one should not also drop the long phrase about the knife in the last sentence—"like the knife with which he dispatches so many victims." The knife is not extraneous; it symbolizes the man's character, thereby supporting the notion of brutality.

Notice that the paragraphing in the source was not shown in the excerpt. No purpose would be served by that nicety. It is better to maintain the flow of thought.

An ellipsis is indicated by three dots, separated from each other and the surrounding text by spaces. Today, if you are using MLA style documentation, you must sometimes surround the three dots with square brackets—[ ]. When *you* have chosen to leave out part of a quotation, the brackets must be used. When the ellipsis occurred in the source, the dots alone are used. This difference tells the reader who made the decision to use an ellipsis, you or the source.

You chose to omit
some words.
However, the mating of a horse and a donkey [. . .] yields a mule, which is always sterile.

Source chose to omit
some words.
The major sign would be a "period of deepening corruption . . . when the devil would make more violent assaults than usual" on humankind (Levy 33–34).

Note the placement of the parenthetical reference at the end.

If the ellipsis occurs at the very end of your sentence, add a fourth dot immediately after the second bracket, indicating the period that ends the sentence. If a parenthetical reference appears at the end of the quotation, place it ahead of the fourth dot (the period).

For Mather, "denial of the Devil's power in this world implied the denial of other spirits, including angels [. . .]" (Levin 200).

If you are omitting a whole sentence or more, consult the *MLA Handbook for Writers of Research Papers*, Fifth Edition, for guidelines.

Caution: If you replace part of a sentence with an ellipsis, make sure you have not inadvertently changed the meaning of the sentence.

Problem 4:   One last problem occurs when you want to quote a remark that was quoted by your source. The possible danger here is that when you review your notes you may become confused. You must clearly indicate whether the quotation marks enclose your source's words or those of the person your source was quoting. Devise a format that will leave no doubt in your mind when you review the notes. We believe the easiest solution is to add a parenthetical note on your card if there is any chance of mistake. (See Figure 12-4.)

Working with Sources

> Loren Eiseley, "Man against the Universe,"
> The Star Thrower (New York: Harcourt, 1978), p. 212
>
> RWE/SCIENCE/FAITH
> Religion vs. Science
>
> Emerson knew a good deal about current scientific advances, e.g., Sir Charles Lyell's geological theories. E. believed that «Christian chronology had become a mere "kitchen clock" compared with the vast time depths the earth sciences were beginning to reveal. "What terrible questions we are learning to ask,"» said E., who realized Americans were moving away from the «theism of our fathers.»
>
> (NOTE: « » indicate Eiseley's words; " " indicate Emerson's)

these words help make it clear, but note at bottom leaves no chance for error

Figure 12-4   An example of quotations whose sources are clearly distinguished.

student's source   Of all the Concord circle, Emerson was perhaps the most widely read in science. He was familiar with Sir Charles Lyell's work in geology and was well aware that Christian chronology had become a mere "kitchen clock" compared with the vast time depths the earth sciences were beginning to reveal. "What terrible questions we are learning to ask," brooded the man sometimes accused of walking with his head in the clouds. He saw us as already divesting ourselves of the theism of our fathers.

An Extended Example of Effective Note-Taking

As Paul Oster was researching the topic *dangerous effects of ozone layer depletion,* he was shown a source by a fellow student who was working on the same subject. The article's title, "Study of Cloud Patterns Points to Many Areas Exposed to Big Rises in Ultraviolet Radiation," is interesting in itself because it does not mention ozone. Paul might not have found this source under *ozone layer* in a periodical index unless the indexer had actually read the article and therefore knew it dealt with the ozone layer. Some indexers will go entirely by the title when it seems as specific as this one. But Paul would have been able to find this item if he had in mind various subjects related to his topic (in this case, *ultraviolet radiation*).

As he read the article, Paul realized that his understanding of the role of the ozone in the dangers of ultraviolet radiation had been incomplete. Paul's working hypothesis was "Although measurements of the ozone layer are not very precise at this time, it seems likely that the ozone layer is being depleted, and that the causes are man-made." Previously, he had imagined that wherever the ozone layer became too thin, the ultraviolet radiation would immediately affect all those living directly under the "hole" in the layer. From the article, he learned that some parts of the Earth are protected from ultraviolet injury by their cloudy climates. Tropical jungles and rainy London, as well as Seattle and the American Northwest, will experience the effects of ozone depletion quite a bit later than sunny southern California and the Saharan lands in North Africa. This news created a new subtopic for Paul's research — *the role of climate (or clouds).*

Now let us watch Paul closely as he takes notes on this article.

Working with Sources

Study of Cloud Patterns Points to Many Areas Exposed to Big Rises in Ultraviolet Radiation

By WILLIAM K. STEVENS

This paragraph states the article's thesis; no note is needed.

Depletion of the earth's protective ozone layer is exposing some areas of the world, including parts of the United States, to biologically harmful doses of ultraviolet radiation, but some other areas will not become vulnerable for another 20 to 50 years, according to a new study.

The paragraph provides new information on the role of clouds. (card 1)

The reason for the variance, the authors of the study say, is that patterns of cloud cover vary from one area to another. Clouds as well as ozone block ultraviolet radiation, and the actual pattern and amount of radiation reaching the ground cannot be calculated globally unless this is taken into account.

The list of affected places may be useful. (card 2)

By making the calculation in that manner, experts in California have concluded on the basis of satellite data that large parts of North America, most of central Europe, the Mediterranean, New Zealand, South Africa and the southern half of Australia, Argentina and Chile are now being subjected to significant increases in harmful radiation. In the United States, the affected areas are the Midwest, the Southwest including southern California, and part of the Northeast. Hawaii is also being affected, according to the study.

This shows the researchers' expertise; Paul may want to consult the source of the information, given at the end of the paragraph. (card 3)

The research was done by Dr. Dan Lubin, a research physicist at the California Space Institute at the Scripps Institution of Oceanography in San Diego, and Elsa H. Jensen, an aerospace engineer

note
card 1

EFFECT OF CLIMATE

Clouds also block UV rad—this effect must be considered
in measuring danger.

note
card 2

DANGER—LOCATIONS

Satellite info shows areas subject to "significant
increases" in UV rad—
    Cent. Eur.; Medit. area; N.Z.; S. Africa; southern
Australia; Argentina & Chile
        in U.S.: Midwest; Southwest (inc. S. Calif.); parts of
Northeast; Hawaii

note
card 3

A BIBLIOGRAPHICAL NOTE

Dr. Dan Lubin, res. physicist, Calif. Space Inst.
Elsa Jensen, aerospace engineer, Sea-Space Corp.
(satellite instrument co.)

See report in Brit. j. Nature Oct. 26, 1995

note
card 4

EFFECT OF UV-B

UV-B causes skin cancer & cataracts; injures immune sys.;
also upsets natural ecosystems.

Working with Sources

A clear, brief statement of the dangers of radiation. There is no need to note the role of the ozone layer, which Paul already knows. (card 4)

The date is important; the rest is familiar to Paul. (card 5)

This needs to be paraphrased for possible use. (card 6)

A paraphrase is needed; absolute accuracy is important. Key words: *calculated, estimated, average, 2.5% per decade, five years.* (card 7)

The paragraph gives more specific information about the future threat. (card 8)

Paul needs to paraphrase the description of the relationship between cloud cover variance and UV exposure, including a quotation, to ensure *accuracy.* (card 9)

with the Sea-Space Corporation, a satellite instrument and software company in San Diego. Their report appeared in the Oct. 26 issue of the British journal *Nature.*

Ultraviolet-B from the sun, a form of radiation that can cause skin cancer and cataracts, damage the immune system and disrupt natural ecosystems, is normally blocked by a layer of ozone in the stratosphere. Industrial chemicals, principally chlorofluorocarbons used as refrigerants, destroy stratospheric ozone.

Under an international agreement, the production of chlorofluorocarbons is to cease at the end of this year. But because the chemicals persist so long in the atmosphere, ozone depletion is expected to continue for decades.

"Whether or not you can assert that ozone depletion is an environmental problem" at any given time "depends very much on where you are," Dr. Lubin said.

He and Ms. Jensen calculated that at the estimated average global rate of ozone depletion, about 2.5 percent per decade, large parts of continental Europe, North and South America, Australia and Southern Africa would be bathed in increased UV-B radiation in five years.

But the British Isles and Ireland, for instance, are not expected to experience a significant increase for another 30 years, and it is not expected for 20 to 50 years in parts of central Russia, most of China, Japan, North and South Korea and the Indian subcontinent. Mexico, northern Australia, New Guinea and areas of South America north of São Paulo, Brazil, are also not expected to experience increases for decades.

In the United States, the South and Pacific Northwest should not experience increases for another 20 years, according to the calculations.

A major factor in determining whether biologically significant amounts reach the earth, Dr. Lubin said, is the natural variability of cloudiness in a given area. When cloud cover varies widely from one year to the next, the ultraviolet radiation that people and other organisms are exposed to also varies. Increases in the radiation because of the depleted ozone layer probably do not

BAN ON CFCS

Internat'l agreement calls for end to CFC prod'n by end of 1996.

DANGER—LOCATIONS

Dr. Lubin: danger to environment from loss of ozone varies from place to place.

DANGER—LOCATIONS

Lubin & Jensen: areas listed on card 2 will feel increase in UV-B rad. in 5 yrs if present estimated avg. rate of ozone depletion remains constant—2.5% depl. per decade.

DANGER—LOCATIONS

Some areas are in less danger:
      Brit. & Irel. safe for 30 yrs
      Cent. Russia, China, Japan, Korea, India—20 to 50 yrs.
      Mexico, n. Australia, n. S. America safe for decades

Working with Sources

(Note cards continued on page 141)

This material is important for telling how the theory was derived. (card 10)

Here is important information on the measurement of UV radiation from place to place. (card 11)

have a biological effect until they exceed this natural variability, Dr. Lubin said.

To calculate natural variability, Dr. Lubin and Ms. Jensen combined satellite data on global ozone trends from 1978 to 1993 with satellite data on solar radiation reflected from clouds from 1985 to 1990. This produced a base line of natural variability, against which the researchers compared trends in UV expected from ozone depletion. The comparison enabled them to determine how long it takes for the expected UV trend to become significant.

In determining the present amount of UV-B striking the earth, an indirect analysis of this sort would not be necessary if there were abundant UV detection instruments around the world. But the instruments are sparse, and most have not been in position long enough, over a broad enough area, to detect any trends, especially in the temperate zones where most people live.

Instruments have shown for certain that UV-B has risen significantly in Antarctica, where ozone depletion has been the most severe. A few measurements in temperate zones also indicate an increase.

EFFECT OF CLIMATE

Dr. Lubin: How much UV rad. reaches earth is greatly
affected by amount of clouds covering area throughout
the year. If this changes much from yr to yr, danger also
varies. Increases due to ozone depl. "probably do not have
a biological effect until they exceed this natural
variability."

EFFECT OF CLIMATE

Lubin & Jensen came to their theory this way: They took
(1) satellite info on global ozone 1978–93 and (2) sat. info
on solar rad. reflected by clouds 1985–90. Putting these
together, they saw how cloud cover affected UV rad.
Then they could predict variation in rates of rad.
increase from place to place.

MEASUREMENT

At present we have very few rad. measuring devices
around the earth; the few in operation have not been
working long enough to yield reliable data, esp. in
temperate zones, where pop. is concentrated.

Only Antarctica has given definite results; ozone depl. is
most severe there.

Working with Sources

Distinguishing Very Useful Information from Not-So-Useful Information

Paul Oster now went to another source, an article titled "Russian Spy Plane Is Turning Its Sights from U.S. to Ozone." Judging by its title, the article seemed unlikely to offer as much information as the previous one had. But Paul did not want to chance missing something valuable.

Russian Spy Plane Is Turning Its Sights from U.S. to Ozone

By MALCOLM W. BROWNE

No note is needed; there is no specific information here, and the use of the plane will be shown.

No note is needed; the plane's features are irrelevant to the hypothesis.

The note needs to mention that the plane reaches 67,000 feet and carries more than U.S. planes. (The information lets readers know that we can expect better measurements in the near future.)

No note is needed; Paul already knows the 1975 date, and the hole's existence is Paul's research topic.

For the first time since the end of the cold war, a Russian high-altitude spy plane has been put at the disposal of Western European scientists, who will use it to study depletion of the protective ozone layer over Arctic regions.

The European Science Foundation announced this month that Russia would provide a specially modified Myasishchev M-55 airplane for high-altitude Arctic studies during the winter and spring months of 1996 to 1998. The M-55 Geophysika is roughly equivalent in purpose and performance to America's U-2 reconnaissance plane, which has been renamed the ER-2 and flies research missions for NASA.

However, it can carry much heavier loads than the American plane, enabling it to fly large analytical instruments to altitudes up to 67,000 feet.

Depletion of the earth's stratospheric ozone, which protects human beings and animals from dangerous solar ultraviolet radiation, was detected in 1975 by a high-flying U-2. Since then, depletion of the ozone layer has progressed to the point at which a gigantic hole in the ozone layer opens over Antarctica every southern spring. Less

No note is needed unless noncompliance seems important, for Paul knows about these pollutants from his background reading; he also knows the date of the U.S. ban on Freon.

No note is needed; Paul already knows that the effect of CFCs is long-lasting, and the very general description of chemical reactions is familiar from his background reading.

The note needs to mention ice clouds' role in the chemical action. (This is news to Paul.)

The note should mention how the plane's data will be used.

severe but marked depletion of the ozone layer has also begun to occur over the Arctic during the northern spring, and there has been pronounced thinning of the ozone shield even over temperate regions in recent years.

Most atmospheric scientists attribute the ozone depletion to increasing quantities of chlorofluorocarbons and similar Freon compounds released into the atmosphere by human activity. Freons have been used for many years as refrigerant gases in refrigerators and air-conditioners, as foaming agents in plastic, as insulators, as solvents for cleaning computer components and in many other applications. Although the United States banned Freon propellants in aerosol sprays in 1978, some nations continue to manufacture Freon-propelled sprays.

Although production of these chemicals is now prohibited in most industrial nations, their effects on the ozone layer are expected to increase and linger for many years. At high altitudes, Freons are broken down by ultraviolet radiation from the sun, producing chlorine compounds that react with ozone. This initiates a chain reaction, in which the destructive chlorine compounds are regenerated, becoming available to destroy still more ozone.

According to the European Science Foundation, which is based in Strasbourg, France, the M-55 provided by the Mya-sishchev Design Bureau, the Russian Central Aereological Center and Aviecocenter will be able to study the chemical reactions believed to occur on the surfaces of fine ice particles that make up polar stratospheric clouds. These clouds, which appear in early spring, seem to play a pivotal role in catalyzing the chemical reactions that lead to the destruction of ozone.

The leader of the scientific team, Dr. Leopoldo Stafanutti of the Italian National Research Council, hopes to combine measurements made by the M-55 with mathematical models of possible physical and chemical changes occurring in the stratospheric clouds. This, he hopes, will lead to methods by which forecasts can be made regarding changes in the ozone layer.

Working with Sources

A note is needed; the precise information on areas being investigated is useful. Paul already knows the sources of aerosols (natural/human).

Participants in the Airborne Polar Experiment include some 20 research institutions in Russia, Italy, Germany, Britain, Finland, Norway, Sweden and Switzerland. The group plans particularly to study lee wave clouds, clouds of ice particles that form downwind of mountain peaks, in Scandinavia and the Urals. The plane will also analyze the chemistry and physics of polar stratospheric clouds in the Siberian Arctic, where no comparable measurements have ever been made, the foundation said.

No note is needed; Paul already knows the sources of aerosols (natural/human).

A secondary object of the flights, each of which may last up to six hours, will be to catalogue all types of aerosol particles present in the European and Arctic atmosphere up to the plane's operational ceiling. Aerosols come from both natural sources (like volcanoes) and human activity (such as the burning of soft coal).

No note is needed; this is not relevant to Paul's research.

The M-55 has been scrutinized by Western observers only a few times since NATO intelligence experts spotted it at a Soviet airfield in 1982. Six of the planes were built, five of which remain in military service. The civilian version, the Geophysika, is a single-seat airplane with two jet engines, twin tail booms and wings 133 feet long, and it has a huge instrument bay that can carry more than 3,000 pounds.

As you can see, much of the material in the article was not very helpful, but the several notes Paul recorded would become pieces in the final analysis of his topic. Of course, someone who read this article as a first source would not have been familiar with some of the information that Paul had already read about and, therefore, would have taken more notes than Paul needed to take.

Working with Sources

13

Avoiding Plagiarism

The subject of plagiarism can be very perplexing because students often have trouble seeing it from the instructor's point of view. Many tend to feel that instructors exaggerate the seriousness of the offense, and some instructors think students treat the problem lightly because avoiding plagiarism sometimes takes a lot of effort. But the fact of the matter is that instructors (as well as readers and writers in general) do consider plagiarism a serious offense, and therefore, you need to beware of getting into trouble through carelessness.

The problem is essentially one of trust and personal integrity. Instructors want to believe that you will give proper credit where it is due, and they want to give you credit for your own judgments concerning the significance of the evidence you gathered. Readers assume that all ideas and judgments that are not accompanied by a note are yours. Only when instructors have good reason to doubt that an idea is yours will they raise the question of plagiarism. As a matter of personal integrity, you must acknowledge any idea that comes from a source as well as the wording that was used to express that idea.

Plagiarizing Ideas

By "acknowledging" sources, we mean that when you use an idea — for instance, a critical judgment that appeared in one of your sources — you must give that writer credit in the form of a note telling readers (1) who proposed the idea and (2) just where you found it. Even if you arrived at the same judgment on your own, you need to acknowledge that the writer had the same idea.

It is possible to plagiarize by accident. If you forget to insert a sourcenote, it will appear that the idea is your own. Such an oversight is easy to correct. Simply reread your paper, with your notes at hand, and check each significant idea or fact to see whether you have given proper credit. Add any source citations you omitted. (*Note:* Chapter 9 provides specific guidelines for determining what kinds of information require notes.)

Plagiarizing Language

The problem of plagiarizing an author's language may not be so easy to deal with. Many of your notes will consist of paraphrases and summaries; therefore, you might accidentally treat a direct quotation as though it, too, had been written in your own words. If in taking notes you followed our suggestion and marked off the quotations with large quotation marks, or « and », you can easily check the paper against the notes to be sure all quotations have been identified as such. If the markings on your note cards are not clear, however, you must go back to the actual sources to determine which words in your notes are quotations and which are your own.

The problem of plagiarizing language, however, usually goes beyond copying full sentences or even paragraphs from a source without inserting quotation marks and adding notes. Sometimes a student is suspected of plagiarism because the wording of his or her paraphrases is so close to that of the wording in source materials that it is practically a quotation. Only a few words have been changed, and the sentence patterns are virtually identical to those in the sources.

Here is an example involving a description of George Washington's plan for saving his forces from the British army, which had trapped him into defending a fortress on the shore of Long Island. The only means of escape required moving the men in small boats.

original passage | The other necessity, and this seemed the impossible one, was for Washington to find some way to get his army away without tremendous loss. The problem was that, when part of the force was on water, the rest, unable adequately to defend the fortifications, would become easy prey for the enemy. Unless he could somehow slip secretly away, Washington would have to sacrifice half his army.

Works Cited entry | Flexner, James T. The Young Hamilton. Boston: Little, 1978.

a case of laziness, or deliberate plagiarism? | The other need, which seemed to be impossible, was for Washington to discover some means of getting the army away without enormous losses. His problem

was that, when some of the soldiers were on the
water, the others would be unable to defend their
land position adequately and could be easily
defeated by the British. Unless Washington could
manage to slip away in secret, he would lose half his
forces (Flexner 110).

Perhaps the only crime here is laziness, but the fact remains that this
student relied heavily on the original sentence structure and only "trans-
lated" the passage by finding synonyms for a few words. The flow of
thought is a direct echo of the original. Although the note tells the reader
where the information came from, there is no indication that the wording
is not entirely the student's own work.

Perhaps this plagiarism was unintentional. The student may have
thought that since the two versions are not *exactly* the same, no plagiarism occurred. But his version sounds too much like the original. To re-
pair the damage, he would have to rewrite the entire paragraph,
changing the sentence structure and finding different word choices. (Remember that a paraphrase restates the author's idea in your own words.)

acceptable paraphrase   Washington's brilliance as a field commander is
shown by his plan for the army to escape by water
before the British knew what was happening.
Obviously, the soldiers could not simply board boats
and sail away, because if the British attacked in the
middle of the operation, most of the troops would be
in no position to defend themselves (Flexner 110).

This paraphrase is distinctly different from the source, as it should
be. Of course, a note is still essential — to credit the author as the source
of the information. (Remember that ideas, opinions, and judgments all
must be acknowledged, even after you express them in your own words.)

Paraphrasing without Plagiarizing

It is not always easy to know how different from the original your
paraphrase must be if you are to avoid plagiarism. A possible rule would
be to enclose any words taken from a source in quotation marks, but this
could lead to absurdities in many common situations. For instance, how

would you paraphrase the following sentence without using the italicized words?

original
: The typical *Inuit igloo* offers superior insulation against *temperatures* that fall as low as *–50° F.*

There are no synonyms for most proper nouns, such as *Inuit,* just as there are no synonyms for most numbers (exceptions: *dozen* for *twelve; score* for *twenty; decade* for *ten years*). As for *igloo,* the substitution of *ice house* or *house made from blocks of hard-packed snow* would be either inaccurate or very clumsy, and *temperature* can be replaced only by a slightly different idea, such as *coldness* or *freezing weather.* If you put quotation marks around these words in your paraphrase, the result would look rather silly:

absurd use of
quotation marks
: A well-made "Inuit igloo" protects its occupants even when "temperatures" outside reach "–50° F."

Obviously, any rule must be flexible enough to prevent this ugliness. In general, then, you can safely repeat specific numbers *(–50° F., 21 percent, 5,280 feet, 7 million people, $524.52),* special terms for which there are no simple synonyms *(igloo, gross national product, income tax, influenza, touchdown, amphetamine),* and even very simple words that would require bizarre substitutions *(horse, ocean, atmosphere, lung, father, high school, temperature).*

Remember, however, that sometimes even a single word taken from a source requires quotation marks if it is especially colorful or represents the writer's judgment. The following summary of an article quoted just two isolated words, *ridiculous* and *absurd.*

student summary
of article
: In 1912, H. H. Goddard, director of research at Vineland Institute for Feeble-Minded Girls and Boys in New Jersey, was commissioned by the U.S. Public Health Service to survey mental deficiency among immigrant populations at Ellis Island. According to paleontologist Stephen Jay Gould, Goddard's study employed "ridiculous" criteria which led to "absurd" conclusions regarding the native intelligence of Jews and other unpopular European minorities. Goddard's work played a significant role in the

passage of the Restriction Act of 1924, which, according to Allan Chase, author of The Legacy of Malthus, barred millions of Jews from entering the United States and thereby escaping the Nazi holocaust (Gould 14–15).

Works Cited entry   Gould, Stephen Jay. "Science and Jewish Immigration." Natural History Dec. 1980: 14–19.

As you can see, the problem of plagiarism concerns not only individual words but also the flow of thought and the presentation of ideas, all of which combine to give a piece of writing its style and originality. The research paper assignment measures, among other things, your ability to express ideas effectively. Although this challenge can be frustrating at times, you will be expected to maintain a personal integrity that will prevent your surrendering to the temptation to borrow even "just a little bit here and there" from sources.

Working with Sources

Reviewing Part Three

Questions

1. What is a working bibliography? How does it differ from the final list of Works Cited or References?
2. Briefly outline the different but related processes of skimming a book and skimming a periodical article.
3. Explain how you can tell whether a potential source is likely to be useful to you. Mention several specific criteria.
4. What signs might warn you that a topic is probably too narrow? Too broad? What steps can you take to resolve both problems?
5. After you have found what seems to be an adequate *number* of sources, and you are *looking over the titles and the authors' names*, what should you be looking for if you are concerned that the list may not be adequate?
6. How does a hypothesis help you read sources and take good notes?
7. What kind of information *must* you record in every note entry to avoid problems at later stages in the process?
8. Why do successful notetakers keep each note as brief as possible?
9. What is the difference between a summary and a paraphrase? How are they similar?
10. What are the advantages of paraphrasing and summarizing rather than copying passages from sources?
11. When paraphrasing, do you have to change every word that appeared in the original? Explain your answer.
12. For what reasons might you quote rather than paraphrase a statement found in a source?
13. Why might plagiarism become a problem even for honest writers of research papers?

Exercises

1. Write out the information for the following sources as you would on a bibliography card:
   - a 1952 book published in New York by Harcourt, Brace & World called A History of Western Philosophy and written by W. T. Jones.

- an article about the Japanese economy called How Japan Does It, written by Christopher Byron, published in Time magazine on March 30, 1981, and running from page 54 through page 60.
- an article in The Sixteenth Century Journal by N. M. Sutherland called Catherine de Medici: The Legend of the Wicked Italian Queen, running from page 45 through page 56 and published in volume 9 in 1978.

2. If you are currently working on a research project and have developed a topic and hypothesis, follow the suggestions in this chapter to put together a working bibliography and evaluate the potential sources by skimming them. Turn in your notes.

3. In a popular magazine of your choice, read an article about a topic of current interest, such as *new energy sources, genetic engineering, political problems in Central America,* or *space probes of distant planets.* Then, using an appropriate periodical index, find an article on the same topic in a professional journal and read it. Write a paragraph or two contrasting the approaches used by the authors of the two articles.

4. Choose a nationally controversial topic, such as *the war on drugs, Medicaid payments for abortion, sexual harassment in the workplace,* or *affirmative action programs,* or any important issue facing your area of the country. Find articles in two different periodicals (newspapers included) that take opposite sides on the issue. Write a summary that points out the major differences in their views and the general tone of each article.

5. Take a full set of notes on the following excerpt from a lecture. Be sure to follow the direction indicated by the hypothesis when deciding what information belongs in your notes. Remember not to put too much information on individual cards. If you quote something, mark it clearly, and, in parentheses, give a reason for quoting — accuracy, memorable words, conciseness, authority.

Topic: *the causes of violence in America today*

Hypothesis: "Although some observers blame violence on television and the economy, the cause may lie in our past, going back to the lawless West and to Prohibition."

It is commonly assumed that violence is part of our frontier heritage. But the historical record shows that frontier violence was very different from violence today. Robbery and burglary, two of our most common crimes, were of no great significance in the frontier towns of the Old West, and rape was seemingly nonexistent.

Bodie, one of the principal towns on the trans-Sierra frontier, illustrates the point. Nestled high in the mountains of eastern California, Bodie, which boomed in the late 1870s and early 1880s, ranked among the most notorious frontier towns of the Old West. It was, as one prospector put it, the last of the old-time mining camps.

From Roger D. McGrath, "The Myth of Frontier Violence," *Harper's* Feb. 1985: 26–28, an excerpt from a lecture given November 1984 at California State University, Long Beach.

Like the trans-Sierra frontier in generally, Bodie was indisputably violent and lawless, yet most people were not affected. Fistfights and gunfights among willing combatants — gamblers, miners, and the like — were regular events, and stagecoach holdups were not unusual. But the old, the young, the weak, and the female — so often the victims of crime today — were generally not harmed.

Robbery was more often aimed at stagecoaches than at individuals. Highwaymen usually took only the express box and left the passengers alone. There were eleven stagecoach robberies in Bodie between 1878 and 1882, and in only two instances were passengers robbed. (In one instance, the highwaymen later apologized for their conduct.)

There were only ten robberies and three attempted robberies of individuals in Bodie during its boom years, and in nearly every case the circumstances were the same: the victim had spent the evening in a gambling den, saloon, or brothel; he had revealed that he had on his person a significant sum of money; and he was staggering home drunk when the attack occurred.

Bodie's total of twenty-one robberies — eleven of stages and ten of individuals — over a five-year period converts to a rate of eighty-four robberies per 100,000 inhabitants per year. On this scale — the same scale used by the FBI to index crime — New York City's robbery rate in 1980 was 1,140, Miami's was 995, and Los Angeles's was 628. The rate for the United States as a whole was 243. Thus Bodie's robbery rate was significantly below the national average in 1980.

Perhaps the greatest deterrent to crime in Bodie was the fact that so many people were armed. Armed guards prevented bank robberies and holdups of stagecoaches carrying shipments of bullion, and armed homeowners and merchants discouraged burglary. Between 1878 and 1882, there were only thirty-two burglaries — seventeen of homes and fifteen of businesses — in Bodie. At least a half-dozen burglaries were thwarted by the presence of armed citizens. The newspapers regularly advocated shooting burglars

on sight, and several burglars were, in fact, shot at.

Using the FBI scale, Bodie's burglary rate for those five years was 128. Miami's rate in 1980 was 3,282, New York City's was 2,661, and Los Angeles's was 2,602. The rate of the United States as a whole was 1,668, thirteen times that of Bodie.

Bodie's law enforcement institutions were certainly not responsible for these low rates. Rarely were robbers or burglars arrested, and even less often were they convicted. Moreover, many law enforcement officers operated on both sides of the law.

It was the armed citizens themselves who were the most potent — though not the only — deterrent to larcenous crime. Another was the threat of vigilantism. Highwaymen, for example, understood that while they could take the express box from a stagecoach without arousing the citizens, they risked inciting the entire populace to action if they robbed the passengers.

There is considerable evidence that women in Bodie were rarely the victims of crime. Between 1878 and 1882 only one woman, a prostitute, was robbed, and there were no reported cases of rape. (There is no evidence that rapes occurred but were not reported.)

Finally, juvenile crime, which accounts for a significant portion of the violent crime in the United States today, was limited in Bodie to pranks and malicious mischief.

If robbery, burglary, crimes against women, and juvenile crime were relatively rare on the trans-Sierra frontier, homicide was not: thirty-one Bodieites were shot, stabbed, or beaten to death during the boom years, for a homicide rate of 116. No U.S. city today comes close to this rate. In 1980, Miami led the nation with a homicide rate of 32.7; Las Vegas was a distant second at 23.4. A half-dozen cities had rates of zero. The rate for the United States as a whole in that year was a mere 10.2.

Several factors contributed to Bodie's high homicide rate. A majority of the town's residents were young, adventurous, single males who adhered to a code of conduct that frequently required them to fight even if, or perhaps especially if, it could mean death.

Courage was admired above all else. Alcohol also played a major role in fostering the settlement of disputes by violence.

If the men's code of conduct and their consumption of alcohol made fighting inevitable, their sidearms often made it fatal. While the carrying of guns probably reduced the incidence of robbery and burglary, it undoubtedly increased the number of homicides.

For the most part, the citizens of Bodie were not troubled by the great number of killings; nor were they troubled that only one man was ever convicted of murder. They accepted the killings and the lack of convictions because most of those killed had been willing combatants.

Thus the violence and lawlessness of the trans-Sierra frontier bear little relation to the violence and lawlessness that pervade American society today. If Bodie is at all representative of frontier towns, there is little justification for blaming contemporary American violence on our frontier heritage.

6. For each of the following topics/hypotheses, prepare a set of note cards based on the accompanying newspaper article. In both cases, be sure to follow the direction indicated by the hypothesis when deciding what information to record in the notes.

Remember not to crowd information onto the cards. If you decide to quote, mark the quoted words off clearly. Then, in parentheses, state your reason for quoting—accuracy, conciseness, authority, memorable language.

Topic 1: *possible genetic basis for schizophrenia*

Hypothesis: "Recent research reveals that schizophrenia is probably caused by a defective gene."

Topic 2: *genetic bases of human behavior*

Hypothesis: "Just as research has located genetic sources of many diseases, so it will find genetic causes for behavior patterns such as addiction, schizophrenia, and criminality."

Gene Hunters Pursue Elusive and Complex Traits of Mind

By NATALIE ANGIER

It was just a handful of years ago that biologists were waving their spears, shields and pipettes in the air, boasting with full-throated glory of their success in capturing the legendary prey of molecular genetics. In a series of widely publicized discoveries, geneticists announced the isolation of the cystic fibrosis gene, the gene for Lou Gehrig's disease, the gene for Huntington's disease and a gene linked to the familial form of breast cancer.

Some of those great gene hunts had taken a decade or more, and had been a Ninth Circle of Hell for many a graduate student and postdoctoral fellow. But molecular geneticists now look back on such triumphs, shake their heads and say, boy, did those lucky devils have it easy.

The field of genetics is moving into a new and much more difficult phase: the search for genes that may contribute in some partial and numbingly convoluted way to complex traits of the mind, the stuff of private psyche and inner life. A fat set of reports being published today in the journal *Nature Genetics* includes two studies that cover this territory.

One confirms an earlier report that had linked male sexual orientation to a spot on the X chromosome.

Another package of papers from several international teams of scientists identifies the rough location of a gene that may play a role in schizophrenia. The reports are accompanied by an editorial that tells biologists how to discriminate between a real finding in the complex field of complex traits, and an experimental coincidence no more meaningful than, say, flipping five heads in a row.

This new work in genetics is riddled with scientific, intellectual and sociocultural mine fields. Many of the straightforward disease genes have been isolated, or are on the verge of being so. These are the genes that hew to the tidy laws of Gregor Mendel, the father of modern genetics. These are the genes that almost surely cause illness in people born with defective versions of them. Inherit the cystic fibrosis mutation, for example, and you are at grave risk of chronic, debilitating lung infections. About 4,000 diseases are thought to be so-called single-gene disorders. Most are very rare in the population, but they have appealed to human geneticists because they are linked to one gene apiece, and are therefore open to molecular dissection.

Scientists are now moving on to the dread complex traits. They are looking for the genes that may predispose people to high blood pressure, heart disease, diabetes and most adult cancers. And on a far more incendiary scale, some researchers are seeking the genes that may put one at risk for a serious mental disease like manic-depressive illness, schizophrenia or alcoholism. They are looking for genes that influence sexual orientation, or the hunger for novel experiences, or the tendency toward introversion, or a taste for nicotine. And the only thing they are sure of in their various hunts is that no single gene can explain any of the behaviors they study, and that they will spend their professional lives qualifying every claim and cautioning audiences to please, please, please, not overinterpret the results.

Nevertheless, after a long period of setbacks and missteps, the field of behavioral and psychiatric genetics is lately picking up steam and enthusiasm, reflected in the studies just published and the commentary on them. With humorous didacticism, Dr. Eric Lander of the Whitehead Institute for Biomedical Research and the Massachusetts Institute of Technology in Cambridge, and Dr. Leonid Kruglyak of the Whitehead Institute warn their fellow biologists in the *Nature Genetics* editorial that while they may often greet statistics with "glazed-eyed indifference" (and you thought scientists liked that stuff!), they are going to have to knuckle under and take statistics more seriously in this new era of mapping complex traits.

Good statistics are essential on two counts. If a disease or trait has multiple causes, including many genes and that squishy business known as "the environment," then it will take a sound use of mathematics to find an interesting genetic connection in the first place. And once that connection has been identified, a rigorous statistical analysis will assure one that it is real before one rushes it into print.

"We wrote the commentary to try to put statistics in simple terms, so people can understand why we have to have a strict threshold before declaring linkage," Dr. Lander said. "We're going to see hundreds of papers on complex traits over the next few years, and we don't want people to be crying wolf."

In fact, the field of psychiatric genetics has only begun to emerge from a slump in which a number of wolves turned out to be dogs. In the late 1980's, several research teams reported finding genes for manic depression and schizophrenia, which either were never confirmed by other researchers, or were proved wrong and had to be retracted.

But the incentive to move forward was too great to be deterred by a flub or two. For one thing, the illnesses are extremely common, each affecting about 1 percent of the population. They are devastating: for example, 30 percent of the hospital beds in the nation are occupied by schizophrenia patients, said Dr. Kenneth S. Kendler of the Medical College of Virginia in Richmond, an author with Dr. Richard E. Straub, a colleague there, of one of the schizophrenia papers appearing today. And scientists have had scant success trying to understand the illnesses through a nongenetic approach. "Psychiatry is still pretty much in the dark ages," said Dr. David Curtis of the Institute of Psychiatry in London, who contributed to the section on schizophrenia in *Nature Genetics.* "We have no idea about the basic biochemical abnormalities that occur in the course of the illnesses," and a genetic angle on the diseases may offer new insights into their cause.

Moreover, the evidence for a genetic contribution to these mental disorders is quite strong. Studies of twins, for example, showed a hereditary contribution of anywhere from 30 percent to 50 percent for schizophrenia, somewhat more for manic-depressive illness. Researchers also said that the tools they had used before in searching for genes involved in complex mental disorders were too crude for the task.

"At the beginning of using linkage analysis to study schizophrenia, we used monogenic models," like those applied to the analysis of cystic fibrosis, said Dr. Hans W. Moises of Kiel University Hospital in Germany, an author on another of today's reports. "These models are inappropriate where complex diseases are involved."

Recognizing the muddy history of their specialty, the psychiatric geneticists reporting today on their discovery of an intriguing link to schizophrenia are resolutely cautious. What the groups have found is that there appears to be a gene on the upper arm of chromosome 6 (out of the 23 pairs of chromosomes all humans have) that may play a part in some unknown percentage of cases of the disease. But everybody involved admit-

ted the evidence for chromosome 6p, as the region is known, is not overwhelming. Four teams found the association; and because independent replication is a benchmark for any scientific finding, the work is considered quite exciting. But in none of the individual studies was the result overwhelming, meaning that the chain of evidence is built of rather fragile links. Moreover, two other teams reported no connection at all between schizophrenia and 6p, and one of those scientists, Dr. Curtis, believes the finding will turn out to have been yet another false positive.

Dr. Ann E. Pulver of the Johns Hopkins University School of Medicine in Baltimore, who obtained one of those positive results, said that if the gene on chromosome 6 was involved in only a limited number of cases of the disease — say, 25 percent or less — there was no reason to expect every researcher to find it active in their sample of patients. She and others said the real test would come when researchers got their hands on the gene proper, rather than its approximate location; and then look to see whether the gene is mutated in patients with schizophrenia.

That will take some doing. The 6p region of the chromosome contains many hundreds of genes. Just getting to that general neighborhood had been an extraordinary task. Dr. Kendler and his colleagues, who first identified the tantalizing chromosomal association, tried to make their work tenable by going to Ireland and collaborating with researchers in Dublin and Belfast. The Irish make a good study population for a number of reasons. They have large families, making it easier to trace genetic patterns and compare one relative with another. The Irish are more genetically similar than a comparable group of, say, Americans, and that makes it easier to home in on particular genes of interest. They are also more culturally homogenized, which means most people are exposed to relatively similar environmental conditions, an important consideration for a disease thought to have some environmental component. And finally, Dr. Kendler said, the Irish use very few recreational drugs beyond alcohol, which rules out the complicating factor of those drugs thought to induce a psychosis-like state.

The scientists identified 265 families with two or more people suffering from schizophrenia. They drew blood from as many of the 1,408 individuals as they could — patients and their nonafflicted relatives alike — and extracted DNA from the blood cells. Dr. Straub then screened the DNA with 200 so-called DNA markers, bits of radioactively tagged genetic material that serve as signposts indicating a location somewhere on the 23 chromosomes. He was looking for patterns of markers that would be found in the DNA of the schizophrenics but not in their nonafflicted relatives. That broadside approach showed chromosome 6 worthy of closer examination.

Dr. Straub then coordinated a collaborative effort with other teams known to be studying the genetics of schizophrenia. He told them about the tantalizing 6p connection, and asked them to scrutinize the DNA of their family groups to see if the link held up. In some cases, it did.

Other researchers have also detected promising links to chromosomes 8 and 22. But in all cases, they are far, far from singling out the genes themselves. Moreover, even if they isolate a gene and it proves to be involved in some cases of schizophrenia, it will never be as clean an association as the Huntington's gene is with Huntington's disease. Any one gene can only tell a minor part of the somber tale of madness.

Part Four

Writing the Paper

Writing the Paper

14

Organizing and Outlining

Now that you have completed most of your research and have produced a full set of notes taken from a variety of sources, you are ready to start planning the actual writing of your paper. Of course, you may have to go back and reexamine one or more sources if you suspect that you missed some useful information. Or, after you have begun to write the paper, you may hear of another relevant source and want to check it out. Research is seldom a straightforward procedure. Retracing your steps is frequently necessary.

The writing of the paper is complicated by the large amount of information that must be organized into a logical sequence. To gain control over all this material, you need to review the notes and the ongoing outline to gain an overview of all that your research has produced.

Organizing Your Notes

An easy way to get such an overview is to lay all your note cards out on a table, arranging them into groups according to subtopics. (If you took notes in a notebook or on a computer, just do the same thing with your notebook pages or printouts.) Now you can see the advantage to having each note on its own card—you can shift a note from one group to another as you try to find the best way to organize the information. The ongoing outline can serve as the basis for the full outline that you will need as you undertake the writing of the rough draft.

The number of subtopics you have at this stage will vary greatly from one research project to the next, but you can probably expect to find yourself faced with somewhere between ten and twenty groups of note cards on the table before you. In an effort to organize these materials, try to form a picture of the research paper as it will look at the end. In all likelihood, the paper will consist of several divisions, each made up of several subtopics.

For his paper on Cotton Mather, Fred Hutchins took five subtopics and placed them in a major subdivision:

> **Subtopics:** the millennium's proximity; visits from an angel; the Puritan colony and the New Jerusalem; a total system — God, Devil, angels, witches; Mather's belief in his closeness to God
>
> **Major Subdivision:** Mather's personal religious views

(This was not Fred's final arrangement of this information. He later broke this large subdivision into two smaller ones: Mather's special place in God's eyes; and the Puritan colony and the Second Coming.)

Fred continued to organize his subtopics until they were all grouped into major subdivisions.

Another objective of forming an overview is to determine whether your research is complete. If you find you do not have enough evidence from which to draw a valid conclusion, you need to do more research — either find more sources or go back and get more information from sources you have already examined.

A student writing on *dinosaur extinction* saw she had just one brief note on a theory that is not widely held. Her research would not have been considered complete without a reasonably thorough account of that theory, which would give readers a fair chance to judge its validity. So back she went to the library.

Writing the Introduction

After you have arrived at your thesis and arranged the note cards into a rough preliminary outline for the paper, your next step is to write the introduction. The introductory paragraph or paragraphs not only state your thesis but also indicate the major subdivisions of the paper and the general nature of the sources. By putting together your major subtopics in what amounts to a preview of the whole paper, you gain a sense of control over the writing. This feeling of control will help you see the significance of each detail as you try to find a place for it in the overall essay.

Before writing the introduction, jot down the major points you expect it to include. In the case of Cotton Mather, the main points were these:

Topic: *Cotton Mather's belief in witchcraft*

Major Subtopics: modern view — humane, not cruel; defense of the social order; possible antifeminism; personal religious views

Sources: modern historians

From these materials, Fred wrote a rough draft of his introduction:

> Many people today are amazed by how strongly people in colonial New England believed in witches, and by the fact that they went so far as to burn or hang witches out of fear. They especially wonder how intelligent, educated ministers could be so superstitious. Why would ministers believe witches were the agents of the Devil, and why would they be so afraid of some people as to accuse them of being witches? Many uneducated people might blame the Devil and witches for their bad luck, but educated religious leaders like Cotton Mather should have been setting them straight, not leading them on. No one seems to agree on the reasons why this prominent Puritan minister supported the witch-hunts, but most historians today say he was not just a cruel persecutor of innocent victims. They think he saw witches as part of God's creation and that he was concerned that the trials be conducted fairly. He was mostly worried that the witches could undermine the society, for they were supposed to be the Devil's secret agents.

Fred realized that this rough paragraph would have to be made a bit more elaborate and polished, but he also saw that it achieved the basic aims of an introduction — a clear view of the ideas he wanted to present. Fred did not write the final version, which grew to three short paragraphs, until he had written the rest of the paper. Take time to note the structure of this revised introduction, which is shown below.

In the first paragraph, Fred sets up the problem he was investigating: "Why did intelligent Christian ministers believe in witches to the extent of killing those accused of witchcraft?" The next paragraph provides several explanations for Mather's behavior. The third paragraph presents Fred's thesis: "Mather's belief in witchcraft stemmed from his perception of his own personal relation to God and that of the Puritans' place in God's master plan for humanity."

Thus his introduction serves as an overview of the full paper.

introductory
paragraphs

In 1692, a series of trials held in Salem, Massachusetts, resulted in the execution of twenty people for practicing witchcraft. Over the years, many historians have tried to explain both the outbreak of witchcraft hysteria at that time and the motives of certain community leaders who played important roles in hunting down and convicting

reference to source
for background
information

people who were considered to be witches.[1] One such leader was Cotton Mather, a prominent Puritan minister and theologian, whose complex life and voluminous writings have provided historians with ample material for attempting to understand both the man and his times.

more background
material—nature of
sources for this paper

Early critics of Mather painted him as a cruel witch-hunter and tormentor of innocent people. And while this negative image of Mather has not entirely disappeared, modern historians have largely ruled out the interpretation that Mather's involvement in witch-hunting stemmed from a deliberate desire to inflict suffering on innocent victims. Indeed, some historians have all but absolved Mather of any unusual responsibility for the trials. He was a person of the times, these writers argue; in late-seventeenth-century America, it was a rare person who did not believe in and fear the existence of witches. Other historians see Mather's general support of the trials growing out of his desire to defend the authority of the civil judges and protect the Puritan social system. Yet another interpretation views Mather's role as that of a champion of the patriarchial social order. This idea may explain why Mather supported the trials of accused witches, the overwhelming majority of whom were women.

narrowing of Fred's
chief argument

statement of thesis

Cotton Mather was a complicated human being, and there may be some truth in all of these ideas. However, the ultimate explanation for his behavior during this fascinating if terrible moment in American history may well lie in his unique view of himself and the Puritan colony. His belief in witches, along with his need to identify and punish them, seems to have supported both his belief that he enjoyed a special, personal relationship with God and his view that the New England Puritan colony was destined to play the central role in God's plan for the future of humanity.

Refining the Outline

Once you have drafted your introduction, your attention turns to the structure of the paper. A fairly detailed outline is essential if you hope to control all the information that has been collected. The preliminary outline you have been working with during the note-taking phase, and which you have gradually fleshed out by creating major subdivisions and subtopics, needs to be further broken down into specific points representing information from individual cards. Such an outline allows you to place each note card in its assigned slot, waiting to be incorporated into the rough draft. As we shall soon see, an outline can take one of several formats.

Broadly speaking, a research paper has three parts:

- *an introduction*—in which the topic is introduced and the thesis stated
- *a body*—in which the topic is developed and relevant information presented
- *a conclusion*—in which the paper is summed up and the thesis restated).

This three-part structure is the framework on which you build your outline. By the time Fred began writing his first draft, the preliminary outline for his paper (the beginnings of which we saw in Chapter 11) looked like this:

Writing the Paper

Introduction

1. The cruel portrait has been updated to show Mather's humaneness.
2. Mather tried to assure fairness of the trials.
3. Mather wrote and preached against witchcraft.
4. Several theories focus on Mather's defense of the social order.
5. One writer believes Mather was antifeminist.
6. Mather's personal religious views led to his belief in witches.

Conclusion

A short outline such as this gave Fred a chance to think about the shape of his paper without being confused by the details he had come across in his research. As he thought over the items in this outline, he realized that point 2 was one of the examples of Mather's humaneness; that is, it fit better in point 1.

Fred also noticed that point 3 did not belong in the outline because Mather's writings are referred to throughout the paper by the historians as they try to explain his character and motivation. However, Fred wanted to mention Mather's influence on the Salem community, so he reworded this item.

Finally, point 5 referred to one aspect of the social order Mather was defending, so it belonged under point 4.

The revised short outline follows:

Introduction

1. Mather was more humane than originally portrayed. (Murdock; Hofstadter; Hansen; Levy)
2. Whatever his motives, Mather did influence the witch-hunting. (Silverman; Levin)
3. Mather was deeply committed to maintaining the Puritan social order. (Hansen; Levy; Karlsen; Pestana)
4. Mather's personal religious views necessitated his belief in witches. (Levin; Silverman; Levy; Middlekauff; Miller)

Conclusion

Notice that Fred listed the sources that contributed each idea to the development of his research paper.

The next stage, constructing a detailed outline, depends on a careful evaluation of your materials.

1. First, *arrange the piles of note cards in the same order as the subtopics in your brief outline.*

2. Next, *read through your notes again to be sure they are both relevant and usable.* You may want to eliminate a note that no longer seems relevant, to reassign a minor subtopic to a different major subtopic, or perhaps even to return to the library and look for information on an important subtopic about which you have not uncovered enough information.

3. Finally, *put your full set of cards in the precise order you expect to follow when writing the paper.* Start by arranging the minor subtopics within the major subtopic to which you have assigned them. Then sort all the note cards within each minor subtopic in a logical sequence.

By arranging your entire collection of notes in this way, you will have laid out on the table an organizational pattern for your paper. This is, in effect, a physical outline, and from it you can prepare the detailed written outline that will guide your writing of the first draft.

The Matter of Balance

As you put your groups of note cards into sequence, look for possible imbalance. No subtopic should outweigh or overshadow other equally important subtopics.

For example, suppose you were writing about Martin Luther King Jr. and had arrived at the thesis "Martin Luther King's success resulted from three major factors — his courage, his intelligence, and his charisma." Your outline, which determines the shape of the paper, would be strongly unbalanced if you devoted one section to "courage," one to "intelligence," and then six sections to "charisma." If your general impression from reading the sources was that all three factors contributed equally to King's success, then you would need to return to your sources or find new sources, looking for more information about the two briefly covered factors. If, however, you now realized that most of the sources had indeed emphasized charisma, you would have to revise your thesis. It might well read: "Martin Luther King's success depended on three factors — courage, intelligence, and charisma — of which charisma was by far the most important."

Whatever direction you take, be sure to correct an unbalanced outline before you start to write. You will find it much harder to make such a change later.

The Traditional Outline Format

In constructing an outline, use whatever format you feel comfortable with, unless your instructor specifies a particular one. A commonly used format combines letters and numbers to designate the various levels of classification. Even if you are already familiar with this format, take time now to be sure you understand the subtle distinctions between those levels.

This list indicates the relative difference between levels:

Roman numerals (I, II) represent major subtopics, each covering a large section of the paper.

Capital letters (A, B) represent minor subtopics, each occupying at least one, sometimes several, paragraphs.

Arabic numerals (1, 2) represent major details that support a minor subtopic.

Small letters (a, b) represent minor details that support a major detail.

The longer the paper you are writing, the broader the area covered by the highest category (Roman numerals) and the greater the chance that you will need a fifth set of symbols to represent the smallest details in the paper (small Roman numerals — i, ii, iii).

Many writers follow two sensible rules for constructing outlines:

Rule 1: *Never break down a category into just one subdivision. To do so is illogical.*

wrong; only one detail
supports subtopic A

I. Difficulties faced by Diego Rivera in early years
  A. Childhood problems
    1. Grave illness from typhus and scarlet fever
  B. Adolescent problems

At some point, childhood problems must have seemed an important subtopic, but in this outline it looks trivial. Perhaps information about another childhood problem has been assigned to a different subtopic and could be moved into this one. Or perhaps another trip to the library would produce information about a second childhood problem accidentally omitted during note-taking. The outline might then look like this:

correct

I. Difficulties faced by Diego Rivera in early years
  A. Childhood problems

1. Grave illness from typhus and scarlet fever
2. Dangers arising from father's radical politics
B. Adolescent problems

On the other hand, if Rivera's only significant childhood problem had been illnesses, the outline might be revised to look like this:

correct I. Difficulties faced by Diego Rivera in early years

A. Childhood illnesses

B. Adolescent problems

(It is not necessary to add Arabic numerals under A for the specific illnesses unless your note cards treat them extensively and you mean to discuss them in detail.)

Rule 2: *Use the same grammatical form for words at the same level of classification. By doing so, you produce parallel structure — that is, a pleasing and easy-to-understand ordering of ideas.*

wrong; the subdivisions are not grammatically parallel

A. Symptoms of senility

1. Forgetting recent events

2. Mistakes in simple arithmetic

3. Occasional hallucinating

4. Inappropriate responses in social situations

correct; each subdivision is a gerund phrase

A. Symptoms of senility

1. Forgetting recent events

2. Making mistakes in simple arithmetic

3. Hallucinating occasionally

4. Responding inappropriately in social situations

Phrase and Sentence Outlines

The outlines presented in the previous section are examples of *phrase outlines,* in which each category is expressed in a phrase. Some instructors may require you to submit a *sentence outline,* in which you must express each category as a complete sentence. A sentence outline usually takes more time to write than a phrase outline, but it offers you an important

Writing the Paper

advantage. The sentences that make up the outline can often be used almost word for word when you start to write your paper.

The opening section of Fred's outline for his Cotton Mather paper is an example of a sentence outline. Note that in addition to using complete sentences, this outline also lists the source for each major detail at the point where it will be used.

Cotton Mather's Necessary Witches

Introduction

    1. Historians have tried to learn about Mather's role in witchcraft hysteria and the Salem trials.

    2. The old view of Mather as a cruel persecutor has given way to more favorable interpretations of his personality.

    3. THESIS: Mather's belief in witchcraft was based on private religious beliefs.

I. Historians' opinions of Mather's role in the witch-hunts and his motives for playing that role have changed in recent years.

    A. Mather's belief in witchcraft was normal for the times, and he was more humane than originally portrayed.

        1. The old harsh view of Mather was due to misinterpretation. (Murdock)

            a. He was actually more humane than most people think.

            b. Almost everyone in seventeenth-century America believed in witches.

        2. Modern historians may be biased against intellectuals of that era. (Hofstadter)

            a. They "encouraged greater tolerance."

            b. They opposed unenlightened trial judges.

        3. Mather tried to ensure fairness of trials. (Hansen)

            a. He warned against dangers of accepting "spectral evidence."

            b. He trusted judges to listen to him, but often they did not.

        4. Witchcraft really works in communities where everyone believes in it. (Hansen; long quotation)

        5. Mather also believed in witches because the Bible warns against them. (Levy)

Note: This example shows just one major division of the paper. The full outline was much longer.

Whichever outline form you use, be consistent. Do not mix phrases into a sentence outline or sentences into a phrase outline. (For an example of a complete phrase outline, see the sample student paper on Emily Dickinson in Chapter 21.)

Unconventional Outlines

The major reason for constructing an outline is to organize your thoughts and notes into a logical pattern before you write your research paper. The outline formats you have studied thus far have been used for many years by many writers to organize their thoughts before undertaking an extensive piece of writing. However, some writers prefer to devise their own approaches to outlining that both satisfy their personal sense of organization and work well as guides to creating logical essays.

Some writers prefer to use combinations of the traditional outline formats. For example, someone might use a very precise phrase outline (including many lettered and numbered subsections) to outline a section that included many details and then switch to a sentence format to outline theoretical or explanatory sections.

What kind of outlining procedure is best for you? The one that best guides you in planning an effective essay — the kind of procedure that leads to a logical expression of your ideas and knowledge in essay form. Fred Hutchins used a sentence outline whereas Shirley Macalbe and Susanna Andrews went for a more conventional phrase format. David Perez used yet another approach. All four students produced successful research papers.

You may have to do some experimenting before you hit on an outlining approach that best suits your particular talents for planning and writing essays. In general, if you have had problems with writing well-organized essays in the past, a tighter, more conventional form will probably serve you best. On the other hand, if you are the kind of person who finds that writing comes easily, then you might experiment with unconventional forms that allow you freer range in planning your research paper. After seeing samples of your writing in the course, your instructor can probably give good advice about which path you should take.

15

Writing the Rough Draft

After you have developed a logical outline and written an introduction, you are ready to write the paper itself. This task will consume a good deal of time because you must plan to write at least three versions of your paper: a rough draft, a revised draft, and a polished final manuscript suitable for submission to your instructor. Many writers feel the need for even further revision, but three drafts are the absolute minimum.

The basic steps involved in drafting your paper are the same whether you are using pen and paper or working with a computer's word-processing program. However, use of a computer can make some of the work go faster and more smoothly. If you will be using a computer for part or all of your work, you may find the following section helpful.

Working on a Computer

Just as the computer has greatly facilitated the search for materials in the library, so has it made writing papers much easier and less time consuming. It does this through *word-processing programs*, which turn a computer into a super-typewriter. Because most college instructors require that papers be typewritten, you would do well to become familiar with the typewriter keyboard. Proficiency is by no means necessary. Once you acquire the knack of two-finger typing, you will be able to write faster than with a pen or pencil, and the "pages" will never become cluttered with notes, and smaller notes, and arrows leading to the backs of pages.

Of course, many people still prefer to write by hand when they are taking notes and brainstorming, and some even like to handwrite their first draft. But when the time comes for revising, almost everyone who has tried word processing agrees that it beats wrestling with sheets of paper covered with barely legible changes and corrections. And, as we have mentioned in earlier chapters, using a computer for the note-taking and drafting stages as well can make the transition from rough notes to complete draft much easier.

As you plan the various steps of writing your research paper, you should take into account whether or not you will have frequent, easy access to a computer. More and more students own personal computers, and virtually all colleges today provide rooms equipped with computers for students to use. However, scheduling access to these computers can be difficult. If you have your own computer, you can use it for much of your note-taking and outlining (although you will need to handwrite work that you do far from your computer). If you must rely on a public computer, you may want to handwrite the early stages of your paper. When you have a complete rough draft, input (type) it, print it out, revise it at home by hand, and return to the computer to input your changes. Be sure to allow ample time in your work schedule for the several computer sessions you will probably need in order to arrive at a final draft.

If you want to use a word-processing program but find that owning a computer is too expensive, you may want to buy a *word processor*, a typewriter-like machine that costs less than a computer but is able to store your text on a diskette and to move text from one part of a document to another, or from one file to another. Word processors are less cumbersome than computers; however, they cannot store large amounts of information or connect you to online resources. Finally, if you are planning to type just the last draft or drafts of your paper, you can use a regular typewriter.

If you do use a computer or a word processor, you will find yourself making changes. When your words appear on the screen, you will, perhaps unconsciously, apply a more critical eye to your handiwork. And making changes is easy with a computer. You can move or remove whole paragraphs with a few keystrokes, and even transfer text from one file to another—for example, from the NOTES file to the DRAFTONE file. You can also keep track of the length of your paper as you go.

Once you have a rough draft on the computer, print it and read it over. You'll notice how much easier it is to think about the overall structure and to see the connection, or lack of connection, between consecutive ideas or paragraphs when reading a clean copy. You'll see how easy it is to judge the flow of your sentences when you don't have to struggle with messy handwriting and squint at tiny insertions. For basic term paper or research paper writing, a word-processing program such as WordPerfect or Microsoft Word will do just fine. Only if your field of study requires that you present graphs, charts, or other complicated elements will you need a software program that allows you to design such elements.

Preparing the finished copy is also easier with a computer. If you forget to insert parenthetical notes, find a need to cross out or insert words or phrases, or spot a misspelled word, everything can be fixed quickly and with perfect neatness. If your command of spelling is a bit shaky, most word-processing programs offer a spell-checking feature that goes through the paper, word by word, stopping at each suspicious-looking combination of letters to ask if you made an error. If you express doubt, one or more correctly spelled, similar-looking words appear on the screen for you to choose from. Some programs also contain a grammar-checking feature, but these programs do not work as well as spell-checkers. Although they catch some mistakes, they miss many more. Even worse, they label as wrong many sentences that are perfectly acceptable.

Another important point about word processing is that your paper is stored on a diskette, and, if the paper becomes lost or soiled, the machine can print another copy in a few minutes. On the other hand, when you are using a computer, you may "lose" your text because of a blunder, a sudden electrical power surge, or a blackout. To avoid such an accident, stop and "save" the text every fifteen or twenty minutes, especially if you are interrupted and leave the machine unattended. *Never* drowsily turn off the machine without first saving the text.

If you own or have access to a computer, you can use its enormous memory to store information that would ordinarily fill many notebooks. Lists of sources, collections of memorable quotations, notes taken on topics closely related to your major field of interest, all would be hard to find and put together if you ever wanted to incorporate them into a future paper. A computer allows you to set up your own filing system so that all your notes on, say, *dyslexia, the CIA, Hillary Rodham Clinton, the Beatles,* or *affirmative action* can be called up at the touch of a few keys. The great potential of computers provides just one more reason to enter the new age of high technology.

Filling In the Outline

Writing the rough draft of a research paper can be thought of as "filling in the outline" because the outline provides a structure not just for your own ideas and conclusions but for the many research notes you have taken. If you try to write your rough draft by working only from the note cards, you will find it much harder to keep in mind the relationships among them. Hardest of all is trying to write the draft from memory, off the top of your head. That approach may work well when writing essays based on personal experience, but if used for a research paper, it absolutely guarantees mistakes and omissions.

While writing the rough draft, you may think of a better way to present your case than you had planned. If that happens, stop writing, go back and revise your outline, or even construct a new one. Remember that if you change one part of your outline, you will probably have to change other parts as well, in order to maintain balance and an orderly and logical presentation of ideas.

Because the first draft is not meant to be seen by anyone but you, don't worry if some sentences are weakly written and some word choices are not as apt as you would like. Concentrate on expressing your ideas clearly. Let your ideas and sentences flow as freely as you can, getting everything down on paper in a form that reflects your thinking, however roughly. When you write the second draft, finding the right words for what you want to say will be considerably easier.

Here are three pieces of advice for the format of the first draft:

1. *Leave plenty of space between the lines* for later insertions and changes—about two lines of space for every line of writing

2. *Don't slow yourself down by copying out each quotation, paraphrase, or summary from your cards.* When you come to a place where you need to use a note, simply make a memo to yourself that says "copy from card" or "see card."

3. *Be sure to note briefly in the margin the source of each note you use in the paper,* no matter if the note is a direct quotation, a paraphrase, or a summary. You can simply note the author's name or a key word or two from the title, plus the page numbers. If you fail to make a note, you may later forget to add a source note.

Integrating Your Sources

Although you are by now familiar with your notes, you are for the first time trying to blend them into a coherent whole. As you are writing the first draft, some situations may arise that cause special kinds of problems. The following situations occur fairly frequently.

No One Source Tells the Whole Story. Often you will have to draw details from different sources in order to deal with a subtopic fully. Then you must be careful to keep track of which facts come from which sources. If you simply combine all the details into one account, with just one source note, your readers may not realize that the picture is a composite, its parts coming from various sources.

Several Sources Disagree over a Question of Fact. Here you have several options:

- Simply report the disagreement, especially if you have no basis for trusting one source more than the others.
- Choose one source, if it seems more trustworthy than the others: it may be more fully documented, or the most recent.
- Try to verify the fact by further research.

The student writing about Emily Dickinson found that various sources gave the number of poems published during the poet's lifetime as six, seven, eight, and ten. Because the most up-to-date source, a review of three recent scholarly books about Dickinson, said the number was ten, the student simply used that number in her paper and disregarded the other sources' claims. After all, she was in no position to verify the fact herself, and the exact number was not crucial to her thesis.

Some Sources Disagree in Their Interpretation of a Fact or Facts. Such differences occur all the time; in fact, they help make research interesting. If the purpose of your paper is not to argue for a particular conclusion but to report the current state of knowledge, you may simply report the disagreement. If, however, your thesis states a definite position regarding your topic, you must not only report the disagreement but also draw your own conclusion as to which interpretation seems most soundly argued or based on the most complete or most reliable evidence. In reporting the disagreement, you must be fair to the writers whose interpretations you reject by presenting their views with enough detail for your readers to be able to agree or disagree with your preference.

Making the Draft Your Own

Finally, remember that your goal is not merely to weave together information and ideas from various sources but to interpret these findings in a way that is logical and meaningful for you and your readers. Although using sources and crediting them appropriately is important to your paper, you should never lose sight of the fact that what you are writing is *your* paper, and that the conclusions in it are, and should be, *yours.*

As you can see, writing the first draft involves a great deal of thinking about the ideas and information in your notes in order to draw reasonable conclusions about them. It is this thinking, and not the physical act of writing down your thoughts or keeping track of your sources, that makes the first draft a time-consuming and challenging task. This is why we encourage you not to get bogged down trying to express your thoughts in exactly the right words. You have enough to do without worrying about that just now.

Ending It All

When the body of your paper is complete, you must compose a suitable conclusion. As a general rule, the conclusion should not introduce any new ideas or information. Instead, it should restate your thesis in terms that reflect the evidence you have presented. (If you use the same words that you used to state your thesis in your introduction, your readers may feel that you haven't taken them anywhere.) Above all, your conclusion should bring your paper to a satisfying close with a statement that sums up what you think your research has shown. Don't be afraid to commit yourself in this respect: you ought to be able to stand confidently behind your research.

Now that you have completed a first draft of your paper, set the project aside for at least a few hours and do something else. It would be best if you could take at least a day's vacation from your paper. During the time you are not consciously working at the research project, your unconscious mind will be digesting, synthesizing, and generally working with what you have done. Then, as you tackle the second draft, not only will you feel refreshed, but you may also find yourself brimming with new ideas.

Writing the Paper

16

Revising the Rough Draft

Once you have brought your outline to life by writing a rough draft, the nature of your job changes significantly. You must now become your own toughest critic. Read closely what you have written, as if for the first time, so that you can find those parts that communicate most effectively as well as those that work poorly or not at all. Then you can become the author again, rewriting and, if necessary, reorganizing the weaker passages so that they become as strong as the best ones. Finally, you must examine the revised draft very closely in order to correct the spelling, punctuation, and other mechanical details.

Approach your revision in an orderly way, by thinking of the task at four levels of organization: the whole paper, paragraphs, sentences, and individual words and phrases.

1. *The whole paper.* Reconsider the order of the major and minor subtopics as presented in your outline, and see if this arrangement still serves your purposes well. Satisfy yourself that these larger elements of the paper have been presented in an effective sequence.

2. *Paragraphs.* Reexamine the structure of each paragraph and revise where necessary. Consider whether any paragraphs seem disjointed and could be reorganized, seem too long or complex and could be divided into shorter paragraphs, or seem too skimpy and could be combined. In addition, make sure that the transitions between paragraphs and between sentences within each paragraph are clear and appropriate.

3. *Sentences.* Look for sentences that could use some improvement. Long, cumbersome sentences, for example, can be broken down

into simpler, more easily digested units, but sometimes your revision will work in the other direction — combining a series of short, choppy sentences into longer, smoothly flowing sentences. Still other sentences must simply be recast to make them clearer.

4. *Wording.* Devote some time to studying individual words and phrases. Changes in wording can be made at any stage of your revision, even when you are repairing weak paragraph organization or faulty sentence structure. But you should still give yourself one last chance to improve your choice of words just before writing the final, polished version.

Reconsidering the Organization

As you arranged your note cards and constructed your outline, you carefully thought about the best order in which to present the information and ideas that would support your thesis. While writing the first draft, however, you may have felt that your plan was not completely practical. On rereading your draft, you may be more dissatisfied than ever. What can you do?

Perhaps you decided, when constructing the outline, to present the evidence supporting your thesis first and the evidence against it afterward. This strategy is effective if your case is so strong that it will make the opposing arguments seem weak. On rereading your paper, however, you found that the opposing case did not seem weak; instead, it seemed to rebut much of your case point by point. One way to reverse that effect would be to switch the order of those two parts of the paper, stating the opposing case first and rebutting it with your case. At this stage of the revision, you would not need to do any rewriting. You would simply cut the two passages out of the paper and reinsert them in the new order. Later you would rewrite them and revise the transitions to make the new order effective.

Rearrangements sometimes require more revision than simple adjustments in paragraph or sentence structure: you may occasionally find it a good idea to rewrite extensively and thereby produce a new "first" draft to work with. More often, however, you will find your outline a good guide, and no major reorganization will be necessary. You can then go on to revising the individual paragraphs.

Revising Paragraphs

Think of a paragraph as a group of sentences that work together to support a controlling idea — the idea expressed in the *topic* (or *main idea*) sentence. Ask yourself if a reader would be able to grasp easily the controlling ideas in your paragraphs, either because you have provided clear topic sentences or because you have so carefully constructed your paragraphs that the controlling ideas can be inferred readily from all the sentences taken together. Although you should not feel that you must impose a single rigid concept of paragraph structure on your writing, you should be certain that your paragraphs contribute to a logical progression of ideas in your paper. To the extent that they do not, you must revise.

If you think that one or more of your paragraphs might be confusing to a reader, the first thing to do is to see if the rewriting (or addition) of a topic sentence will clarify your thoughts. If a paragraph remains confusing even after you have improved its topic sentence or created a new topic sentence for it, you must focus on two additional features of paragraph structure:

- the order in which you have presented the details in support of your topic sentence
- the smoothness with which you have moved from one sentence to the next or from one idea to another

As you review your work, try to read each paragraph as though you were a reader unaware of what the writer intended to say. If you find a paragraph confusing, rearrange the details until you have found the most effective order for them. If the progression from one detail to the next still is not smooth, pick up your composition book or rhetoric text and read about achieving coherence, or logical sequence, in paragraphs. Pay special attention to what the book says about using *transitional words and phrases* and other *devices for linking ideas* smoothly and logically. A short review of this kind can enable you to improve the flow of thought within your paragraphs and throughout your paper as a whole.

Revising Sentences

Writing effective sentences is primarily a matter of style, and style develops only through a great deal of practice. Even when you recognize that a sentence calls for improvement, you may have trouble deciding just what changes would make it better. As you revise your paper, you can help yourself by being alert to a few common weaknesses in sentence construction. Pay particular attention to sentences in your rough draft that may be either too complex or too simple and to patterns of construction that may be monotonously repetitive.

Fixing Overly Long Sentences

Some sentences may be too long and complicated for readers to follow comfortably. Usually such sentences can be broken down into more easily digested sentences, as the following example illustrates:

too long a sentence	Throughout the war, many Southerners came to think of Lincoln as a power-hungry autocrat, who, in spite of the public speeches in which he advocated peace and reconciliation, was in reality determined to destroy anyone, in the North or South, who stood in the way of his gaining absolute control of the nation he had been elected to govern.
improvement	Throughout the war, many Southerners came to think of Lincoln as a power-hungry autocrat, in spite of the public speeches in which he advocated peace and reconciliation. They believed that he was in reality determined to destroy anyone, in the North or South, who stood in the way of his gaining absolute control of the nation he had been elected to govern.

Fixing Overly Short Sentences

Short sentences are easy to understand, but a series of five or six very short, choppy sentences actually may be more difficult to read than two or three sentences of average length. When you find such a series in your draft, consider combining several of them into longer sentences. Save your short sentences until they can be used most effectively — for example, when emphasizing a particularly important point.

too many short sentences	Throughout the war, many people detested Lincoln. They considered him to be power-hungry. His speeches called for peace and reconciliation. But these people did not believe him. They included Northerners as well as Southerners. They believed that he intended to destroy anyone who opposed him. They thought he desired to gain absolute control of

Writing the Paper

the country. They saw his election as part of his plan to rule as a dictator.

improvement

Throughout the war, many people detested Lincoln, whom they considered power-hungry. Although his speeches called for peace and reconciliation, these people did not believe him. Both Northerners and Southerners thought that he intended to destroy anyone who opposed him as he sought dictatorial control of the country he had been elected to govern.

Fixing Repetitious Sentence Patterns

Check the patterns of your sentences to see if you have repeated one pattern monotonously. Such repetition may needlessly bore your readers.

repetitous pattern

Hartman says that . . . Anna Freud states that . . . Mahler claims that . . . And recently Kohut stated that . . .

improvement

Hartman says that . . . This idea gained support from Anna Freud, who believes . . . Mahler agrees, for the most part, claiming that . . . Recently, Kohut added further support to this idea when he stated . . .

The second example is an improvement over the first not only because it is more varied but also because the writer has taken a set of ideas from different sources and blended them into a smoothly flowing passage that shows how these ideas relate to each other.

Revising Word Choice

When you revise your word choice, keep in mind three elements:

1. *Variety*—Find appropriate synonyms for words that appear often (except for technical terms, which do not allow substitutes).
2. *Accuracy*—Avoid vague, loose terms that may be misinterpreted.
3. *Slang*—Avoid words that are not appropriate to the formal context of a research paper.

Writing the Paper

Finding Variety

This example illustrates ways to revise to eliminate monotonous repetition of terms:

lacking variety

A young, idealistic anthropologist, on first venturing into a primitive society, is likely to suffer severe disillusionment. For one thing, most such societies live under physical conditions that no one coming from American society can possibly anticipate. But far more dispiriting is the fact that these societies often practice customs radically opposite to the ideal life in nature that naive students like to imagine: a society of simple folk, yes, but a society that knows the true value of love, kindness, sharing, and mutual respect. The Yanomamo society provides an example that could try the soul of any young idealist searching for simple, natural virtues. Their social practices include . . .

improvement

A young, idealistic anthropologist, on first venturing into a primitive society, is likely to suffer severe disillusionment. For one thing, most such people live under physical conditions that no one coming from America can possibly anticipate. But far more dispiriting is the fact that these communities often practice customs radically opposite to the ideal life in nature that naive students like to imagine: a society of simple folk, yes, but one that knows the true value of love, kindness, sharing, and mutual respect. The Yanomamo tribe provides an example that could try the soul of any young idealist searching for simple, natural virtues. Their social practices include . . .

Achieving Accuracy

Here are some examples illustrating ways to revise to eliminate the emptiness of vague words:

Writing the Paper

vague	Napoleon was a great man.
	Meryl Streep is an outstanding actress.
	Einstein was a fantastic thinker.
	<u>Oedipus Rex</u> is a first-rate play.
improved	Napoleon was a brilliant military strategist.
	Meryl Streep has played a variety of roles to perfection.
	Einstein's theories reshaped the world of modern physics.
	The play <u>Oedipus Rex</u> provides profound insights into human behavior.

Of course, you cannot entirely avoid vague terms, but you can keep them to a minimum and use them with care. In short, say exactly what you mean, or at least come as close as possible.

Avoiding Slang and Colloquialisms

The following are examples of revisions of word choices not appropriate to the formal context of a research paper:

inappropriate	The women in Rubens's paintings are very sexy.
	The CIA has been blasted recently for failing to perform its duties with sufficient restraint.
	The prosecutor called on a well-known shrink to testify that the defendant was not really crazy.
improved	The women in Rubens's paintings appear very sensuous.
	The CIA has been sharply criticized recently for failing to perform its duties with sufficient restraint.
	The prosecutor called on a well-known psychiatrist to testify that the defendant was not legally insane.

Writing the Paper

Beware the thesaurus: When revising word choice, be careful if you decide to use a *thesaurus,* or collection of synonyms. Books of synonyms can be valuable in helping you remember a word whose meaning you know well; they can be dangerous if you use them to select high-sounding words that are unfamiliar to you. The connotations of such words may not be appropriate to the contexts in which you place them. You may find a *dictionary of synonyms* more useful than a thesaurus because the former defines and illustrates the different shades of meaning between synonyms.

Avoiding Sexist Language

Over the last few decades, many people have come to realize that some fairly familiar conversational words and phrases tend to diminish the contributions of women to various areas of our society, especially the workplace. Common examples of sexist nouns include *policeman, businessman, congressman, spokesman, cleaning lady, stewardess, poetess, housewife.* A slightly different situation involves using pronouns referring to a particular sex—especially *he, his,* and *him* in sentences referring to people in general. For example: "A pilot should be concerned about *his* passengers' safety." If in writing formal papers you use such language, readers may feel that you are being sexist, or at least inconsiderate of this important social issue.

To avoid sexist language, you can either substitute neutral words or rephrase your sentences. Here are some suggestions.

Using Substitutions

You may feel that as long as you use words such as *chairwoman, congresswoman,* and *policewoman* when appropriate, you are not being sexist. That, however, is not the case because you are likely to end up using the male formations much more often, leaving the subtle impression that these positions belong in the male domain. Usually an inoffensive substitute can be easily called to mind. In some cases, a little reflection is required. Follow the general idea behind this partial list, and you will have no problems.

TV anchorman	anchor (*Anchorperson* seems a bit heavy-handed.)
chairman	chair, chairperson
clergyman	member of the clergy, minister, rabbi, priest, etc.
fireman	firefighter
policeman	police officer
garbageman	trash collector

Girl Friday	administrative assistant
salesman	salesperson
spokesman	representative, spokesperson
weatherman	meteorologist
workman	worker
congressman	representative, legislator, member of Congress
stewardess	flight attendant
cleaning lady	house cleaner, office cleaner
businessman	businessperson (or choose a more specific term: *business executive, executive, retailer, manager, business owner, shopowner, shopkeeper*)

Feminine endings, such as the *-ess* in *poetess,* sound condescending and should generally be avoided. Use *poet* (not *poetess*); *sculptor* (not *sculptress*); *dressmaker* (not *seamstress*); *suffragist* (not *suffragette*); *heir* (not *heiress*); and *host* (not *hostess*).

Avoiding Sexist Use of Pronouns

The common sentence construction that uses single-sex pronouns when referring to a group that includes both men and women presents a somewhat greater challenge to you as a writer. Examine these sentences:

A doctor needs to consider *his* patients' feelings before presenting *his* diagnoses.

When a teacher reads a student's essay on a controversial issue, *she* should try to be objective.

You can, of course, take the easy way out by substituting *his or her* or *he/she;* but these constructions may detract from the smoothness of your sentences and, worse yet, call attention to the pronoun problem and thereby distract readers from your line of thought. We recommend two more artful remedies.

Switch to plural: Doctors need to consider their patients' feelings before presenting their diagnoses.

Avoid using any pronouns: When reading a student's essay on a controversial issue, a teacher should try to be objective.

We hope these hints will help you handle this sensitive issue.

Writing the Paper

An Example of Revision

Here is how one student, Anita, moved from rough draft through the various revisions of her opening paragraphs:

Increasing Maximum Life Expectancy:

Myth or Reality?

opening paragraph
rough draft

> For a long time, people have dreamed of extending their life spans. In fact, Juan Ponce de Leon is said to have discovered Florida in 1513 when he was searching for the Fountain of Youth. By now we have pretty much given up hope that there is a fountain of youth or a marvelous herb that can extend our life spans. But gerontologists (people who study aging processes) are working on the problem. They are carrying out experiments that may or may not help us to extend our lives. However, many gerontologists are optimistic that they are on the right track.

Anita realized that this opening paragraph was not particularly effective as an introduction to her paper. The reference to Ponce de Leon — intended as an "interest grabber" — was left hanging, leaving it to the reader to determine precisely why she had used this reference. She saw the possibility that some readers might interpret "For a long time" as meaning from 1513 to the present, when she had actually intended to suggest that the desire to extend life span has been a dream of human beings for as long as there have been human beings. In addition, she saw that the "problem" gerontologists are working on could be interpreted by some readers as the problem of finding a fountain of youth or a marvelous herb. The last two sentences, intended as her thesis statement, were vaguely worded and did not help pull the paragraph together. All in all, she concluded, her paragraph was badly in need of rethinking and rewriting.

After some thought, Anita decided to write a two-paragraph introduction. In the first, she would expand on the Ponce de Leon reference to create a broad introduction to her topic and to generate reader interest. In the second, she would introduce her topic more specifically and present a clearer statement of her thesis. This strategy differed somewhat from her original plan for the paper, but Anita saw that the change was necessary to ensure that her paper got off to a good start.

Writing the Paper

revised introduction

Every American schoolchild is told that Juan Ponce de Leon discovered Florida in 1513 while searching for the Fountain of Youth. He believed the waters of the fountain would make him young again. But he never found the fountain. Instead, he found death by an Indian arrow. Today, we know how silly Ponce de Leon was for believing in a fountain of youth provided by a beneficent nature. But his dream of extending his life span was one that many people have had throughout the ages. It is still very much with us today.

By now we have pretty much given up hope that somewhere in nature we may discover the Fountain of Youth or a marvelous herb that can relieve us of the problems associated with the process of aging. Instead, our hopes of extending life expectancy are in the hands of scientists. Gerontologists (people who study aging) are attempting to slow down — and perhaps even overcome — nature's timetable for human aging. Not all scientists think that it is possible. But many do. Many gerontologists and knowledgeable commentators are optimistic about our chances for increasing the life span. Gerontological researchers are optimistic because of the promising results they have obtained from experiments with animals and cell cultures. These experiments might well lead us to a "fountain" of extended, healthy life, if not to eternal youth.

Now Anita felt that she had used her Ponce de Leon example successfully to present a broad introduction for her paper. She had not been too concerned with her writing style because she was mainly interested in improving the organization and content of the introduction. Her second paragraph also drew some ideas and wording from her original brief introduction.

Her next step was to take a closer look at her sentences and her word use to see if the writing itself could be improved. Her self-criticism, along with some advice from her instructor, led her to make the following changes.

a bit more accurate — Ponce de Leon did not want to be restored to childhood	Every American schoolchild is told that Juan Ponce de Leon discovered Florida in 1513 while searching for the Fountain of Youth. ~~He believed the~~ *, whose waters,*
sentence combining for variety and to lessen repetition of *fountain*	~~waters of the fountain would make him young again.~~ *he believed,* *restore him to youthful manhood.*
unfortunately works better than *but* to prepare reader for following sentence	*Unfortunately,* ~~But~~ he never found the fountain. Instead, he found death by an Indian arrow. Today, we know ~~how silly~~ *smile at the naivete of*
silly isn't a fair word to describe the explorer's search — in his day, many people believed that nature held the secret to extended life	Ponce de Leon ~~was~~ for believing in a fountain of youth provided by a beneficent nature. But his dream of extending his life span was one that many people have had throughout the ages. ~~It is~~ still very much *, and it is a dream that is* with us today.
again, combining for variety and to clarify *it* as referring to *dream*	By now we have pretty much given up hope ~~that somewhere in nature we may discover~~ the *of discovering*
unnecessary and wordy	Fountain of Youth or a marvelous herb that can relieve us of the ~~problems~~ associated with the *anxieties and debilities*
vague word in this context	process of aging. Instead, our hopes of extending life expectancy are in the hands of scientists.
more precise	Gerontologists (~~people~~ who study aging) are *scientists* attempting to slow down — and perhaps even
rewritten to improve clarity and style of thesis	overcome — nature's timetable for human aging. ~~Not all scientists think that it is possible. But many~~ *Although not all scientists think that increasing the life span is possible*
wordy and repetitious	~~do. Many~~ gerontologists and knowledgeable *in the near future, many* commentators are optimistic about our chances ~~for~~
unclear pronoun reference	~~increasing the life span. Gerontological researchers~~ ~~are optimistic~~ because of the promising results ~~they~~ *researchers*

have obtained from experiments with animals and cell cultures. These experiments might well lead us to a "fountain" of extended, healthy life, if not to eternal youth.

Writing the Paper

Understanding Abstracts

Some instructors require students to write abstracts for their research papers. An abstract is a concise summary that allows a reader to grasp the purpose and major ideas of a paper without having to delve into all the details.

Abstracts are more commonly encountered in science papers and are usually required for papers using the APA documentation format.

The idea behind the use of abstracts is simple: an abstract saves time for other researchers who want to determine quickly whether or not an article will be useful for their own research project. Thus, an abstract must present a complete picture of what the article covers but be brief enough to let readers know quickly whether reading all of it will be worthwhile.

The research paper on the fire ant, *Solenopsis invicta,* is preceded by an abstract. When you read the paper (in Chapter 21), take time to consider how well its writer summarized his work in his abstract.

Writing the Polished, Final Draft

Equipped with a carefully revised draft, you are ready to produce the polished, final version of your research paper. As you write the final version, you may continue to make changes in wording to improve the clarity of your paper. You may also make minor alterations in your paragraphs and sentences to improve the flow of thought. However, if at this time you find yourself making major changes in the organization or the content of your paper, you have embarked on the final draft without being fully prepared. If this is the case, consider this draft as another revision and work out your problems before again attempting to produce the final draft.

There are two more jobs you must do before you begin to prepare the manuscript of your paper. You must prepare a complete set of notes acknowledging the source of each quotation or paraphrase in the paper, and you must ready a final version of your Works Cited or References. The next chapters discuss the form and placement of these source citations.

Reviewing Part Four

Questions

1. Why should you review all your note cards before beginning to write? What problems might you discover at this stage, and how might you deal with them?
2. A thesis is a far more comprehensive statement than the hypothesis you started with. What additional features go into the thesis to make it more inclusive?
3. What are the usual objectives of an introductory section?
4. What is the function of an outline? What are some problems that you might encounter when constructing an outline?
5. At least how many versions of a research paper must you write? Why?
6. What should you do when your sources disagree about factual matters?
7. Briefly outline the steps in revising a rough draft.

Exercises

1. Read the following introductions, keeping in mind that an effective introduction should state the thesis, point out the major questions addressed by the research, and indicate the kinds of evidence used in reaching the paper's conclusions (thesis). Which introduction best fulfills these objectives? Explain your choice.

Title: Jefferson Davis as President: A Confederate Asset

Version I

Jefferson Davis became president of the Confederate States of America in 1861, shortly after the Civil War began, and remained its leader until 1865, when the war ended and he was imprisoned, only to be released two years later. Davis, as senator from Mississippi before the war, had staunchly advocated the states' rights movement, which had arisen largely as a defense of slavery. A graduate of West Point, Davis had served in the Mexican War and as secretary of war under Franklin

Pierce. His background made him a strong candidate for the Confederate presidency once the war was under way.

At the beginning of the Civil War, the two sides seemed evenly matched. The North enjoyed a seeming advantage in numbers and a definite industrial superiority. The South, on the other hand, was better able to mobilize its potential manpower, since much of the work back home was being performed by slaves, and its military leaders far outshone those of the North. Eventually, the North's material edge and the emergence of General Ulysses S. Grant were able to wear the South down, but some people blamed the defeat on the South's leader, Jefferson Davis, who they believed had mishandled his responsibility as commander in chief. Other observers defend Davis as an intelligent man fated by history to a tragic end.

Version 2

As a new millennium dawned, the Stars and Bars of the Old South still flew over the state capitol of South Carolina, in memory of the heroic although doomed struggle for a people's right to choose its own economic and social system. Bloodier than all other American wars, producing more dead than all of them combined, the Civil War has fascinated later generations of Americans in both the North and the South.

For the South, humiliated in defeat, no explanation for its devastating loss, given the brilliance of its field officers, especially General Robert E. Lee, could salve its wounds. For the North, its superior moral position sufficed as explanation, but survivors in the South looked to more concrete scapegoats, and Jefferson Davis, its president, stood out like a sore thumb among the crowd at the Confederacy's funeral. His vice president later wrote a scathing account of the debacle, placing full blame on Davis, and many historians thereafter have placed much, if not all, of the blame on his shoulders. But maybe they were wrong.

Version 3

For many years after Robert E. Lee surrendered at Appomattox, historians tended to lay much of the blame for the South's crushing defeat on the president of the Confederacy, Jefferson Davis. One writer, however, in comparing Davis to Abraham Lincoln, claims that Davis's reputation would have been quite different if he had been on the winning side. When a leader fails to achieve victory, even if his cause is doomed from the start, his "errors and defects and limitations of character... stand out as do a few spots of ink on a white sheet of paper" (Patrick 44–45). This does not mean that Davis had no faults. Almost all historians agree that the man suffered from character flaws. He spent far too much time on administrative details; he often interfered in military matters; and he allowed himself to be drawn into bitter controversies with other political leaders.

The question all Civil War analysts must answer is this: To what extent did Davis's failings contribute to the defeat of the Confederacy? A survey of modern studies of Davis and the Civil War reveals a softening in the historical judgment of Davis as a leader. Most historians today conclude that Jefferson Davis was probably the most capable president the South could have chosen. Indeed, given the enormous problems the Confederacy faced, Davis was a definite asset in the struggle to secede from the Union.

2. Revise three consecutive paragaphs in your rough draft until you are satisfied with the entire sequence. Show every stage of your revision, and explain your reasons for making each change.

Part Five

Documenting Sources

17

Understanding Documentation Requirements

After you have written, revised, and polished your research paper, one essential step remains: documenting the sources. Although there are various methods of documenting sources, all of them involve two elements:

1. *A list at the end of the paper,* in a section titled Works Cited or References or Bibliography, of all the sources of material you have used in your paper.
2. *Notes inserted within the text* to tell readers where you found the various ideas and information that form the backbone of your paper.

Although citation of sources can be tedious, it serves several important purposes, and you should take it as seriously as you do the work of researching and writing the paper. These purposes include:

- *Giving credit where credit is due*—namely, to the work of researchers who have gone before you. (If another writer were to use an interesting idea from something you had written or placed on the Internet, you would surely want your work acknowledged as its source.)
- *Telling your readers where to find more information about your topic.* You may have raised some questions that would send a curious reader back to your sources for answers. Or a reader might want to verify your interpretation of what you read; for instance, someone might want to be certain you had not quoted out of context.

For example, in a paper on the "fallacy of statistical 'truth,'" a student claimed that a survey of Long Island women that showed the incidence of breast cancer in that area to be abnormally high, supposedly because of environmental pollution, should be discounted because Long Island's population included an unusually large number of Ashkenazi Jews, a group the student said is known to suffer from an abnormally high rate of breast cancer. A skeptical reader went to one of the sources cited in the paper. The source stated that these researchers were studying Ashkenazi women "all with family histories of breast cancer." Later, the reporter noted that the rate of breast cancer is no higher among Ashkenazi Jews than any other group, but that their genetic codes are easier to probe for the cancer gene because the cancer gene in their DNA strand is always in the same position, which is not the case for other women. This information in part undermined the student's claim about the original Long Island study.

- *Giving knowledgeable readers some idea of how authoritative a particular statement is*—that is, whether the author of the source is an expert in the field or simply a reporter summarizing recent developments for the general public.

- *Providing the date of initial publication.* For instance, Sigmund Freud spent more than forty years developing the psychoanalytic theory of personality, and over that period he revised some of his earlier ideas considerably. Therefore, a well-informed reader might want to know just when Freud made a statement that you quoted in your paper. For this reason, you must be careful to find out the year the source was published. Don't stop when you learn the year in which the copy of the book that you have in your hand was *printed* because many books are printed more than once and by more than one publisher.

- *Giving an overall sense of how thoroughly you carried out your research.* The list of Works Cited reveals at a glance the range of your investigation of the topic; the notes indicate how thoroughly you have read the sources.

Types of Material That Require Source Notes

While writing the rough draft, you noted in the margins or elsewhere in your draft the sources of all ideas and information that came from your notes. Now you must formally incorporate the notes into your text, clearly indicating those sources for your reader. Before we discuss how to go about preparing these notes, an important question needs to be answered:

Is it necessary to indicate the source of every piece of information that goes into your paper?

For instance, you might wonder whether it is essential to state where you came across simple facts such as these:

The Battle of Chickamauga was fought on September 19 and 20, 1863.

Nitrogen makes up 78 percent of Earth's atmosphere.

The capital of the African nation Chad is Ndjamena.

Depending on the nature of your research topic, identifying the source of every such fact could clutter the paper with distracting and unhelpful notes. To prevent this, it is generally agreed that you do not have to identify the sources for information considered "general knowledge," that is, information readily available in the reference section of any library, even a small one. The facts regarding Chickamauga, nitrogen, and Ndjamena clearly fall under the heading of general knowledge.

Naturally you will sometimes be unsure whether a particular fact is general knowledge. In that case, to be safe, insert a note. Before you begin any research paper, however, it is best to ask your instructor what kinds of information do not call for documentation.

Looking at the problem the other way around, we can say: *Documentation is required for any information that falls into one of these categories:*

- opinions, judgments, theories, and personal explanations
- "facts" that are open to dispute, and virtually all statistics
- factual information gathered by a small number of observers, no matter how expert they may be (for example, the results of a recent scientific test)

Opinions, Judgments, Theories, and Personal Explanations

Encyclopedias are filled with facts that are considered general knowledge, but that does not mean that all information found in an encyclopedia can go into your paper without a note. In the following encyclopedia entry, the annotated passages constitute opinions. If you used them in your paper, they would require notes *unless* you determined, by reading several expert sources on the topic, that these opinions were shared by virtually everyone writing about Mary Cassatt and her art.

"influenced by her . . . French contemporaries" is an inference; "greatly" indicates a judgment	**CASSATT,** Mary (1845–1926). American figure painter and etcher, b. Pittsburgh. Most of her life was spent in France, where she was greatly influenced by her great French contemporaries, particularly Manet and Degas, whose friendship and esteem she enjoyed. She allied herself with the impressionists early in her career. Motherhood was Cassatt's most frequent
"refreshing simplicity," "vigorous treatment," and "pleasing color" reflect personal observations and judgments	subject. Her pictures are notable for their refreshing simplicity, vigorous treatment, and pleasing color. She excelled also as a pastelist and etcher, and her drypoints and color prints are greatly admired. She is well represented in public and private galleries in the United States. Her best-known paintings include several versions of *Mother and Child* (Metropolitan Mus.; Mus. of Fine Arts, Boston; Worcester, Mass., Art Museum); *Lady at the Tea-Table* (Metropolitan Mus.); *Modern Women,* a mural painted for the Women's Building at the Chicago Exposition; and a portrait of the artist's mother. See catalog by A. D. Breeskin (1970); biography by J. M. Carson (1966).

"Facts" Open to Dispute

This category includes commonly accepted "facts" based largely on inference. When new evidence is discovered, new inferences may have to be made. For example, the significance of a particular fossil bone is definitely a matter of judgment, and the nature of the astronomical phenomenon known as a "black hole" has not by any means been as definitively established as many popular accounts suggest. Much of the work done by behavioral scientists consists of collecting statistical information (the average number of children in Chinese-American families, the rate of juvenile crime in Boston, and so on). Although the statistics you encounter in your research may seem to be hard facts, these facts can be disputed. Indeed, theories and conclusions based on such facts are continually debated by the experts. Therefore, almost all information in the behavioral sciences must be documented except historical facts about individual persons and events in the field.

Factual Information Gathered by a Small Number of Observers

Information gathered by observation and experimentation is subject to dispute. The results of similar experiments may vary, or different researchers may interpret identical results differently. Accordingly, such information should be documented so your readers know its source.

For example, you might read in a newspaper or magazine this week that "scientists at the Murphy-Weiss Laboratories in Ipswich, Mass., have shown that cola drinks cause liver cancer in rats and monkeys." The headline might even have read: "Soda Pop Causes Cancer." The experiment may have been honestly and carefully executed, and the information may *eventually* be accepted as fact. But until other scientists have duplicated these scientists' work and arrived at the same results, this information is just a "possible" fact, and therefore it definitely needs to be documented.

Now for one last question:

Is it necessary to provide source notes for ideas and information that you were already aware of before undertaking the research paper?

If the information falls into one of the three categories just discussed, you must take the time to locate a source for it. Readers have a right as well as a need to know of a reliable source for the information in question. Furthermore, finding a source protects you against misremembering what you have previously heard or read. Thus it is always wise when reading sources to take notes on everything that is relevant to your hypothesis, even when you are familiar with the information.

General Information about Source Notes

Notes can take one of two forms: *parenthetical notes* or *numbered notes.* This book concentrates on the Modern Language Association's preferred format, which uses parenthetical notes. For examples of this system, which is followed by most instructors of language and literature, see pages 201–26 and the papers on the "new immigrants" and "Emily Dickinson" in Chapter 21. The traditional numbered endnote/footnote format, which many history instructors prefer, is briefly explained (see pages 227–32) and then illustrated in the paper on Cotton Mather, also found in Chapter 21. (The MLA offers one version of this style; the version we present, often called "Chicago style," is described in the fourteenth edition of *The Chicago Manual of Style,* published by the University of Chicago Press.) A third system, devised by the American Psychological Association (APA) and used in most of the social sciences, is discussed on pages 232–41 and exemplified by the paper on "fire ants," also in Chapter 21. Yet another system, the number system used for scientific research, is briefly explained on pages 241–42.

Because scholars in various fields have not yet agreed on a standard system of documentation, for every paper you are assigned be sure to ask your instructor which system you should use. Then consult a guidebook such as this one for the proper format.

General Information about the List of Sources

A list of all your sources must appear at the end of your paper, in a section titled *Works Cited* or *References* or *Bibliography*, depending on which citation system you use. Arrange the items alphabetically according to the authors' last names. If a source has no known author, list it alphabetically according to the first word of its title (ignoring *A*, *An*, and *The*). A look at the sample papers in Chapter 21 will show you that all the major citation systems alphabetize the list of sources.

Do not inflate your list of sources by including items that were not direct sources of the information in your paper. This means that, *as a rule, no item should appear among your sources unless at least one note in the paper refers to it.* To be useful to your reader, a list of sources must answer several basic questions about each source.

- What is its full title?
- Who wrote or created it?
- Where and when was it published? By what publisher?
- If the source is an article in a periodical or an essay in a book, on what pages can it be found?

Occasionally other kinds of information will have to be added. For books, there may be translators and editors, or volume numbers; for periodicals, the handling of dates and of volume and issue numbers varies according to the type of periodical (annual, monthly, weekly, daily); and for nonprint sources, such as films, recordings, television programs, and online sources, yet other kinds of information must be included.

18

Using the MLA Parenthetical System

In general, the MLA's main documentation system requires that you identify the source of any idea or information you discovered through research by placing a brief parenthetical reference within the appropriate sentence, most often directly following the words being cited. Such a note should contain the page number(s) on which the information was found, plus any additional information needed to identify the source, such as the author's name or the title of the work. (A list of all the sources you cite, titled Works Cited, should appear at the end of your paper.) The amount of information required in a parenthetical note depends on what you have said about the source within the text.

Basic Formats for Parenthetical Notes

1. If you have mentioned the author's name in your text, the note usually consists of just the page number(s) on which the information was located.

   This fact led the critic Owen Thomas to conclude that Emily Dickinson "was well aware of the world outside her little room, that in fact she used the language of this outside world to create some of her best poetry" (523).

2. If you have not mentioned the author's name, the note must include that information.

But an economist who predicted the recession of the early 1990s a year in advance fears the price of gold will decline slowly for at least ten years (Goodserve 143).

3. If the author has written more than one of the sources in your Works Cited, your note must include a shortened form of the particular title unless it is mentioned in your text.

Chomsky claims that all humans inherit the same basic linguistic structural framework on which their community's particular language is fitted (Language 29-41).

The Works Cited in this case also includes Chomsky's *Syntactic Structures*.

4. If the author is unknown, as in many newspaper accounts, the title must appear in the note, if not mentioned in the text. (Titles may be shortened.)

Only Mayor McCarthy expressed the least optimism regarding the city's fate ("Rebirth" 2).

The Works Cited entry for this source would be:

"Rebirth of a City." News-Times [Danbury, CT] 6 Sept. 1977: 2.

Spacing and Punctuation

1. Leave a space before the opening parenthesis. If a punctuation mark follows the citation, place it *outside* the closing parenthesis and leave a space after the punctuation mark.

Morgan believes the whale stands for God (132), whereas Kay claims it "embodies all that is evil" (19-20). This controversy derives largely from . . .

2. The parentheses are placed *inside* a sentence, directly following the quotation or paraphrase they refer to, and *outside* quotation marks. (See previous example.)

3. When a quotation ends with a question mark or an exclamation point, the question mark or exclamation point goes *inside* the quotation marks. A period is still needed *after* the parentheses.

Dickinson's letter to Higginson contained a question: "Are you too deeply occupied to say if my Verse is alive?" (Letters 2: 403).

Note that this parenthetical note refers to a multivolume collection of Dickinson's letters: 2: 403 means "volume 2, page 403."

4. If you quote *more than four lines* from a source, set the quotation off from the rest of the text by *indenting ten spaces* or one inch (or two paragraph indents) from the margin. Place the parenthetical note *after* the final mark of punctuation, separated by a space.

> Catton also suggests that Davis's attempt to lead his people to independence was somehow doomed to failure from the start.
>
> > He had done the best he could do in an impossible job, and if it is easy to show where he made grievous mistakes, it is difficult to show that any other man, given the materials available, could have done much better. He had courage, integrity, tenacity, devotion to his cause, and, like Old Testament Sisera, the stars in their courses marched against him. (279)

Numbered Notes for Special Purposes

Once in a while, you will find something that might interest your readers but is not essential to whatever idea you are developing in the paper at that point. If that happens, insert a note number directing readers to a footnote or endnote. Endnotes, if you use them, are placed on a separate page between the end of the paper and the Works Cited.

Insert the note number immediately after the final mark of punctuation for the sentence that led you to think of adding the additional information. Raise the number half a line.

> Literary critics, serious biographers, and writers of fictionalized accounts of her life created an image of Emily Dickinson as a timid, reclusive, mystical thinker who was too absorbed in personal sorrows and ecstasies to be concerned with literary recognition. And this image persists, to a great extent, in the public mind today.[1]

The endnote or footnote would read:

> [1]For a full discussion of sources leading to the "Emily myth," see Ferlazzo 13-21.

(This note offers readers more information than they could get from the simple parenthetical note "Ferlazzo 13–21.")

Variations on the Basic MLA Formats

Sources with More Than One Author

If a source has more than one author, a parenthetical note should give the last names of all the writers. If there are more than three authors, you can use the first author's last name followed by "et al."—Latin for "and others"—but this form of citation diminishes the importance of the other authors. Whichever method you choose, you should consistently use the same method in text references as you do in the Works Cited.

> Davis took the position that "the President was entrusted with military leadership, and he must exercise it" (Randall and Donald 271).

> A recent investigation of iridium levels in the Dolomites revealed traces insufficient to justify Alvarez's hypothesis (Sapperstein et al. 12).

Works Cited would show:

> Randall, J. G., and David Donald. The Divided Union. Boston: Little, 1961.
> Sapperstein, M. L., et al. "Iridium Levels in the Dolomites." Astronomy Today Sept. 1983: 12-15.

Two or More Sources for One Note

Sometimes a piece of information or an idea will appear in more than one of your sources. Usually, especially with purely factual information, you choose one of the sources and refer only to it. Occasionally, however, when each source offers some interesting additional commentary that a curious reader might enjoy investigating, you should mention each of them in your note, separating them with semicolons.

> Many of Davis's personal troubles grew out of his ill health (Catton 121-22; Nevins 3: 86-89).

Indirect Source: A Source Quotes Another Writer

Frequently, your source will quote another writer's work, and you may want to quote that second writer. When this happens, you must make every reasonable effort to find the original source in order to verify the accuracy of the quotation. For one thing, you should check to be certain it was not quoted out of context (see pages 129–30). When you have seen that source, you can add it to your list of Works Cited and refer directly to it in a parenthetical note.

However, sometimes you will find it impossible to locate the original source. In that case, you will be forced to rely on your first source, but your parenthetical reference must indicate, with the abbreviation "qtd." (for *quoted*), that you used an indirect source.

In this example, the author was quoting from an out-of-print book, *Criminal Man,* that was written in Italian.

> Lambroso's racism becomes apparent in his remark that "[criminals']
> physical insensibility well recalls that of savage peoples who can
> bear, in rites of puberty, torture that a white man could never endure.
> All travelers know the indifference of Negroes and American savages
> to pain: the former cut their hands and laugh in order to avoid work;
> the latter, tied to the torture post, gaily sing the praises of their tribe
> while they are slowly burnt" (qtd. in Gould 18).

The Works Cited page would show:

> Gould, Stephen Jay. "Criminal Man Revived." Natural History Mar.
>   1976: 16-18.

Reference to an Entire Work

If you refer to an entire source by way of a summary or paraphrase of its thesis, you do not need a parenthetical note as long as you mention author and title.

> Gore Vidal's Lincoln presents a very readable reconstruction of the
> president's approach to problems, both personal and political.

Summary of a Chapter or an Essay

Occasionally you will make a statement that summarizes a major idea from an article or essay or a chapter in a book. For a chapter, you may use the chapter number instead of page numbers.

> Chomsky claims that all humans inherit the same basic linguistic
> structural framework on which their community's particular language
> is fitted (Language ch. 2).

If you are referring to an entire essay or article, do not use a parenthetical note. Just mention the author within your text. A reader will know from the nature of your statement that it covers a good deal of ground and will expect no note.

> Gould settled the perplexing question as to whether a Portuguese man-of-war is an organism or a colony by approaching the problem from a new point of view, that of overlapping, evolving categories rather than rigidly fixed definitions.

The author's name is enough to lead a reader to the right source in your Works Cited:

> Gould, Stephen Jay. "A Most Ingenious Paradox." Natural History Dec. 1984: 20-29.

Quotation from Literary Works

When writing on literary topics, you will usually quote from the plays, poems, or prose works under discussion. For works of prose reprinted in many editions (novels, short stories, and most plays), indicate the page numbers, as with other sources, but also include chapter, book, act, or scene number so readers can locate the quoted material in any edition. For poems and long poetic works that consist of "books" or "cantos," indicate the quoted material not by page numbers but by line numbers. For long poems, like *The Iliad*, give the canto or book number plus the line numbers. For verse drama, use act/scene/line notation.

novel
> It would seem that Captain Ahab has forever rejected God as he commences his final soliloquy in Moby-Dick with "I turn my body from the sun [. . .]" (468; ch. 135).

poetry
> Along the same lines, given her deliberate decision to forgo publication rather than compromise her art, the first lines of another poem become significantly clear: "Publication--is the Auction / Of the Mind of Man" (lines 1-2). And there can be no doubt that when she wrote the following stanza, Emily

Dickinson had accepted the fact that true fame
would not be hers in her lifetime.

Some--Work for Immortality--
The Chiefer part, for Time--
He--Compensates--immediately
The former--Checks--On Fame--
(lines 1-4)

drama (reference
to *Othello*)

Once again, Shakespeare deftly shifts images, this
time in Othello's speech over the sleeping Desdemona, from lightness of color (Desdemona as compared to Othello) to light as a symbol of life (5.2.3-13).

If you do not mention the title of the verse drama or long poetic work in
your text, add the title — which you may abbreviate — to the note. Underline the abbreviation as you would a full title.

(quotation from
Doctor Faustus)

I see there's virtue in my heavenly words;
Who would not be proficient in this art?
How pliant is this Mephistophilis,
Full of obedience and humility!
Such is the force of magic and my spells:
Now, Faustus, thou art conjuror laureate,
That canst command great Mephistophilis. (Faustus
1.3.30-36)

long poetic work
(quotation from
Paradise Lost)

Thus Adam to himself lamented loud
          [. . .] on the ground
Outstretcht he lay, on the cold ground, and oft
Curs'd his Creation, Death as oft accus'd
Of tardy execution, since denounc't
The day of his offence. Why comes not Death,
Said he, with one thrice acceptable stroke
To end me? (PL 10.845-56)

Notice the difference between the punctuation of this note and the punctuation for volume and page numbers: 10.845-56 reads "book ten, lines
845-56"; 3: 203 reads "volume 3, page 203."

If you are citing a sacred text, give the title, the book, and the chapter and verse. Spell out the names of books mentioned in your text. In a parenthetical citation, use an abbreviation for books with names of five or more letters.

> She ignored the admonition "Pride goes before destruction, and a haughty spirit before a fall" (<u>New Oxford Annotated Bible</u>, Prov. 16.18).

Blending Notes into Your Text Smoothly

This system of documentation encourages you to name your sources as you refer to them in the essay and to put as little information as possible in the parenthetical notes. Keep in mind that your notes should avoid, as far as possible, breaking a reader's concentration. The example shows how an obtrusive parenthetical note can be made less obtrusive.

obtrusive

> Certainly, then, the woman who has been called "one of the greatest lyric poets of all time" (Winters 40) was all but unknown as a poet during her lifetime.

less obtrusive

> Certainly, then, the woman Yvor Winters has called "one of the greatest lyric poets of all time" (40) was all but unknown as a poet during her lifetime.

Notice that the parenthetical note was placed directly after the quoted phrase. If it had been put at the end of the sentence (to reduce the interruptive effect), the note would seem to cover the whole idea, not just the part that belonged to Yvor Winters.

When paraphrasing, you will sometimes find it difficult to slip in the source's name, especially when the paraphrase deals with factual matter rather than a judgment, as in this example.

> During her later years, Emily Dickinson had virtually no direct contact with anyone outside her immediate family. While she was still connected to her circle of friends, the poet made at least one tentative attempt to find an audience for her poetry. But only a handful of verses were published anonymously, most of them in a local newspaper, and these were subjected to considerable editing. On the poet's death at

fifty-six, her sister discovered more than a thousand poems and
initiated an effort to publish them. Beginning four years later, in 1890,
these poems finally appeared in print (Sewall 1: 4-11).

Clearly you would have had no reason to introduce Sewall's name in the
text because the information is both factual and very general; nothing
seems to be particularly the work of a specific biographer.

Both of the following examples are well-constructed passages using
the same sources; both make good use of the parenthetical note format.
The differences are due to a shift of purpose on the writer's part. The
comments that follow the examples explain the effect of the variation.

Example 1

Recent studies show that anorexia can be successfully treated by
psychotherapy (Kline; Evans et al.; Yaster and Korman). These studies
dealt mostly with young persons who came to therapy voluntarily and
continued treatment for at least six weeks. The authors of the studies
concluded that anorexia is a "socially induced disorder" (Kline 214) and
not a biologically caused illness.

Example 2

Recent studies show that anorexia can be treated successfully by
psychotherapy. Kline achieved an 85 percent cure for twenty cases
in adolescent women. A group of Illinois therapists found that "most
victims underwent marked improvement following four sessions"
(Evans et al. 35). In California, Oscar Yaster and T. G. Korman,
working with a population of males and females ages 16-30,
produced "significant remission rates" among those completing
five sessions or more of group and individual treatment (17-18).

Notice that in Example 1 the writer did not intend to make a specific
statement about each of the sources. Therefore, she cited all three of them
after the introductory sentence of the paragraph. However, when she decided to quote a phrase from one of the three sources, which she felt
spoke for all three, she then cited that one study.

If, on the other hand, the writer had wanted to say something about
each source, she might have constructed Example 2. In that case, she
would delay citing the sources until she got to each one individually. No
special note was needed for Kline because the writer was summarizing

the full study. But with Evans et al., she introduced a quotation, and that called for a note indicating the page number. Although the last of the three sources was quoted very briefly, a note was still needed to show where the phrase could be found. (Putting that note directly after the quoted phrase would have created an unnecessary interruption.)

General Guidelines for Listing Sources in Works Cited

A list of all your sources must appear at the end of your paper, in a section titled *Works Cited*. Arrange the items alphabetically according to the authors' last names. If a source has no known author, list it alphabetically according to the first word of its title (ignoring *A, An,* and *The*). See the Works Cited lists for the papers on the new immigrants and Emily Dickinson in Chapter 21.

Our sample entries cover the most common variations, dividing them into four categories: *books, periodicals, electronic sources* (which may include online books and periodicals), and *other kinds of source materials.* Later in your college career, advanced research may lead you to rarer kinds of publications. At such times, you may need to check the *MLA Handbook for Writers of Research Papers,* Fifth Edition, for the correct format. But because you will often discover these unusual sources through specialized indexes or in bibliographies attached to other sources, you will often see the correct entry form before picking up the source itself.

See page 241 for a list of abbreviations commonly used in source citations.

Group 1: Sample Entries for Books

Basic Format

Follow these guidelines, noting spacing and punctuation:

1. The first line of each entry starts flush with the left margin; each subsequent line indents five spaces.
2. Periods separate the main parts of an entry: Author. Title. Place of publication: Publisher, date.
3. Each period is followed by *one* space.
4. Titles of books are underlined. (If your word-processing program allows you to type italics, *check with your instructor* to see whether you should use underlining or italics for your paper.)

5. Titles of essays and other short works contained within books or periodicals are placed in quotation marks. (Exception: See "Critical Review," page 218.)

6. The first letters of all major words in titles are capitalized.

7. Publishers' names are shortened; terms such as *Inc., Co., Publishers,* and *Press* are dropped. Only the first surname is used when the publisher's name is made up of one or more individual's names: *Norton* for *W. W. Norton and Company, Farrar* for *Farrar, Straus and Giroux. University* and *Press* are abbreviated for university presses: *Oxford UP, U of Chicago P.*

A Single Author

Author of a Book

note punctuation and
indentation; *Graphics*
is a shortened form of
The Graphics Press

Tufte, Edward R. Envisioning Information. Cheshire, CT: Graphics, 1990.

Author of an Essay in a Collection

Ed. stands for *edited
by:* pages on which full
essay appears are
shown, even if only a
page or two are used
as sources

Brooks, Gwendolyn. "The Rise of Maud Martha." Invented Lives: Narratives of Black Women 1860-1960. Ed. Mary Helen Washington. New York: Anchor-Doubleday, 1987. 429-32.

Notice that if all the essays in a collection are by the same author, you do not need to include the individual essay title in the Works Cited entry. But if the collection contains essays by various authors — as in the preceding example — the essay title should be cited.

If you use more than one essay from the same collection, you do not need to repeat the full information for the collection with each essay.

essays in collection
are listed by essay
author, essay title,
collection editor's
name, and page
numbers of essay

Sullivan, Patricia A., and Donna J. Qualley, eds. Pedagogy in the Age of Politics: Writing and Reading (in) the Academy. Urbana, IL: NCTE, 1994.

Bleich, David. "The 'Kinds of Language' Curriculum." Sullivan and Qualley 195-213.

Two or More Authors

authors' names are in order in which they appear on title page of source; for two or three authors, list all names; for four or more authors, either list all names or list just the first author, followed by the abbreviation "et al."

Bar-Adon, Aaron, and Werner F. Leopold. Child Language. Englewood Cliffs, NJ: Prentice, 1971.

Dugan, James, Robert C. Cowen, Bill Barada, and Richard M. Crum. World beneath the Sea. Washington: Nat. Geographic Soc., 1967.

Dugan, James, et al. World beneath the Sea. Washington: Nat. Geographic Soc., 1967.

Two or More Sources with Same Author

line of three hyphens is used in place of author's name for all entries after the first; works listed alphabetically by title

Thomas, Lewis. The Lives of a Cell. New York: Viking, 1974.

---. The Medusa and the Snail. New York: Viking, 1979.

Author of Several Sources Having Different Coauthors

Chomsky, Noam. Language and Problems of Knowledge. Cambridge: MIT P, 1988.

coauthored books follow singly authored books alphabetically by coauthor; repeat the first author's name in each entry

Chomsky, Noam, and Morris Halle. The Sound Pattern of English. New York: Harper, 1968.

Chomsky, Noam, and George A. Miller. Analyse formelle des langues naturelles. No. 8 of Mathematiques et sciences de l'homme. The Hague: Mouton, 1971.

Special Cases

Afterword

A commentary coming at the end of some books: see "Introduction, Preface, Foreword, or Afterword," page 214.

Anonymous Author

Classical Literature

The Song of Roland. Trans. Frederick B. Luquines. New York: Macmillan, 1960.

MLA

Unsigned Book or Pamphlet

both writer and
publisher unknown

Latchkey Kids. Huntingdon, NY: n.p., 1989.

Corporation as Author

Phillips Petroleum. 66 Ways to Save Energy.
Bartlesville, OK: Phillips Petroleum, 1978.

Editor

Editor's Ideas Are Cited

Gardner, Martin, ed. The Annotated Alice. Alice's
Adventures in Wonderland and Through the
Looking Glass. By Lewis Carroll. New York:
Potter, 1960.

The Work Itself Is Cited

Carroll, Lewis. The Annotated Alice. Alice's
Adventures in Wonderland and Through the
Looking Glass. Ed. Martin Gardner. New York:
Potter, 1960.

Encyclopedia Article

although article's title
is "Isaac Newton," it
is entered under
"Newton," under
which a reader would
look it up; second
example shows form
for signed article;
publisher's name is
not necessary

"Newton, Isaac." The New Columbia Encyclopedia.
1975 ed.

Kaufmann, Walter. "Friedrich Nietzsche." New
Encyclopaedia Britannica. 1989 ed.

Enlarged Edition

See "Revised or Enlarged Edition," page 215.

Foreword

A commentary at the beginning of some books: see "Introduction,
Preface, Foreword, or Afterword," page 214.

Government Agency as Author

note abbreviations
Cong. (for *Congress*),
House (for *House of
Representatives*),
sess. (for *session*);
GPO (Government
Printing Office) is
publisher
for many federal
documents

United States. Cong. House. Committee on Ways and
   Means. Background Material and Data on
   Programs within the Jurisdiction of the
   Committee on Ways and Means. 102nd Cong.,
   2nd sess. Washington: GPO, 1992.

United States. Bureau of the Census. Statistical
   Abstracts of the United States: 1994.
   Washington: GPO, 1994.

United Nations. Centre on Transnational
   Corporations. World Investment Report
   1991. New York: United Nations, 1991.

Introduction, Preface, Foreword, or Afterword

reference here is to
Edel's rather than
Wilson's writing; had
Wilson's text also
been cited, book
would be entered
twice, once under
each author's name

Edel, Leon. Foreword. The Thirties. By Edmund
   Wilson. New York: Farrar, 1980. vii.

Preface

See "Introduction, Preface, Foreword, or Afterword," above.

Reprint

note distinction
between reprint and
revised edition:
revision means that
changes were made,
and only new version's
publication date is
given; *reprint* includes
no changes, and both
dates are given (date
of first printing
follows title, reprint
date follows
publisher)

Boys, C. V. Soap Bubbles and the Forces Which
   Mould Them. 1916. New York: Doubleday, 1959.

Revised or Enlarged Edition

editions other than first must be identified by number (2nd ed., 3rd ed., etc.), by name (rev. ed., enl. ed., etc.) or by year (1995 ed., etc.)—whatever information is shown in book

University of Chicago Press. The Chicago Manual of
    Style. 14th ed. Chicago: U of Chicago P, 1993.
Chomsky, Noam. Language and Mind. Enl. ed. New
    York: Harcourt, 1972.

See also "Encyclopedia Article," page 213.

Title within a Title

Especially in the field of literary criticism, titles of books and essays often contain titles of other works. When a book's title includes the title of another *book*, do not underline the interior title.

The Theological Underpinning of Moby-Dick.

When a book's title includes the title of a *poem* or an *essay*, underline the interior title and place it within quotation marks.

The Anthropological Background of "The Waste
    Land" of T. S. Eliot.

Translation

Translator's Ideas Are Cited

Fitzgerald, Robert, trans. The Iliad. By Homer. Garden
    City, NY: Anchor, 1974.

Only the Work Is Cited

Homer. The Iliad. Trans. Robert Fitzgerald. Garden
    City, NY: Anchor, 1974.

Volume Numbers

For works that are published in more than one volume, you must indicate which volume(s) you used in your paper.

More Than One of the Volumes Is Cited

bibliographic entry
indicates that all three
volumes have been
used

Dickinson, Emily. The Poems of Emily Dickinson. Ed.

Thomas H. Johnson. 3 vols. Cambridge:

Belknap-Harvard UP, 1955.

Just One Volume Is Cited

Manchester, William. The Last Lion: Winston Spencer

Churchill. Vol. 2. Boston: Little, 1988.

a volume will often
have its own title; if
so, it is cited first

Nevins, Allan. The Organized War, 1863-64. Vol. 3 of

The War for the Union. New York: Scribner's,

1971.

Group 2: Sample Entries for Periodicals

A periodical entry contains two titles: that of the article (within quotation marks) and that of the periodical (underlined, like the title of a book).

Volume numbers are needed for periodicals that do not carry specific dates — month, or day and month. Academic journals are especially likely to go by volume and issue rather than by date.

Page numbers of the full article are placed at the end of the entry.

Basic Format

Pay close attention to spacing and punctuation for each case. In general, however, follow these guidelines:

1. Periods separate main parts of an entry: Author. Article title. Periodical title and date.
2. Page numbers are preceded by a colon and a space.
3. Names of periodicals are underlined.
4. Titles of articles are placed in quotation marks.

A Single Author

Berthoff, Ann E. "Problem-Dissolving by Triadic

Means." College English 58 (Jan. 1996): 9-21.

Article in an Annual, Semiannual, or Quarterly Periodical

Flynn, Elizabeth A. "Feminism and Scientism." College Composition and Communication 46.3 (1995): 353-68.

when author's name is not given, source is listed by title

"Do Cities Change the Weather?" Mosaic 5 (Summer 1974): 29-34.

Notice that some periodicals do not number each issue's pages separately. For periodicals with consecutive page numbering, you must include the issue number (as in the Flynn entry above).

Article in a Monthly Periodical

do not give volume number; "+" indicates article is not printed on consecutive pages

Damasio, Antonio R., and Hanna Damasio. "Brain and Language." Scientific American Sept. 1992: 88-109.

Sahgal, Pavan. "Idiot Geniuses." Science Digest May 1981: 12+.

Article in a Weekly Periodical

issue is identified by date, month, and year

Dorschner, John. "Look Out! Here Comes the Sahara!" Tropic 29 Dec. 1974: 34-45.

"Women's Bank: A Modest Profit." Newsweek 20 Apr. 1981: 16.

Article in a Daily Newspaper

when only writer's initials are known, they follow normal order (not "K., J."); note quotation marks within quotation marks in third example; section number or letter, if there is one, is included; when paper's title does not include name of city, that information is shown in brackets (the Daily Worker *was a national newspaper)*

Roughton, Roger. "Barber's Bust with Loaf on Head." Daily Worker 8 Apr. 1936: 7.

J. K. "Explodes an Illusion." Daily Worker 30 Dec. 1936: 7-8.

"Presidential Panel Holds Hearings on 'Right to Die.'" New York Times 12 Apr. 1981, late ed., sec. 1: 24.

"Rebirth of a City." New-Times [Danbury, CT] 6 Sept. 1977: 2.

Special Cases

Critical Review of Another Work

> Yorke, Edmund. Rev. of History of Africa, by Kevin
> Shillington. Journal of African History 32 (1991):
> 339-40.

Notice that "Rev. of" is neither underlined nor enclosed within quotation marks. If the review has its own title, list it in quotation marks before "Rev. of."

Issue Numbers

Some journals do not publish in "volumes"; they assign issue numbers only. Treat the issue number exactly as you would a volume number. In this example, *94* is the issue number.

> Pritchard, Allan. "West of the Great Divide: A View of
> the Literature of British Columbia." Canadian
> Literature 94 (1982): 96-112.

If a journal assigns both volume and issue numbers, place the issue number directly after the volume number and a period (for example, 21.3).

Reprint of a Journal Article

> Mazzeo, Joseph A. "A Critique of Some Modern
> Theories of Metaphysical Poetry." Modern
> Philology 50 (1952): 88-96. Rpt. in Seventeenth-
> Century English Poetry. Ed. William R. Keast.
> New York: Oxford UP, 1962. 63-74.

Title within a Title

Underline the titles of books, plays, and long poems.

> "Hawthorne's Reaction to Moby-Dick."

Place single quotation marks around the title of an essay, short story, or short poem.

> "A Psychoanalytic Interpretation of 'America.'"

Group 3: Sample Entries for Electronic Sources

Going back to electronic sources you have consulted can be much harder (for you and your readers) than looking up printed books and periodicals listed in your Works Cited. By *electronic sources* we mean information that is stored in a computer or in a computerized format and must be accessed by computer.

Some electronic sources are relatively easy to cite because they are stored in a permanent format. CD-ROMs, for example, will not change their content once they are manufactured and arrive at the bookstore or library. Like books, they may be reissued in a new edition, but on the whole you can cite them much as you would a book. (In fact, some CD-ROMs are actually based on books — for example, the works of Mark Twain — whereas others hold databases, various other educational materials, or even games.)

However, not all electronic reference materials reach you in a permanent format. Electronic sources that you access online (whether through online information services or on the Internet) need to be cited in special ways because the contents of such documents can be changed at any time (by the author or by someone managing the online archive in which a document is stored). When you are examining such documents, *it is very important that you*

1. print out a copy of any material you think you may use in your paper.
2. note on the copy the date on which you accessed the material.

The following list includes sample citations for the most common kinds of electronic sources. Some electronic sources are available in several formats — for example, a popular magazine might be available on CD-ROM, through an online subscription service, and on a World Wide Web site. To cite such a source, use the format in which *you* found the source.

In general, if the online source is also published in print format, you should include the print publication information in the citation. But if you cannot find this or other kinds of information shown in the examples and guidelines (such as the author's name or date of electronic publication), just include what is available and try to give readers as much information as you can. If no page numbers are shown, for example, you can mention other numbered sections if there are any, such as "para. 4" or "14 screens." For online documents containing only one screen's worth of text, you do not need to give a location reference.

CD-ROM

Book

include the information you would for a printed book, adding the CD-ROM designation

The Oxford English Dictionary. 2nd ed. CD-ROM. Oxford: Oxford UP, 1992.

Periodically Revised Database

print publication information is given first; final items are the vendor's name and the date of electronic publication

Natchez, Gladys. "Frida Kahlo and Diego Rivera: The Transformation of Catastrophe to Creativity." Psychotherapy-Patient 4.1 (1987): 153-74. PsycLIT. CD-ROM. SilverPlatter. Nov. 1994.

Diskette

SPSS/PC+ Studentware Plus. Diskette. Chicago: SPSS, 1991.

Scholarly Project or Information Database

Complete Project

title is followed by date of electronic publication and sponsoring institution

The Victorian Web. 1996. Brown U. 27 Jan. 2000 <http://www.landow.stg.brown.edu/victorian/victov.html>.

Short Work within Project

note URL is that of specific work

Pyle, Forest. "'Frail Spells': Shelley and the Ironies of Exile." Romantic Circles. Ed. John Morrillo, Orrin N. C. Wang, and Deborah Elise White. 1999. 27 Jan. 2000 <http://www.rc.umd.edu/praxis/irony/pyle/frail.html>.

Anonymous Article from Information Database

"Zeugma." A Handbook of Rhetorical Devices. Ed. Robert Harris. 1997. Vanguard of Southern California. 27 Jan. 2000 <http://www.sccu.edu/faculty/R_Harris/rhetoric.htm>.

Online Book

Complete Book

> Hauben, Michael. Netizens: On the History and
> Impact of UseNet and the Internet. IEEE
> Computer Society Press, 1997. 27 Jan. 2000
> <http://studentweb.tulane.edu/~rwoods/netbook/
> contents.html>.

Short Work within Book

citation includes
information about
scholarly project of
which book is a part

> Dickinson, Emily. "The farthest thunder that I heard."
> Poems by Emily Dickinson: Third Series. Boston,
> 1896. Bartleby.com: Great Books Online. 1999.
> Columbia U. 28 Jan. 2000 <http://bartleby.com/
> 113/dickinson1.html#26>.

Online Periodical Article

Journal Article

include the
information you
would for an article in
a print periodical,
adding the date of
access and the URL

> Bostock, William W. "The Global Corporatisation of
> Universities: Causes and Consequences."
> AntePodium 3 (1999). 27 Jan. 2000
> <http://www.vuw.ac.nz/atp/>.

Newspaper Article

> Uchitelle, Louis. "Productivity Gains Help Keep
> Economy on a Roll." New York Times on the
> Web 22 March 1999. 24 March 1999
> <http://www.nytimes.com/yr/mo/day/news/
> financial/econ-sustain.html>.

Newswire Article

> "Bertha Advances toward Bahamas." CNN World
> News 9 July 1996. 9 July 1996 <http://cnn.com/
> WORLD/9607/09/bertha.update>.

Magazine Article

> "Prisons in America: An Online Conference with
> Robert Worth." Hosted by Scott Stossel. The

Atlantic Unbound 14 Nov. 1995. 22 March 1999
<http://theAtlantic.com/unbound/aandc/trnscrpt/
worth.htm>.

Posting to a Discussion Group

Mailing List (listserv) Posting

include the subject line and date of the posting, the name of the list, the date of access, and the URL of the list or the e-mail address of its moderator or supervisor

Sherwood, Matthew. "Writing Process and Self
Discipline." Online posting. 15 Feb. 1995.
CompLit. 19 Feb. 1995 <eng13764@ebbs
.english.vt.edu>.

Newsgroup Posting

include the subject line and date of the posting; the date of access; and the name of the newsgroup in angle brackets

Kuchinsky, Yuri. "Original Homelands of
Polynesians." Online posting. 14 Mar. 2000.
17 Mar. 2000 <sci.archaeology>.

General Web Site

first and second examples list persons who created the sites; third example lists date given in the site and institution associated with it (second date is date of access)

Dawe, James. Jane Austen Page. 15 Sept. 1998
<http://nyquist.ee.ualberta.ca/~dawe/austen
.html>.
Lancashire, Ian. Home page. 1 May 1998 <http://
www.chass.utoronto.ca:8080/~ian/>.
Romance Languages and Literatures Home Page.
1 Jan. 1997. Dept. of Romance Langs. and Lits.,
U of Chicago. 8 July 1998 <http://humanities
.uchicago.edu/romance/>.

Real-Time Communication

if you are citing a specific posting, start with the name of the speaker

Seminar discussion on netiquette. 28 May 1996.
LambdaMOO. 28 May 1996 <telnet://lambda.
parc.xerox.edu:8888>.

FTP, Gopher, or Telnet Site

substitute *ftp, gopher,* or *telnet* for *http* at the beginning of the URL

Matloff, Norm. "Immigration Forum." Online posting. 28 May 1996. Immigration. 31 May 1996 <ftp://heather.cs.ucdavis.edu/pub/Immigration/ Index.html>.

Smith, Charles A. "National Extension Model of Critical Parenting Practices." Online posting. 1994. Parenting Group. 28 May 1996 <gopher:// tinman.mes.umn.edu:4242/11/Other/Other /NEM_Parent>.

E-Mail Message

if e-mail was sent to someone other than you, substitute person's name for "the author"

Garretson, Kate. "CUNY Proficiency Exam." E-mail to the author. 22 Feb. 1999.

Article without a URL from an Online Subscription Service

Your Own Subscription

"Romanticism." Compton's Encyclopedia Online. Vers. 3.0. 1998. America Online. 17 Mar. 2000. Keyword: Compton's.

Library's Subscription

end with the URL of the service's home page

Epstein, Robert. "Examining the Nation's Psyche." Psychology Today Mar./Apr. 1999: 20. ProQuest. Rutgers U Lib., New Brunswick, NJ. 17 Mar. 2000 <http://www.proquest.umi.com>.

Other Electronic Sources

Work of Art

Picasso, Pablo. Woman Seated in an Armchair. ca. 1938. PaceWildenstein Gallery, New York. 28 Jan. 2000 <http://www.pacewildenstein.com/ images/picasso/armchair/jpg>.

Interview

Stipe, Michael. Interview. Fresh Air 16 Oct. 1998
<http://whyy.org/cgi-bin/FAshowretrieve.
cgi?2469>.

Group 4: Sample Entries for Other Material

Film or Video Recording

film can be entered
either by title or by
director, depending
on how used as a
source: when studying
film itself (as art form
or as adaptation of a
novel) title is used;
when studying
director's work, name
is given first; for other
visual materials,
include original
release date (if
applicable) and name
of medium

Howard's End. Dir. James Ivory. Sony, 1992. Based on
E. M. Forster's Howard's End.

Kurosawa, Akira, dir. Rashomon. 1950. Videocassette.
Embassy, 1986.

Interview

the first citation
refers to a private
interview, the second
to a broadcast one

Boxer, Barbara, Sen. Personal interview. 17 Mar. 2000.

Schickele, Peter. Interview with Margaret Juntwait.
Weekend around New York. WNYC Radio. New
York. 2 June 1996.

Lecture

Thomas, Lewis. "Notes of a Biology Watcher."
Princeton Club, New York. 21 Feb. 1978.

Letter

Entwhistle, Jacob, M.D. Letter to the author. 28 May
2000.

Microform

Sharpe, Lora. "A Quilter's Tribute." Boston Globe
25 Mar. 1989. NewsBank: Social Relations
(1989): fiche 6, grids B4-6.

Sound Recording

Leadbelly (Huddie Ledbetter). Rock Island Line. Notes by Frederick Ramsey Jr. LP. Folkways, 1956.

Television Program

Marshall was program's narrator

"Gorilla." National Geographic Society. Narr. E. G. Marshall. PBS. WNET, New York. 15 Apr. 1981.

Testimony, Official

note absence of underlining or quotation marks

Bell, Mark. Testimony before the Subcommittee on the Environment and the Atmosphere. Committee on Science and Technology, House of Representatives, 22 May 1975.

How to Cite Sources of Illustrative Materials

A final matter regarding documentation concerns the layout and labeling of graphs, tables, and other illustrative materials. In general, these items should be placed as close as possible to the text to which they relate. For tables, place a label and title over the table and a source note below it; for figures, place the label, title, and source note below the figure. Double space all of the text. (See the examples below and on page 226.)

Table 1

U.S.-Japan Merchandise Trade: 1975-78

Year	U.S. Domestic Exports to Japan	U.S. General Imports from Japan
1975	$9,421,000,000	$11,268,000,000
1976	10,027,000,000	15,504,000,000
1977	10,422,000,000	18,550,000,000
1978	12,689,000,000	24,458,000,000

Source: U.S. Bureau of the Census, Statistical Abstract of the United States: 1979 (Washington: GPO, 1979) 920.

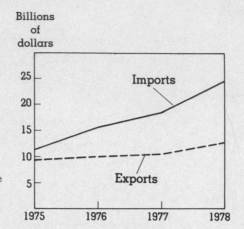

figure shows same
information as
preceding table; figure
number and caption
are placed below
figure

Fig. 1. U.S.-Japan Merchandise Trade: 1975-78, from:

U.S. Bureau of the Census, Statistical Abstract of the

United States: 1979 (Washington: GPO, 1979) 920.

Tables are referred to as "Tables," but graphs, pictures, diagrams, and other kinds of illustration are all referred to as "Figures" (usually abbreviated "Fig."). Each kind of item is numbered consecutively throughout the paper with Arabic numerals (Table 1, Table 2; Fig. 1, Fig. 2, Fig. 3). In addition to the source note that accompanies the table or figure itself, do not forget to include a citation in the Works Cited list. The citation for either the table on page 225 or the figure above would be as follows:

United States. Bureau of the Census. Statistical Abstract of the United

States: 1979. Washington: GPO, 1979.

19

Using Other Documentation Systems

Instructors in fields other than English will often require that you document sources using a system other than the MLA parenthetical system explained in Chapter 18. This chapter explains three other systems that are widely used and then discusses the preferred system in each academic discipline and any distinctive features of that system as it is used in that discipline.

The Chicago (Endnote/Footnote) System of Documentation

Some instructors, particularly those in the fields of history, philosophy, and religion, may prefer that you document your sources by inserting numbers in your text to refer to notations on a separate page of endnotes (called simply *Notes*) or at the foot of each page. The following guidelines pertain to one such documentation system, known as Chicago Style because it is based on the *Chicago Manual of Style,* Fourteenth Edition, published by the University of Chicago Press.

If you are using this system, insert a superscript (raised) number at all points where you would have used a parenthetical note. These numbers must run in sequence throughout the paper: 1, 2, 3, and so on. If you find you have left out a note after inserting all the numbers within the text, you must change all the succeeding numbers. Do not create "5a," for instance, when inserting an entry between 5 and 6.

After all the numbers have been placed within the text, make a list of notes. Next to each number, enter the bibliographic information that precisely identifies the source of the quotation, paraphrase, or summary. Occasionally an instructor may ask you to place footnotes at the bottom of each page, rather than compile a list of endnotes. The rules for punctuating footnotes are the same as those for endnotes, but whereas endnotes are double-spaced within and between notes, footnotes are double-spaced between notes but single-spaced within each note.

Insertion of Numbers within the Text

1. Type each number *half a space* above the line (many word-processing programs place superscript numbers on command), and directly (no space) after the final punctuation of the sentence it refers to.

2. For quotations that end in the middle of a sentence, place the number directly after the final quotation mark.

Here are examples in which numbers replaced parenthetical notes in the paper on Emily Dickinson.

> Dickinson sent Higginson four poems, along with a letter containing this question: "Are you too deeply occupied to say if my Verse is alive?"[8] This . . .

> Certainly, then, the woman Yvor Winters called "one of the greatest lyric poets of all time"[2] was all but unknown as a poet during her lifetime.

> Paul Ferlazzo, for example, infers that Higginson's response to her first letter must have included some recommendations for altering, or "regularizing," her poems, along with a request for more of her work.[9]

When you quote from a literary work, use a note for the first reference, identifying the specific edition you used and informing your readers that all subsequent notes will be in-text parenthetical notes. After the first note, simply insert the pages or, as in the following quotation from *Paradise Lost*, the book and line numbers.

> Evil into the mind of God or Man
> May come and go, so unapprov'd, and leave

No spot or blame behind: Which gives me hope

That what in sleep thou didst abhor to dream,

Waking thou never wilt consent to do. (PL 5.117-21)

Basic Endnote Format

This format differs from that of entries in the Works Cited list in the MLA parenthetical system, although the same basic questions are answered: Who? What? Where? When?

Works cited	Cook, Blanche Wiesen. Eleanor Roosevelt. New York: Viking, 1992.
Endnote	1. Blanche Wiesen Cook, Eleanor Roosevelt (New York: Viking, 1992), 79.

Here is the basic endnote format:

1. The first line of each note indents five spaces to the note number; each subsequent line flushes with the left margin.
2. Author's name is given in normal order.
3. Commas and spaces replace the periods and one space used in Works Cited. No comma is used before parentheses.
4. Parentheses surround publishing information.
5. Page number(s) are added at the end. Do not use "p." or "pp." A comma comes between parentheses and page number(s).

A few samples of the most common situations should give you an idea of how to handle this system.

Editor and Translator

1. Martin Gardner, ed., The Annotated Alice. Alice's Adventures in Wonderland and Through the Looking Glass, by Lewis Carroll (New York: Potter, 1960), iv-vi.

2. Feodor Dostoevsky, Crime and Punishment, trans. Jessie Coulson, ed. George Gibian (New York: Norton, 1964), 142.

Essay in a Book of Essays

> 3. Gwendolyn Brooks, "The Rise of Maud Martha," in Invented Lives: Narratives of Black Women 1860-1960, ed. Mary Helen Washington (New York: Anchor-Doubleday, 1987), 430.

Introduction, Preface, Foreword, or Afterword

> 4. Leon Edel, foreword to The Thirties, by Edmund Wilson (New York: Farrar, 1980), vii.

Periodical

> 5. Earl G. Ingersoll, "Considerations of Gender in the Dramatic Monologue," Modern Language Review 86 (July 1991): 547.

(Note the colon between date and page number for scholarly journals, unlike the format for books.)

> 6. Stephen Jay Gould, "A Most Ingenious Paradox," Natural History, December 1984, 20.

(A comma rather than a colon separates the date and page numbers for popular magazines and newspapers.)

> 7. John Dorschner, "Look Out! Here Comes the Sahara!" Tropic, 29 December 1974, 38.

(No comma follows a title that ends with a question mark or an exclamation point.)

> 8. "Presidential Panel Holds Hearings on 'Right to Die,'" New York Times, 12 April 1981, late edition, sec. 1.

(Note the quotation within a quotation.)

Shortened Form for Second and Further References to Same Source

After you have produced one complete note for a particular source, you can use a shorter form for all subsequent references to the same source.

> 9. Bernstein, 231.

If the author wrote more than one of your sources, you have to put the title (in a shortened form) in the note. In the next example, earlier notes would have given the complete bibliographic information for Freud's *Interpretation of Dreams* and his *Moses and Monotheism*. A comma goes between the author and title.

> 16. Freud, Dreams, 303.
>
> 17. Freud, Moses, 68.

In this system, as in the MLA parenthetical system, mentioning the source or the author in the text affects the amount of information that appears in the note.

> Jehovah was originally the god of a local volcano, according to Freud.[19]
>
> 19. Moses, 23.

Don't carry this too far, however. Never give just the page number(s) in the shortened notes. Always mention either the author or the title unless a note refers to the same source as the previous one, in which case you can often simply use the Latin abbreviation *Ibid.*

> 17. Freud, Moses, 68.
>
> 18. Ibid.
>
> 19. Ibid., 69.

Do not overuse *Ibid.*, though, because it forces the reader to look back at a previous note to identify the reference. If an extended series of notes all refer to the same source, it is better to make the second and subsequent ones into parenthetical page citations in the text.

Jehovah was originally the god of a local volcano, according to Freud (p. 23).

If you use the endnote system, you may not need to include a Works Cited or bibliography with your paper. However, find out your instructor's preference. For a full example of the endnote system of documentation (including a bibliography), see the sample paper by Fred Hutchins in Chapter 21.

The APA (Author/Year) System of Documentation

Many behavioral science instructors will ask you to follow the system devised by the American Psychological Association (APA), which uses parenthetical notes in the text that correspond to sources listed at the end of the paper under *References*. The APA system is similar in form to the MLA parenthetical-notation system; the major difference lies in the contents of the parenthetical notes.

- In the APA system, you generally give the year of publication in the note, whereas in MLA, you never put the date in the note.
- In the APA system, you give the page numbers only for a quotation, not for paraphrases or summaries, as in MLA.

These differences are not trivial. The APA believes the most important information is the time the idea was presented to the world; the MLA is primarily concerned with precisely locating the information within the source.

The APA system is a variant on a general approach called the *author/year system*. (Some disciplines within the behavioral sciences have arrived at their own slightly different versions of author/year. Several of them are briefly illustrated at the end of this chapter.)

Punctuation of Notes

1. As in the MLA system, parenthetical notes are included within the sentences to which they refer.
2. Commas separate name from date when both appear inside a note.
3. An ampersand (&) is used instead of *and* between authors' names when more than one name appears in a note. (But use *and* when you mention coauthors in your text.)
4. The abbreviations "p." and "pp." are used to indicate *page* and *pages*, except after volume and issue numbers.

APA

Basic Format of Notes

Insert the parenthetical note immediately after the last name of the author. You are strongly encouraged to mention the author's name in your text rather than in the parenthetical note. The note contains just the year of publication.

> Robinson (1986) asserted that child abuse in upper-middle-class homes manifests itself in subtler ways.

If a source has two authors, mention both in all references.

> Martin and Elder (1969) demonstrated that abusive parents were usually themselves abused.

If, for stylistic reasons, you do not mention the authors' names in your text, place them inside the note.

> It was shown in the late 1960s (Martin & Elder, 1969) that abusive parents were usually themselves abused.

You can avoid using a note by mentioning both author and date in your text.

> In 1969, Martin and Elder demonstrated that abusive parents . . .

When you quote a source directly, use a note to indicate the page number as well as the date and author if they are not already clear in the text. For electronic or other works without page numbers, paragraph numbers may be used instead, preceded by the symbol ¶ or "para."

> Rogers (1984) believed that "virtually all female abusers suffered from primary splitting" (p. 67).
> One theorist believed that "virtually all female abusers suffered from primary splitting" (Rogers, 1984, p. 67).
> Denes (1980, ¶1) claimed that psychotherapy is an art that is "volatile, unpredictable, standardless in its outcome, subjective in its worth."

When a source has three, four, or five authors, cite all of the authors' names in the first reference; in later citations, use the first author's name and "et al." If a source has six or more authors, use the first author's surname and "et al." for the first and subsequent citations. But watch out for the situation in which two of your sources have several authors with the same person heading both series of names.

<table>
<tr><td>in third and fourth entries, lead author is same but other authors are different; therefore, later references to either work must list second author as well as first</td><td>Gold, Bache, Cohen, and Arnach (1978) found that . . .

Gold et al. (1978) were not so sure that . . .

Marx, Walcott, Blau, and Johanssen (1985) said . . .

Marx, Martin, and Schuster (1980) were convinced that . . .

A study of college students (Marx, Walcott, et al., 1985) concluded that . . .</td></tr>
</table>

If two authors have the same last name, use initials to distinguish them, both in notes and within the text.

J. Prescott (1983) tried testing infants . . .

A later study (D. Prescott, 1989) could find no . . .

If the author is a corporation or a government agency, place the full name in the first note and the abbreviation in brackets; abbreviate thereafter.

An international agency (Organization for Economic Cooperation and Development [OECD], 1990) took a strong interest in . . .

A hotly contested survey by an international agency (OECD, 1990) came to the conclusion that . . .

If an author contributed more than one source to your list, and two of them were published in the same year, lowercase letters are added to the year numbers.

Freud (1923a) first announced . . .

In a now-famous essay (Freud, 1923b), the idea of . . .

When a source has no author, use a short form of the title in the parenthetical note.

One source ("Supergene Cluster," 1982) predicted that . . .

The References page would list this article as follows. Note that the article is listed without quotation marks, and only the first word is capitalized.

Supergene cluster fights aging. (1982, August). Science Digest, p. 91.

If one of your sources mentioned the work of another author, and you want to refer to that other work, use this form:

Ashkenazi's work (cited in Beatty, 1992) showed . . .

Be sure to list Beatty's work, not Ashkenazi's, in your list of References because that is where you found the information.

If you need to cite an entire Web site, not a specific document on the site, simply give the URL of the site as a parenthetical note. You need not list the site in the References.

Results of recent polls are available on the organization's home page (http://www.gallup.com).

Letters, memos, phone conversations, e-mail messages, and postings to online discussion forums like newsgroups and mailing lists (listservs) are considered *personal communications* and are generally cited only in text, not in the References. However, if a posting is archived, include the source in the References.

S. A. Hatem (personal communication, May 5, 1996) . . .

Punctuation and Capitalization of References

1. Book titles and periodical names and volume numbers are underlined or italicized. Check which format your instructor prefers.
2. Titles of essays and periodical articles are *not* placed in quotation marks or underlined.
3. Only the first word, proper nouns, and proper adjectives in book, essay, and article titles are capitalized. But all main words in names of periodicals are capitalized, as is the first letter of the first word of a subtitle.

4. Commas are used between authors' surnames and initials and between authors. With more than one author, an ampersand (&) is used before the last author's name.

5. Periods separate the main parts of an entry: Author. (Date). Title. Publisher.

Basic Format of References

1. Sources are listed alphabetically by their authors' last names, or, when the author is not known, by the first word of the title, ignoring *A, An,* and *The.*

2. No first names are given for authors, just initials (unless two people have the same last names and initials).

3. When a source has more than one author, all authors' names are entered by last name, followed by initial(s). (This rule applies even to six or more authors.)

4. The year of publication (inside parentheses) follows the author's name. When two or more sources have the same author, list the sources chronologically. If two or more articles appeared in the same year, use letters (a, b, c) to distinguish them, and list them alphabetically. Repeat the author's name in each case.

5. The first line of each entry starts at the left margin. Remaining lines indent five spaces (or one tab) from the margin.

(In this sample list, only authors and titles are shown, so that you can concentrate on the above points.)

Freud, A. (1951). An experiment in group upbringing.

Freud, S. (1905). Three essays on the theory of sexuality.

Freud, S. (1910a). Five lectures on psychoanalysis.

Freud, S. (1910b). Leonardo da Vinci and a memory of his childhood.

Freud, S. (1931). Female sexuality.

Goldstein, J., Freud, A., & Solnit, A. J. (1979). Before the best interests of the child.

Klein, M. (1961). Narrative of a child analysis.

See page 241 for a list of standard abbreviations for bibliographical terms.

Sample List of References for Print Sources

periodical issue numbers are underlined; consecutive page numbers include all three digits for both numbers; state of publication is given only if city is not well known or could be confused with another city (use postal state abbreviations); publisher names keep *Books* and *Press* but omit *Publishers, Co.,* and *Inc.*

Arlow, J. A. (1981). Theories of pathogenesis. Psychoanalytic Quarterly, 50, 488-514.

Berkowitz, M. S. (Ed.). (1985). Peer conflict and psychological growth. San Francisco: Jossey-Bass.

Epstein, A. (1982). Teen parents: What they need to know. High/Scope Resource, 1(2), 6-7.

Foulks, E. F., Persons, J. B., & Merkel, R. L. (1986). The effect of patients' beliefs about their illnesses on compliance in psychotherapy. American Journal of Psychiatry, 143, 340-344.

Freud, S. (1966). Introductory lectures on psychoanalysis (J. Strachey, Trans. and Ed.). New York: W. W. Norton. (Original work published 1917)

Kohn, M. L. (1980). Job complexity and adult personality. In N. J. Smelser & E. H. Erikson (Eds.), Themes of work and love in adulthood (pp. 193-212). Cambridge, MA: Harvard University Press.

Murphy, K. (1989, April 17). The long arm of RICO--is it reaching too far? Los Angeles Times, pp. 1, 19.

Organization for Economic Cooperation and Development. (1990). Foreign direct investment and industrial development in Mexico. Paris: Author.

Steinem, G. (1981, May). The politics of talking in groups. Ms., pp. 43-45+.

Supergene cluster fights aging. (1982, August). Science Digest, p. 91.

Zigler, E., & Muenchow, S. (1992). Head Start: The inside story of America's most successful educational experiment. New York: Basic Books.

References for Electronic Sources

For electronic sources in the list of References, the APA style requires much of the same information as for print sources. The purpose of a citation for both types of sources is to give your reader the necessary information to retrieve the source. For electronic sources, the minimum information needed is the author and the title of the document; the date it was published or posted and, usually, the date you retrieved it; and the URL of the document or the name of the database where you found it.

For sources from the Web, the URL needs to be as specific as possible and should include not only the host name but the exact directory path for the document you are using. Because URLs are often long and complex, it is important to proofread them with particular attention. Remember that the directory path is case-sensitive; be sure to use capital and lowercase letters correctly. If you need to break the URL because it will not fit on one line, do so only after a slash or before a period. Do not add a hyphen at the break, and remove a hyphen added by your word-processing program. The APA recommends testing each URL from your References list frequently to make sure it still leads to the source and updating it if the source has moved to a new location. The APA also recommends omitting sources that no longer exist on the Internet at the time you complete your work.

Specific Documents on a Web Site

a journal article that has an identical print version but that you have viewed only electronically

Hyde, J. S., DeLamater, J. D., & Hewitt, E. C. (1998, September). Sexuality and the dual-earner couple: Multiple roles and sexual functioning [Electronic version]. Journal of Family Psychology, 12(3), 354-368.

an article from an Internet-only source

Hubbard, J. (2000, November 17). Open-sourcing the Apple. Slate. Retrieved May 30, 2001, from http://www.slate.com/tech/review/2000/11/17/hubbard_osx.index.html

an article with no author or no date: begin the citation with the title of the document, or type n.d. in parentheses where the date would normally appear

"Learned optimism" yields health benefits. (1996). Retrieved June 28, 2001, from http://helping.apa.org/mind_body/learned.html

Matloff, N. (n.d.). Immigration forum. Retrieved from ftp://heather.cs.ucdavis.edu/pub/Immigration/Index.html

a document from a
university Web site

Oi, D. H., & Koehler, P. (1996). Imported fire ants on
lawns and turf. Retrieved January 30, 2000, from
University of Florida, Institute of Food and
Agricultural Sciences Web site: http://edis.ifas
.ufl.edu/LH059

an electronic version
of a government
report

California Department of Food and Agriculture.
(2000). U.S. History. Retrieved January 31, 2000,
from http://www.cdfa.ca.gov/pests/fire_ants/
new/history.html

Articles and Abstracts from Electronic Databases.   References for articles and abstracts found on electronic databases, such as Lexis-Nexis or PsycARTICLES, should follow the format for the particular kind of document, such as a newspaper article, an abstract, or a government report. They should also include a retrieval statement that gives the name of the database and the date of the retrieval.

an abstract of a
journal article

Natchez, G. (1987). Frida Kahlo and Diego Rivera: The
transformation of catastrophe to creativity.
Psychotherapy-Patient, 4, 153-174. Abstract
retrieved February 21, 1999, from Psychological
Abstracts database.

a newspaper article

Calloway, E. (1999, December 25). Blues mirrors the
emotions of African Americans. Chicago
Defender. Retrieved March 17, 2000, from
Softline Information: http://www.softlineweb
.com/ethnic.htm

Other Kinds of Electronic Sources.   The APA suggests that you consider omitting online sources such as e-mail and postings to newsgroups and mailing lists (listservs) from your work because they are not connected with recognized scholarly organizations as other sources usually are. If you do cite an e-mail or a posting from a newsgroup or mailing list that does not archive its messages, do not include that source in your list of References: cite it only in the text, as a personal communication, as shown on page 235.

an archived newsgroup posting	Conrad, E. (1996, July 8). Proof of life after death [Msg. 2]. Message posted to news://sci.archeology
an archived electronic mailing list (listserv) posting	Freed, A. (2001, February 24). Language Use, Feminism, and Economics [Msg 2]. Message posted to Feminists in Linguistics electronic mailing list, archived at http://listserv .linguistlist.org/srchives/fling.html

Formats for Other Kinds of Sources

interview (if tape or transcript; if contents are not recoverable, see discussion of personal communications, page 235)	Schickele, P. (1996, June 2). [Interview with Margaret Juntwait]. Weekend around New York. New York: WNYC Radio.
motion picture or video recording	Ritchie, M. (Director). (1972). The candidate [Motion picture]. Los Angeles: Warner.
sound recording	Colvin, S. (1991). I don't know why. [Recorded by A. Krauss & Union Station]. On Every time you say goodbye [Cassette]. Cambridge, MA: Rounder Records. (1992)
television program (single episode)	Kuttner, P. K., Moran, C., & Scholl, E. (Writers), & Chamberlain, W. (Executive Director). (1994, July 19). Passin' it on [Television series episode]. In D. Zaccardi (Executive Producer), P.O.V. New York: Public Broadcasting System.
television series	Zaccardi, D. (Executive Producer). (1994). P.O.V. [Television series]. New York: Public Broadcasting System.
review of a book	Mantel, H. (2001). The monster we know. [Review of the book Interpreter of maladies]. The New York Review of Books, 48, 22–23.

review of a motion picture (retrieved from an online periodical)

> Taylor, C. (2001). Artificial maturity. [Review of the motion picture A.I.]. Salon. Retrieved July 12, 2001, from http://www.salon.com/ent/movies/ feature/2001/06/29/artificial_intelligence/ index.html

Abbreviations for Bibliographical Terms

When using the following list of standard abbreviations for common bibliographical terms, note that APA style capitalizes some of the abbreviations in certain situations (for example, *Ed.* for *editor*, *Rev. ed.* for *revised edition*, *4 vols.* but *Vol. 4*).

chapter	chap.
edition/edited by	ed.
editor	ed.
no date	n.d.
no place of publication/no publisher	n.p.
number	no.
part	pt.
reprint	rpt.
revised edition	rev. ed.
supplement	supp. (MLA), suppl. (APA)
translator	trans.
volume	vol.

The Number System of Documentation

A fourth system, sometimes called the *number system,* is employed primarily in mathematics, computer sciences, chemistry, physics, and engineering. Each source is assigned a number in the list of references, and these numbers—shown in parentheses or as superscripts—are what readers see in text references, instead of page numbers or years.

numbers appear in parentheses

> Widlow (1) discovered that cells injected with . . .
>
> Breitenstein and Forester (2) attempted to convert . . .
>
> Morgan (3) and Stanley (4) both argued that stress . . .

number appears as superscript

> Widlow[1] discovered that cells injected with . . .

Even if you do not mention the author within your text, place only the number assigned to it in the note. If you refer to more than one source at the same time, include the number assigned to each source.

Recent experimentation (5, 6, 7) seems to indicate . . .

In these sciences, writers rarely quote their sources directly; however, if you quote, the page number must be included in the note.

As Johnstone stated (2, p. 18), "The outcome depended on..."

Format Preferences for Various Academic Disciplines

Most disciplines use variations of either the APA (author/year) or the number system of citation. In-text citation styles resemble rather closely the models we have described in this text; there is more variation among different disciplines' approach to listing references. Find out your instructor's preference or consult one of the discipline-specific style guides mentioned later in this section.

When comparing citation styles for listing references in various fields, expect to see differences in these areas:

- placement of publication date
- use of underlining and quotation marks and capitalization for titles
- abbreviation of periodical names
- treatment of publisher's location and name

Sciences

As we mentioned in the preceding section, the *physical and applied sciences* generally use the number system. The biological and earth sciences (including biology, botany, geology, and zoology) mainly use the author/year system, except for the biomedical sciences (medicine, nursing, and health), which employ the number system. (For a complete description of the CBE [Council of Biology Editors] style, see the sixth edition of *Scientific Style and Format: The CBE Manual for Authors, Editors, and Publishers,* published by Cambridge University Press.)

Consider the following examples of citation styles of some specific sciences.

Biology, botany, and *zoology* use the author/year system and list references in alphabetical order. These examples follow basic CBE style for author/year citation.

all author names are inverted; no periods follow abbreviations; initial letters of first words of titles and proper nouns are capitalized; page count is given for books	Hairston NG, Smith FE, Slobodkin LB. 1960. Community structure, population control, and competition. American Naturalist 94:421-25. Ross C. 1995. Writing nature. New York: St Martin's. 650 p.

Chemistry uses the number system and lists references in the order in which they are cited in the paper.

note omission of titles for periodical articles and use of underlining for book titles; journal years of publication are in bold type	(1) Raptolinsky, T. Chemists and the New Technology; Mills Ltd.: Manchester, 1976; pp 102-109. (2) Pauling, L.; Corey, R. B.; Branson, H. R. Proc. N. A. S. **1951**, 37, 205-211.

Engineering follows the same general format as *physics* (see below).

Mathematics uses the number system and lists references in alphabetical order. For more information, see the 1990 edition of *A Manual for Authors of Mathematical Papers,* published by the American Mathematical Society.

note that all titles are underlined	[1.] Paul Bennacerraf, God, the Devil, and Goedel, Monist 51 (1967), 9. [2.] John Allen Paulos, Beyond Numeracy, New York, Vintage, 1991.

Physics uses the number system and lists references in the order in which they are cited. (For more information, see the fourth edition of the *AIP Style Manual,* published by the American Institute of Physics.)

page numbers for books tell which pages are relevant to paper	[1] J. O. Hirschfelder, R. E. Wyatt, and R. D. Coalson, Lasers, Quanta, and Molecules (Wiley, New York, 1989), pp. 801-22, 867-90.

titles of articles are not given; titles of periodicals are not underlined

²J. M. Jauch, <u>Are Quanta Real? A Galilean Dialogue</u> (Indiana University Press, Bloomington, 1973), pp. 72-77.

³D. R. Hofstadter, Physical Review B, <u>14</u>, no. 6, 45-64 (1976).

Social Sciences

The social sciences (business, economics, education, geography, physical education, political science, psychology, sociology, etc.) generally follow APA style, except for history, which follows MLA style or the endnote/footnote system.

Business and *economics* use the author/year system and list references in alphabetical order; a similar alternate style is shown here.

note that last item, although numbered like a periodical, is a pamphlet or small book, and no page numbers are given

Bloomfield, C. L., and Fairley, I. R. (1991). <u>Business Communication: A Process Approach</u>. San Diego: Harcourt Brace Jovanovich.

Easterlin, R. (1973). "Does Money Buy Happiness?" <u>The Public Interest</u>, 30, 1-17.

United States Department of Commerce. (1979). Survey of Current Business, 59, no. 7.

Education uses either a variation of the MLA format or the author/year system and lists references in alphabetical order.

preferred form; note that authors' first names are spelled out

Bruner, Jerome S. (1977). The Growth of Mind. <u>Amer. Psychol</u>. 20, 1007-17.

Pearson, Carol S., Shavlik, Donna L., and Touchton, Judith G. (1989). <u>Educating the Majority: Women Challenge Tradition in Higher Education</u>. New York: Macmillan.

History follows the MLA format or the endnote/footnote system.

Political science usually follows the APA format.

Psychology uses the APA author/year system, but some journals use the number system. Both systems follow alphabetical order when listing references. Ask your instructor which to use.

Sociology uses the author/year system and lists references in alphabetical order. Book and journal titles are not underlined, and article titles are not capitalized (after the first word) or enclosed in quotation marks. Your instructor's preferences may vary somewhat from this.

preferred form

Inglehart, Ronald. 1991. Culture shift in advanced
industrial society. Princeton, NJ: Princeton
University Press.
Maranda, Elli. 1971. "Theory and practice of riddle
analysis." Journal of American Folklore 84:51-61.

Reviewing Part Five

Questions

1. Why do research papers include parenthetical notes? Is the answer the same for all disciplines?
2. When might you use a traditional footnote number while working with the MLA system of parenthetical documentation?
3. Explain why you would or would not cite a source for each of the following pieces of information.
   - the definition of *palindrome*
   - the names of Emily Dickinson's father and mother
   - the latest census data about the size of the average American household
   - the poet T. S. Eliot's interpretation of the river in *Huckleberry Finn*
   - Dr. Elizabeth Kübler-Ross's concept of the appropriate attitudes toward dying patients
   - author Willa Cather's date and place of birth
   - results of a recent study of caffeine's effect on the heart
   - the population of each of the states that used to constitute Yugoslavia
   - American patriot Nathan Hale's last words, "I regret that I have but one life to give for my country."

Exercise

Construct a Works Cited page for the following sources, putting all of the information in the correct order according to the MLA format. If you need help getting started, note that the first five of the following items appear in the bibliography for the Dickinson paper in Chapter 21.

1. Your research led you to a book titled Emily Dickinson: A Collection of Critical Essays, in which you found an essay called Emily Dickinson and the Limits of Judgment. The book was edited by Richard B. Sewall, and the essay was the work of Yvor Winters. The essay begins on page 38 and ends on page 56. The book was

published in 1963 by Prentice-Hall, the location of which was shown as Englewood Cliffs, New Jersey.

2. Your research uncovered an essay, Father and Daughter: Edward and Emily Dickinson, which was published in a journal, American Literature, in January 1960. This is volume 40, and the essay covers pages 510 to 523. The writer is Owen Thomas.

3. When quoting Emily Dickinson's poetry, you used a collection called The Complete Poems of Emily Dickinson, which was published in 1960 by Little, Brown and Company, located in Boston, Massachusetts. The person who edited the poems was Thomas H. Johnson.

4. When quoting the poet's letters, you used a three-volume collection called The Letters of Emily Dickinson, which was published in Cambridge, Massachusetts, by the Harvard University Press in 1958. The editors were Thomas H. Johnson and Theodora Ward.

5. You read a book written by the critic Paul J. Ferlazzo in 1976. The book is titled Emily Dickinson and was published by Twayne Publishers, which is located in Boston, Massachusetts.

6. You read a tribute to the poet, called The First Lady of Mt. Holyoke, which appeared in the South Hadley (Massachusetts) Gazette on December 10, 1984. This unsigned essay appeared on the second and third pages of the second section of the newspaper.

7. You wrote a letter to a professor at Mt. Holyoke College, Joanna Caldwell, who is an authority on the poet and her works. You quote a remark from her reply to you, which was written on November 4, 1983.

8. You read an article in the magazine Psychology Today, written by John Forsyte, Joanna Caldwell, and Edgar Polishook. The article, titled Emily Dickinson: Inhibited Genius?, appeared in the July 1979 issue on pages 68 to 80.

9. You read a review of Ferlazzo's book (see item 5), written by Joanna Caldwell, which was published in PMLA, volume 65, pages 343 to 345. This issue was published in May 1980.

10. You misplaced your notes on the Caldwell article (see item 9) and didn't have access to the print article anymore, so on October 10, 1996, you referred to an online version of the article. The information appeared in the ERIC database, and you accessed it using the DIALOG online service.

Part Six

Preparing the Manuscript

20

Following Format Requirements

As you may already know, presentation is an important part of any research paper. The style in which you communicate strongly influences how well your readers understand what you are trying to say or how willingly they accept your argument.

The first rule in preparing a paper to be turned in is to read it over carefully for spelling, mechanical, or grammatical errors. Corrections should be made before the final copy is printed or completed rather than directly before you turn it in. Written corrections on your work look sloppy and distract readers from your points.

College research papers should be typed. Whether typed on a typewriter or computer, research papers should follow specific formatting rules and guidelines. Your instructor will likely review the format he or she prefers. If not, however, the rules listed here are standard for all academic and professional writing and should serve as basic guidelines for you.

Basic Formatting

1. Use 8 ½-by-11-inch, high-quality white paper.
2. Leave 1-inch margins on all four sides: top, bottom, left, and right.
3. Double space the lines of your paper.
4. If you are using a computer, print the paper with a high-quality print setting. Use a laser printer if possible.

Abiding by these rules will result in professional-looking written work that will be easy for your readers to follow and comprehend. Specific kinds of research papers may call for more specific formatting decisions, but this is something that you will need to discuss with your instructor.

Following a Particular Format

Your instructor will usually tell you if he or she wants you to follow a particular formatting style such as MLA or APA. The format that you work with can determine such decisions as how you list information on a Works Cited or References page and whether you use footnotes or endnotes. Make certain, then, that before you complete your paper you have worked with the format that your instructor recommends.

Creating a Title Page

A separate title page can be useful and pleasing to the eye because it sets off information that is more important to the identification than the content of the paper. In addition to the title of your paper, information that typically appears on the title page includes your name, the class the paper was written for, your instructor's name, and the date on which the paper was handed in, in that order. The title should be centered on the page, and the other information should appear on separate lines, ending 1 inch from the bottom of the page.

Paginating Your Paper

Except for the title page, all pages of your research paper should be numbered, including the list of sources at the end. Unless your instructor tells you differently, page numbers should appear in the upper right corner. If you are using MLA format, precede your page numbers with your last name in case any pages accidentally become separated from the rest of the document. If you are working in APA format, instead of your name, use the first two major words of the title of your paper. You can follow either of these styles automatically by using a header function on many word-processing programs. Headers or page numbers should appear ½ inch from the top of the paper and flush with the right margin, 1 inch from the right side of the page.

Selecting an Appropriate Font

Though your word-processing program may afford you a large selection of fonts, many of them are not acceptable for academic writing. When selecting a font, be sure to:

1. Use a 10- or 11-point size.
2. Choose a font that is as simple and professional looking as possible. In general, use a serif font, in which the characters have fine lines projecting from their ends, rather than a san-serif font like this.
3. Avoid fonts that look like handwriting and *ornate* fonts. They can be difficult to read and will not give your work the seriousness that it deserves.
4. If your word-processing program allows you to use *italics,* check with your instructor to make sure that he or she does not prefer underlining.
5. Keep your font consistent throughout your work unless you have a strong reason for doing otherwise.

Using Color

If you have access to a color printer and to a computer that has color functions as part of its word-processing program, you may want to use color to draw attention to important elements in your paper, such as visuals. Keep in mind, though, that color works much like variation in fonts: it can easily become too much of a good thing. When deciding whether or not to make use of color, consider the following guidelines:

1. Color can draw the reader's eye to specific details and can make images more lively, distinct, and easy to read.
2. Overusing color looks confusing and unprofessional. In general, use italics or underlining rather than color for highlighting important words in the text, and do not print the main text of your document in a color other than black.
3. If you are using color for anything other than reproducing a visual, the fewer and more consistent colors you use, the better.

Including Visuals

Charts, graphs, tables, maps, photographs, and other illustrations can help convey important information to your readers in a manner that is very different from written text and can help make this information more immediate, concise, and memorable. When you are deciding whether or not to include a visual in your paper, ask yourself the same question that you would of any other information you might incorporate in your work: "What is this visual doing to enhance my paper?" If you do not think that it is doing something significant that writing could not, there is no reason to include it. Here are some guidelines for including specific kinds of visuals:

1. *Charts and graphs* illustrate relationships between different sets of data.
2. *Tables* contain numerical information.
3. *Maps* indicate locations and relationships between geographical and numerical information.
4. *Photographs and drawings* can often depict what something looks like more easily and accurately than written description can.

21

Four Sample Research Papers

This chapter contains four sample student research papers. These papers were chosen as samples not only because they demonstrate competence in the research techniques described in this book but also because the students were writing for different academic disciplines and therefore used slightly different approaches to their projects.

The first paper, "The New Immigrants: Asset or Burden?" and the second paper, "Emily Dickinson's Reluctance to Publish," illustrate MLA documentation style and procedures. The third paper, "Cotton Mather's Necessary Witches," illustrates the *Chicago Manual of Style* endnote/footnote method of documentation. The fourth paper, *"Solenopsis invicta:* Destroyer of Ecosystems," illustrates the author/year system of the American Psychological Association (APA), a system used by researchers in various scientific and social science disciplines.

The New Immigrants: Asset or Burden?

by

Shirley Macalbe

Professor Alan Sandalt

Sociology 57

December 11, 20_ _

Outline

THESIS: From the findings of experts on immigration, we can conclude that if the new immigrants have economic effects on the United States similar to those that earlier immigrants have had, then they will prove to be, for the most part, an asset rather than a burden.

Introduction

    I. Background

       · A. Immigration as historically controversial issue in the United States

       B. Immigration as current issue of controversy

       C. Economic issues as principal reasons for resistance to immigration

    II. Consideration of "asset vs. burden" question

       A. Past history of immigration as possible predictor of value of new immigrants

       B. Agreement among many experts that past history bodes well for success of most new immigrants

    III. Student interviews

       A. Purpose

       B. Selection of interviewees

       C. Selection of interviews for analysis

       D. Analysis of interviews

    IV. Controversies on impact of immigrants

       A. Lacey and Crewdson: little or no competition between immigrants and Americans for jobs

       B. Muller and Fogel: evidence of some competition

Macalbe iii

    C. Miles: immigrant pressure as one major cause of the Los Angeles riot in 1992

    D. Question of whether immigrants cause problems or intensify already existing problems

V. Encouraging patterns of immigrant economic history

    A. Fogel: despite some negative effects on low-skill workers, overall impact of immigration strongly positive

    B. Reimers: based on past patterns, optimistic outlook for success of new immigrants

    C. Lacey: immigrants a benefit and "essential" to continued economic health of America

VI. Challenges to claim that immigrants are economic burden on society

    A. Muller on relationship between taxes and immigrants

    B. Crewdson on Mexican immigrants and taxes

    C. Lacey on theory that immigrants "overwhelm" public assistance programs

    D. Seller on growth of self-help organizations in immigrant communities of the past

Conclusion

Preparing the Manuscript

Macalbe 1

The New Immigrants: Asset or Burden?

The ideal image of the United States, symbolized by the Statue of Liberty, is of a country that welcomes immigrants and provides them with opportunities to succeed in their new surroundings. It is certainly true that millions of people from foreign lands have come here and have improved their lives. But a study of the history of immigration to the United States also shows that periods of heavy immigration have caused controversy in this country about the desirability of allowing so many foreigners to enter. And in the midst of such controversy, as Elizabeth Midgley notes, many Americans who voiced opposition to immigration have, from time to time, succeeded in forcing legislation to limit the flow of newcomers to America.

Immigration has once again become a controversial issue in the United States because large numbers of foreigners have been entering the country in recent years. Most of these new immigrants, unlike the great waves of immigrants in the past, are not from Europe. According to the U.S. Immigration and Naturalization Service, of the more than thirteen million people to enter the United States as legal immigrants between 1981 and 1996, the overwhelming number were from Third World countries. More specifically, the INS reports, all of the ten countries that were the largest sources of immigrants during this period were in Latin America, the Caribbean, and Asia. (See Table 1.) In

Introductory background paragraph

Reference to entire work

Controversial nature of subject offers reason for research

Preparing the Manuscript

Macalbe 2

Table 1

Immigration, 1981-96: Top Ten Countries of Birth

All Countries	13,484,275
Mexico	3,304,682
Philippines	843,741
Vietnam	719,239
China	539,267
Dominican Republic	509,902
India	498,309
Korea	453,018
El Salvador	362,225
Jamaica	323,625
Cuba	254,193

Source: United States, Dept. of Justice, Immigration and
    Naturalization Service. Immigration Fact Sheet. 27
    July 1999. 28 Jan. 2000 <http://www.ins.usdoj.gov/
    graphics/aboutins/statistics/299.htm>.

assessing the effect of these numbers, Nathan Glazer, a
professor of sociology, explains that the American
public is undecided about whether these new
immigrants will make the United States a stronger
nation or a weaker one (3).

> **Question behind this research**

In the past, opponents of immigration raised
economic, racial, religious, and nationalistic objections
or questions about large-scale immigration to the United
States (Jones 247-305). Today, however, experts tell us
that opposition to immigration is expressed almost
exclusively in economic terms. For example, Dan Lacey,

Macalbe 3

a workplace consultant, business journalist, and editor, found that "research on immigration attitudes" shows that the fear that some Americans have of losing their jobs to immigrants is the main reason for opposition to immigration in the United States today (41). In the same economic vein, Thomas Muller, an economist with the Urban Institute, points out the widespread concern among Americans that the new immigrants use welfare and other public aid programs to such an extent that they are a "financial burden" on government and, therefore, a financial burden on American taxpayers (126-27).

> Mixture of quotation and paraphrase

> Two sources connected

> *Preparing the Manuscript*

It is, of course, impossible to predict with certainty what permanent economic effects the new immigrants will have on the United States. But sociologists, economists, journalists, consultants, and other experts on immigration affairs have investigated the economic effects of past immigration. From their findings, we can draw the conclusion that if the new immigrants have similar economic effects on the United States as earlier immigrants have had, then they will prove to be, for the most part, assets rather than burdens.

> Nature of sources

> Thesis statement

As part of the background for my research, I took the opportunity to conduct informal interviews on my campus with selected students. The purpose was to gather firsthand impressions about what economic effects the students perceived the new immigrants have had, or might have, on the country. And since I

> Explanation for interview portion of paper—note use of first person when researcher refers to herself

Macalbe 4

attend a community college in New York City—a city with a large population of new immigrants—I had the chance to talk to students for whom the new immigrants were real people, and not just textbook statistics.

In selecting potential students to interview, I looked for U.S.-born American citizens with no direct ties to the Third World groups that make up the great majority of new immigrants. I did this because I wanted to gather impressions and opinions that could be offered with as few preconceptions as possible. From thirty-five attempted interviews, I selected the twenty in which students spoke at some length to the topic and produced fairly complete expressions of how they thought the new immigrants were affecting, or might affect, the economic status and future of the United States. Of the group, six were native-born African Americans; seven were native-born Americans with immigrant roots in northern Europe; seven were native-born Americans with immigrant roots in southern Europe. Twelve of the students were male, and eight were female.

In presenting the following results of my interviews, I selected only those responses that related directly to the topic of this paper. In addition, I selected only those opinions that were expressed, in one way or another, by a majority of the students. Again, my purpose was not to construct a scientific study but to gather impressions from the campus that

Explanation for interviewee selection

Explanation for selection of interviews used in analysis of results

Specific identification of selected interviewees

Criteria for presenting data from interviews

Macalbe 5

would get me started on my projected research and that might offer some chances to compare the opinions of students with the findings of experts.

Presentation
of findings
from interviews

1. None of the students expressed a definite opinion in answering the question "Do you think the new immigrants will be an economic asset or an economic burden to the country?" Some said they had trouble thinking of people as "assets" or "burdens" in an economic sense and did not think they could evaluate the immigrants in that way. A majority (eleven) responded much as one student, Joseph Verano, did: "Everybody here except the native Americans, maybe, came from someplace else. Most of us did OK, so I guess these new people have a chance to do OK."

2. When asked about problems they thought the new immigrants were causing, seventeen were of the opinion that the immigrants were taking away jobs from native-born Americans because the immigrants were willing to work for less money than Americans would accept. Eight complained that the immigrants were even competing with Americans for part-time jobs, such as waiting on tables and pumping gas, the kinds of jobs students look for to earn money while attending school.

"Problem"
identified
through
interviews

Preparing the Manuscript

Macalbe 6

Second "problem" identified through interviews

3. Another problem that a majority (seventeen) brought up had to do with what they called welfare. They claimed that too many immigrants were getting money from the government, causing Americans to pay higher taxes to support them. When asked if they thought the immigrants were only interested in getting welfare and not in getting jobs, seven of the seventeen said they thought that was the case. For these students, welfare was a permanent way of life for many immigrants.

Transition paragraph, including restatement of thesis

With information and impressions from my interviews, I turned to see what the experts had to say about the economic effects the immigrants were having on the United States. As previously stated, my research led me to conclude that the experts generally agreed that, based on the past history of immigration, the newcomers should be a benefit to the economic growth of the United States.

Relationship between interviews and library sources

Subtopic: economic issues as principal cause of resistance to immigration

Interestingly, but not surprisingly, the students brought up a number of points that the experts discuss in their studies of immigration. Lacey, as was shown, points to the fear that immigrants may take away jobs from Americans as the major reason for opposition to the new immigration. However, Lacey does not agree with this perception of immigrant impact on jobs. He claims that research shows "that immigrants generally do not compete with Americans for jobs."

Macalbe 7

Instead, Lacey continues, the record shows that while immigrants take over low-paying jobs, Americans move into better-paying jobs and improve their lives (182). John Crewdson, a <u>New York Times</u> reporter and Pulitzer Prize winner, also minimizes the effect of immigrants on the job market by explaining that many immigrants take jobs that Americans refuse to do (370).

Lacey and Crewdson may be accurate in a general sense, but other research shows that immigrant impact on jobs is more severe than they seem to imply, even if the impact is rather limited. Thomas Muller, for example, has found that immigrants do compete with some "unskilled workers" in certain areas and with "some low-skilled native-born workers unable to improve their occupational status and unwilling (or unable) to move from areas with large numbers of low-skill, low-wage immigrants to other areas" (133). Walter Fogel, a professor of industrial relations, supports Muller's contention. He tells us that late-nineteenth- and early-twentieth-century immigrants joined the oversupply of unskilled laborers in the United States, causing additional economic hardship for Americans who were already doing poorly (98).

Jack Miles, a journalist for the <u>Los Angeles Times</u>, discusses a recent event in relation to the effect of immigration upon the lives of underprivileged Americans. In an <u>Atlantic Monthly</u> article, he argues

Note refers to quoted and paraphrased passage

Paraphrase

Transition to subtopic: possible problems caused by immigration

Use of one source to support another

Periodical mentioned to clarify source of journalist's essay

Preparing the Manuscript

Macalbe 8

that immigration played a large role in the riot that enflamed Los Angeles in July 1992. Miles contends that the "black rage" unleashed by African Americans during that riot was not just the result of the acquittal of a

Partial summary of periodical article in relation to subtopic

number of white police officers who had been charged with use of excessive force in what seemed to be— according to most people who saw parts of a videotape of the incident—a brutal beating of an African-American motorist, Rodney King. For Miles, behind the outbreak of violence was the desperation of "fifteenth-generation African Americans" who were being forced to compete for low-wage jobs and limited community resources with "first-generation Latin Americans and Asian Americans" (51). Miles's article is really aimed at questioning United States immigration policies. He fears that the country may be forced to choose between its humane tendency to admit people who are desperately seeking a new life in America and the obligation to improve the lives of many African Americans who have suffered from a long history of prejudice and neglect.

Presentation of cause/ effect question in relation to immigration problems

In recognizing these problems related to immigration and economic pressures, we should keep in mind professor of social history Maxine Seller's point that periods of intense opposition to immigration in the United States have been "expressions of problems within the nation as a whole" (199). So, we might ask whether immigrants are the cause of the problems we have been discussing, or whether they intensify certain problems

Macalbe 9

that have been simmering within the United States. In
concluding his article, Miles makes clear that in regard
to the Los Angeles riot and the conditions that fostered
it, the nation as a whole may well be responsible. He
talks of "that old and still unpaid debt" that goes back to
the Civil War. He is referring, of course, to the promise
of a nation in which African Americans are finally
afforded their rightful place in a society where prejudice
and fear do not set one group against another (68).

    When we go beyond the particular problems in
which immigration may play a part, however, the
history of immigration in the United States shows
encouraging patterns. Thus even though Fogel
summarizes the negative effects of immigration on low-
skill workers in the past, his overall assessment of the
immigrants' impact on the nation's economic health is
strongly positive: "The economic growth to which
immigrants contributed mightily brought [. . .]
opportunities for millions of Americans and much of
the basis for the high standard of living that most
enjoy today" (98). In addition, David M. Reimers, a
professor of history, sees in past patterns of
immigration a reason "to be fairly optimistic" about
the "economic impact" that the new immigrants will
have on U.S. society. Rather than becoming permanent
drains on the nation's wealth, Reimers says that
research shows that "immigrants, although initially
at a disadvantage, on the whole do rather well

**Transition
to subtopic:
"encouraging
patterns" in
support of
thesis**

**Direct quotation
with ellipsis**

**Summary
of passage
incorporating
paraphrase and
direct quotation**

Preparing the Manuscript

Preparing the Manuscript

Macalbe 10

economically." For example, Reimers points to research "indicating that, all things being the same, immigrant earnings catch up to and surpass those of American-born workers within a few years." Reimers adds that "most economic historians and economists" agree on the positive effect immigration has had on the economic progress of the country (248-49).

Continued support of thesis

In a strong defense of immigration, Lacey denounces those who would restrict the flow of newcomers, going so far as to say that immigration is not only beneficial to America but also essential to its future economic growth. He berates what he calls the "standard wisdom" that says that whenever a new wave of immigrants arrives, the economic wealth of those who are already here will go down.

Indented long quotation used to preserve tone and wording of the passage

> Standard wisdom notwithstanding, those who study the American economy scientifically know that both consumption and immigration add to America's affluence, rather than subtract from it. In a consumption-based economy such as America's, ever-rising consumption has always been the seemingly magical force that makes wonderful things rise from the bare earth. (171)

The second major economic point that my student interviewees showed concern about, and that a number

Macalbe 11

of the experts I consulted commented on, was the
perception that immigrants cause financial burdens
to Americans because immigrants have a great
dependence upon welfare and other government aid
programs. On this point, evidence from the past and
some present indications tend to show that new
immigrants do, initially, put some financial stress on
communities where they are represented in large
numbers. In most cases, however, the stress is usually
temporary, and immigrants, by and large, return more
economic assets to such communities than they received
initially.

Muller, using past evidence and recent data,
explains that taxes will be "somewhat above
average" for established residents in areas where
new immigrants decide to live in numbers. He adds,
however, that the tax money is usually made up for by
the profits the community gets from the economic
activity of the immigrants. "On balance," Muller says,
"the economic benefits of immigration [. . .] tend to
exceed private and in some areas public costs" (133).
Crewdson agrees with Muller, based upon his research
into the effects of Mexican immigration on some areas of
our country. The immigrants, Crewdson reports, "were
making jobs as well as taking them, and were paying
more than their fair share of taxes in return for less than
their share of public benefits" (340). And Lacey, again
attacking standard wisdom, claims that the idea that

Second major objection to immigration challenged

Specific support for challenge in previous paragraph

Preparing the Manuscript

Macalbe 12

"impoverished immigrants" will overwhelm the welfare system is false. He says that "a number of studies have discredited that theory" and have found, instead, that a good number of the new immigrants have cultural "aversions" to seeking public assistance (185). If Lacey is correct, we might expect to see a growing number of self-help organizations in ethnic communities where new immigrant groups have gathered. In the past, Seller explains, these organizations and communities served not only groups of immigrants but also the country as a whole by providing financial assistance and a sense of security for great numbers of desperate people in a period when the United States offered little economic security to anyone (171). If the future is similar to the past in this regard, the growth of such self-help activities should further reduce any possible financial burden the new immigrants might place on Americans.

Speculation on future based on pattern of the past

It is worth keeping in mind that the past does not always accurately predict the future. However, if most of the immigrants who have come to the United States in the recent past follow patterns of economic upward mobility similar to those of immigrants who came to America in the more distant past, then, at the least, the new immigrants will—in the words of one of my interviewees—"probably have a chance to do OK." At best, they may provide the impetus for a new age of economic prosperity and growth in the United States.

Conclusion

Macalbe 13

Works Cited

Crewdson, John. The Tarnished Door: The New
    Immigrants and the Transformation of America.
    New York: Times, 1983.

Fogel, Walter. "Nonimmigrant Labor Policy: Future
    Trend or Aberration?" Papademetriou and Miller
    93-122.

Glazer, Nathan, ed. Clamor at the Gates: The New
    American Immigration. San Francisco: Inst. for
    Contemporary Studies, 1985.

---. Introduction. Glazer 3-13.

Jones, Maldwyn Allen. American Immigration. Chicago:
    U of Chicago P, 1960.

Lacey, Dan. The Essential Immigrant. New York:
    Hippocrene, 1990.

Midgley, Elizabeth. "Comings and Goings in U.S.
    Immigration Policy." Papademetriou and Miller
    41-69.

Miles, Jack. "Blacks vs. Browns." Atlantic Monthly Oct.
    1992: 41+.

Muller, Thomas. "Economic Effects of Immigration."
    Glazer 109-33.

Papademetriou, Demetrios G., and Mark J. Miller, eds.
    The Unavoidable Issue: U.S. Immigration Policy in
    the 1980s. Philadelphia: Inst. for the Study of
    Human Issues, 1983.

Reimers, David M. Still the Golden Door: The Third
    World Comes to America. New York: Columbia UP,
    1985.

Preparing the Manuscript

Macalbe 14

Seller, Maxine. To Seek America: A History of Ethnic Life
    in the United States. Englewood, NJ: Ozer, 1977.

United States. Dept. of Justice. Immigration and
    Naturalization Service. "Immigration, 1981-96: Top
    Ten Countries of Birth." Immigration Fact Sheet. 27
    July 1999. 28 Jan. 2000 <http://www.usdoj.gov/
    graphics/aboutins/statistics/299.htm>.

Verano, Joseph. Personal interview. 8 Mar. 2000.

Emily Dickinson's Reluctance to Publish

by
Susanna Andrews

English 102: American Literature
Section 3c
Professor Ann Leigh
June 2, 20_ _

Andrews ii

Outline

Introductory paragraph, including thesis statement

I. Background of the "myth of tragic Emily"
   A. Life in brief
      1. Retreat from social life
      2. Tentative effort to find an audience
      3. Eventual publication of her work
   B. First biographies
      1. The myth's genesis
      2. Its revision in recent years
   C. Refutation of "unworldly" image through analysis of poems
      1. The vocabulary (Thomas; Howard)
      2. The content (Griffith)

II. The correspondence between Dickinson and Higginson
   A. The beginnings of their dialogue
      1. Higginson's article
      2. Dickinson's approach
   B. Higginson's first letter to the poet
      1. "Surgery" advised
      2. Request to see more poems
   C. Higginson's second letter
      1. Further revision advised
      2. Dickinson's response—disavowal of ambition
   D. Interpretations of Dickinson's reaction
      1. Disavowal questioned
      2. Higginson's blindness noted

Andrews iii

III. Dickinson's view of herself as an artist

   A. Her state of mind

      1. Self-confidence

      2. Realization that the world was not ready

      3. Refusal to compromise

   B. Dickinson's real reason for approaching Higginson

      1. Need for special kind of advice

      2. The painful first publications

   C. Higginson's effect on Emily Dickinson

      1. His limitations recognized

      2. His confusion in face of genius

      3. Her rejection of his advice

IV. Evidence from Dickinson's poetry

   A. Choice between fame and popular recognition

      1. Kher's interpretation of poem

      2. Poem's suggestion of her choice

   B. Choice between publication and artistic integrity

      1. Dickinson's decision to forgo publication

      2. Opposition of immortality and time

Conclusion

Preparing the Manuscript

Andrews 1

Emily Dickinson's Reluctance to Publish

Introduction   At her death in 1886, Emily Dickinson left behind
over seventeen hundred poems. Of this number,
only ten were published while she was alive, and

Note includes page number given onscreen   all of these through the initiatives of others (Benfey 4).
Certainly, then, the woman Yvor Winters called "one
of the greatest lyric poets of all time" (40) was all but

Question behind this research   unknown as a poet during her lifetime. For many
years after her poems first appeared in 1890, her
reluctance to publish was attributed to a supposed
unconcern for worldly matters, including literary

The traditional view   fame. Literary critics, serious biographers, and writers
of fictionalized accounts of her life created an image
of Emily Dickinson as a timid, reclusive, mystical
thinker who was too absorbed in personal sorrows

Extra information offered in an endnote   and ecstasies to be concerned with literary recognition.
And this image persists, to a great extent, in the public
mind today.[1]

Since the late 1950s, however, a new view of the poet
has been emerging. This view, based on close studies of

Nature of sources   Dickinson's life, letters, and poetry, reveals an artist well
aware of her worth, who deliberately chose to withhold

Thesis statement   her poems from the world until they could be valued as
unique artistic creations, even if this meant postponing
fame until after her death.

Subtopic: background of the myth   Beginning in her mid-twenties, Emily Dickinson
gradually retreated from the many stimulating personal
relationships that had filled her early life. By her late

Andrews 2

thirties, her retirement was complete; she passed the rest of her days living with her parents and her younger sister, who managed the household. During her later years, Emily Dickinson had virtually no direct contact with anyone outside her immediate family. While she was still connected to her circle of friends, Dickinson made at least one tentative attempt to find an audience for her poetry, but only a handful of verses were published anonymously, most of them in a local newspaper, and these were subjected to considerable editing. Upon the poet's death at fifty-six, her sister discovered over one thousand poems and initiated an effort to publish them. Beginning four years later, in 1890, these poems finally appeared in print (Sewall 1: 4-11).

Over the years, as her following grew, Emily Dickinson became the subject of a number of highly romanticized biographies. Her admirers were trying to establish a connection between her cloistered existence and the powerful passions that course through much of her finest poetry. Only after scholarly editions of her letters and poetry appeared in the 1950s were literary critics in a good position to produce an accurate picture of the poet's life and her attitude toward her art. Even so, a good deal of the mystery remains with us.

The idea that Emily Dickinson knew very little of the real world has been disputed by recent studies of her

Preparing the Manuscript

Note refers to the entire paragraph, summarizing source

Subtopic: refutation of myth

Andrews 3

life and works. One biographer and critic, Owen Thomas, finds a remarkable number of legal, political, and financial words and expressions in her poetry. This fact leads him to conclude that Dickinson "was well aware of the world outside her little room, that in fact she used the language of this outside world to create some of her best poetry" (523). In the same vein, William Howard points out that the largest group of specialized words in Dickinson's poems reflects the scientific and technological discussions of her day (230). Further disagreement with the image of the poet as a shy, unworldly creature comes from Clark Griffith, who sees her as a person whose sensibility was "responsive to the brutalities which life imposes on the individual, and acutely aware of the nothingness with which existence seems surrounded" (5-6). If we reject the image of Emily Dickinson as a mystical recluse who had little interest in the real world, we must also question the theory that she did not publish her poems out of the same lack of interest.

Perhaps the most substantial evidence regarding Dickinson's reluctance to publish can be found in her letters to a professional writer and social reformer, Thomas Wentworth Higginson. This correspondence began in 1862, after Higginson published an article in the April issue of the <u>Atlantic Monthly</u>, entitled "Letter to a Young Contributor," which offered some practical advice for beginning writers seeking to publish. As a result of reading this article, Dickinson sent Higginson four poems,

---

Preparing the Manuscript (sidebar)

Note clearly refers to Thomas's work

New source identified in text

Connection of subtopic with thesis

Subtopic: correspondence with Higginson

Andrews 4

along with a letter containing this question: "Are you too deeply occupied to say if my Verse is alive?" (<u>Letters</u> 2: 403). This and other early letters in their correspondence reveal the poet's interest in gaining recognition. Later correspondence with Higginson seems, however, to have dampened her hope of achieving critical praise.

Reference to primary source; *Letters* are clearly Dickinson's; note includes title because Dickinson is author of two of the Works Cited

Unfortunately, almost all of Higginson's letters to Dickinson have been lost. Nevertheless, the main points of his answers to her early letters have been inferred by numerous critics, using the poet's replies to Higginson as the basis for these conclusions. Paul Ferlazzo, for example, infers that Higginson's response to her first letter must have included some recommendations for altering, or "regularizing," her poems, along with a request for more of her work (136). Ferlazzo bases this judgment on Dickinson's second letter to Higginson, which says, in part, "Thank you for the surgery—it was not so painful as I supposed. I bring you others—as you ask—though they might not differ—" (<u>Letters</u> 2: 404). The "surgery" surely refers to some changes recommended by Higginson, and Ferlazzo thinks it is significant that the poet admits that she was sending him more of the same kind, for this indicates that she did not intend to follow his advice (137).

Quotation from *Letters* interrupts reference to Ferlazzo; otherwise, one note at end of paragraph [(136-37)] would be sufficient

In a second letter to Dickinson, Higginson must have recommended that she not try to publish for the present time, perhaps suggesting that she rewrite her

Support for thesis

Preparing the Manuscript

Andrews 5

poems along the lines he had prescribed. This can be
inferred from her reply to this letter, which reads, in part:

> I smile when you suggest that I delay "to
> publish"—that being foreign to my thought,
> as Firmament to Fin—If Fame belonged to
> me, I could not escape her—if she did not,
> the longest day would pass me on the
> chase—[. . .] My Barefoot—Rank is better.
> (Letters 2: 408)

Those critics who believe that Dickinson's
reluctance to publish was a deliberate choice on her
part do not take at face value her avowal to Higginson
that publishing was "foreign" to her. Instead, they see
Higginson's inability to recognize the genius in her work
as a major factor in her decision to renounce her desire
to publish. As Richard Sewall says it, Dickinson's

> disavowal about publishing can hardly be
> taken literally. After all, she had sent him
> [Higginson] the poems in response to his
> article on how young writers could get their
> work published. [. . .] What she said [. . .]
> about publishing and fame could perhaps
> mean that, in view of Higginson's hesitance,
> she was renouncing her ambition to be a
> public poet, [. . .] perhaps in the hope that
> some far-off Tribunal would render different
> and unequivocal judgment. [. . .] (2: 555)

In suggesting that Dickinson chose obscurity after
Higginson's "hesitance," Sewall does not mean to imply

Preparing the Manuscript

Note referring to
long, indented
quotation comes
after concluding
punctuation

Extended
quotation; student
felt it was
necessary to
identify "him" in
brackets

Subtopic:
Dickinson's view of
herself as an artist

Andrews 6

that she was unsure of herself as a poet because of his criticism. On the contrary, Sewall states that "in her exalted conception of herself as a poet and in her confidence in her powers, she had no [. . .] reason to be deferential to Higginson [. . .] and one cannot help feeling that she knew it" (2: 555). Thus, it was not a sense of inferiority that moved the poet to her decision. Rather, it was the realization that her poems would not be accepted in the forms she had created for them and that public recognition would require her to alter them to meet public expectations. Robert Spiller, in finding that Dickinson "failed to publish" because she would not accept compromise as a path to recognition, makes much the same point as Sewall:

> The general reading public that asked for
> meter that is smooth, rhythm that is easy,
> and words that are limited to only one
> obvious meaning interested her not at all.
> She was willing to wait. (Spiller 127)

In this same regard, Thomas Johnson remarks that, although Dickinson's early letters to Higginson do indicate an interest in publication, she is also asking for a special kind of advice. "At the time she wrote Higginson," Johnson explains in his biography of the poet, "she does not seem to be trying to avoid publication as such; she is inquiring how one can publish and at the same time preserve the integrity of one's art" (11). This inquiry, Johnson continues,

Support for thesis

Two sources connected

Readers could be confused because Sewall's name precedes quotation, so Spiller's name is added to the note

Mixture of paraphrase and quotation

Preparing the Manuscript

Andrews 7

was a real concern for Dickinson because, prior to her writing to Higginson, two of her poems had been published anonymously in the Springfield Daily Republican, an influential newspaper at that time, and both poems had been altered radically by editors to suit their sense of regularity.

Modern critics and biographers are in almost universal agreement that she was disappointed in Higginson's response to her poetry. They also agree that, as Ferlazzo puts it, the man "lacked discernment as to her purpose as an artist" (139). Johnson, in his appraisal of their correspondence, concludes that Higginson, though somewhat impressed by the working and thoughts in Dickinson's poems, "literally did not understand what he was reading" (Biography 111). By this, Johnson means that Higginson was confronted with the work of an "original genius" and was bewildered as to what to make of it. Throughout his correspondence with her, Higginson was apparently attempting to get Dickinson to write more traditional poetry, or, as Johnson observes: "He was trying to measure a cube by the rules of plane geometry" (Biography 107). There is no evidence, however, that she ever followed any of Higginson's suggestions, despite the fact that she maintained a friendly correspondence with him for many years.

For Emily Dickinson, then, the idea of revising her creations for the sake of achieving quick—and probably fleeting—recognition was what was "foreign" to her, not

Preparing the Manuscript

Here and below it would be difficult to work *Biography* into the text smoothly

Subtopic: evidence from poetry

Andrews 8

recognition based on acceptance of her poems as
unique works of art. This conviction comes through
clearly in several of her poems; for example:

> Fame is the one that does not stay—
>
> Its occupant must die
>
> Or out of sight of estimate
>
> Ascend incessantly—
>
> Or be that most insolvent thing
>
> A Lightning in the Germ—
>
> Electrical the embryo
>
> But we demand the Flame. (lines 1-8)

Reference to primary source

In commenting on this poem, Inder Nath Kher
says that it does not mean that Dickinson is "averse to
genuine fame." It means, he continues, "that she does
not wish to be considered as writing simply for the sake
of some cheap glory" (128). Reinforced by this poem—
assuming "we" in the last line refers to the poet—is the
conclusion that Dickinson would rather have had "the
Flame" of her artistic integrity than the "insolvent thing"
called popular recognition.

Support for thesis

Along the same lines, given the deliberate
decision to forgo publication rather than compromise
her art, the first lines of another poem become
significantly clear: "Publication—is the Auction/Of the
Mind of Man" (lines 1-2). And there can be no doubt that
when she wrote the following stanza, Emily Dickinson
had accepted the fact that true fame would not be hers
in her lifetime.

References to primary sources

Support for thesis

Preparing the Manuscript

Preparing the Manuscript

Andrews 9

Some—Work for Immortality—
The Chiefer part, for Time—
He—Compensates—immediately
The former—Checks—on Fame—
(lines 1-4)

She chose to maintain her artistic integrity and await
that immortality.

Conclusion

    The personality of Emily Dickinson will continue to
fascinate those who enjoy speculating about brilliant
artists whose lives were cloaked in privacy. Since she
said so little about herself outside of her somewhat
enigmatic poetry and her letters, the popular image of a
mystical, romantic Emily Dickinson is likely to coexist
for many years with scholarly appraisals of her life and
work. Her poetry, however, does more than create an
aura of mystery about its author; it reveals a dedicated
genius moved by deep, religious reverence for her craft.

Restatement of the thesis

Yet Emily Dickinson, gifted with the power to create
extraordinary works of art, also felt compelled to
preserve the uniqueness of her creations by refusing to
compromise in order to attain public recognition. She
was willing to trust that future generations of readers
would award her the fame her work deserved.

Andrews 10

Note

[1]For a discussion of the sources of the "Emily myth," see Ferlazzo 13-21.

Andrews 11

Works Cited

Benfey, Christopher. "The Mystery of Emily Dickinson."
Rev. of The Poems of Emily Dickinson: Variorum
Edition, ed. R. W. Franklin; Open Me Carefully:
Emily Dickinson's Intimate Letters to Susan
Huntington Dickinson, ed. Ellen Louise Hart and
Martha Nell Smith; and The Emily Dickinson
Handbook, ed. Gudrun Grabher, Roland
Hagenbüchle, and Cristanne Miller. New York
Review of Books 8 April 1999. 28 March 1999
<http://nybooks.com/nyrev/WWWfeat
display.cgi?19990408039R@p4>.

Dickinson, Emily. The Complete Poems of Emily
Dickinson. Ed. Thomas H. Johnson. Boston: Little,
1960.

---. The Letters of Emily Dickinson. Ed. Thomas H.
Johnson and Theodora Ward. 3 vols. Cambridge,
MA: Harvard UP, 1958.

Ferlazzo, Paul J. Emily Dickinson. Boston: Twayne, 1976.

Griffith, Clark. The Long Shadow: Emily Dickinson's
Tragic Poetry. Princeton: Princeton UP, 1964.

Howard, William. "Emily Dickinson's Poetic Vocabulary."
PMLA 72 (1957): 225-48.

Johnson, Thomas H. Emily Dickinson: An Interpretive
Biography. Cambridge, MA: Harvard UP, 1955.

Kher, Inder Nath. The Landscape of Absence: Emily
Dickinson's Poetry. New Haven: Yale UP, 1974.

Preparing the Manuscript

Andrews 12

Sewall, Richard B. The Life of Emily Dickinson. 2 vols.
New York: Farrar, 1974.

Spiller, Robert E. The Cycle of American Literature: An
Essay in Historical Criticism. 2nd ed. New York:
Free, 1967.

Thomas, Owen. "Father and Daughter: Edward and
Emily Dickinson." American Literature 40 (1960):
510-23.

Winters, Yvor. "Emily Dickinson and the Limits of
Judgment." Emily Dickinson: A Collection of
Critical Essays. Ed. Richard B. Sewall. Englewood
Cliffs, NJ: Prentice, 1963. 38-56.

Preparing the Manuscript

Preparing the Manuscript

Cotton Mather's Necessary Witches

by

Fred Hutchins

History 57: Witchcraft in America

Professor Alfred Wintrol

November 13, 20_ _

Outline

Introduction

1. Historians have tried to learn about Mather's role in witchcraft hysteria and the Salem trials.

2. The old view of Mather as a cruel persecutor has given way to more favorable interpretations of his personality.

3. THESIS: Mather's belief in witchcraft was based on private religious beliefs.

I. Historians' opinions of Mather's role in the witch-hunts and his motives for playing that role have changed in recent years.

  A. Mather's belief in witchcraft was normal for the time, and he was more humane than originally portrayed.

    1. The old harsh view of Mather was due to misinterpretation. (Murdock)

      a. He was actually more humane than most people think.

      b. Almost everyone in seventeenth-century America believed in witches.

    2. Modern historians may be biased against intellectuals of that era. (Hofstadter)

      a. They "encouraged greater tolerance."

      b. They opposed unenlightened trial judges.

    3. Mather tried to ensure fairness of trials. (Hansen)

Hutchins iii

      a. He warned against dangers of accepting "spectral evidence."

      b. He trusted judges to listen to him, but often they did not.

   4. Witchcraft really works in communities where everyone believes in it. (Hansen; long quotation)

   5. Mather also believed in witches because the Bible warns against them. (Levy)

B. Whatever his motives, Mather played a critical role in the witch-hunts.

   1. Mather's influence as preacher and writer may have encouraged the witch-hunting. (Silverman)

   2. However, witch-hunts began as local events, and probably would have occurred without Mather's pronouncements. (Silverman)

   3. Mather did not oppose the trials as such, and that implied approval. (Levin)

C. Mather was deeply committed to maintaining the Puritan social order.

   1. Mather's book Wonders expressed concern for the Puritan church and the Devil's attempt to ruin it.

      a. He defended his friends, the judges. (Hansen)

      b. He later admitted some judges erred, but he never said the trials were wrong. (Levy)

2. Mather may have been an antifeminist. (Karlsen)

    a. History shows that accused witches were mainly women.

    b. He writes of "woman's complicity" in the Devil's plot against the Puritans.

3. Salem trials were symptomatic of women's problems in colonial America. (Karlsen)

    a. A "new woman" was called for; she should take care of the home so her husband could be free to succeed in business.

    b. Many women asserted their spiritual equality with men, based on Puritan creed.

    c. Men feared this equality might threaten their social dominance.

4. By defending the church against the Devil, Mather was defending male superiority. (Karlsen)

5. Puritans closely linked "church, state, and family," and saw the Devil attacking all three. (Pestana)

II. Mather's personal religious views necessitated his belief in witches.

  A. Mather believed he enjoyed a special relationship with God.

    1. Mather had to believe in witches to support belief in good supernatural beings.

      a. Witches were as real as angels. (Levin)

Preparing the Manuscript

Hutchins v

   b. Witches, angels, spirit, God are all linked.
      (Silverman)
2. Denying witches meant denying his whole
   faith.
   a. Mather believed he had been visited by an
      angel, who assured him he was righteous.
      (Levy)
   b. Witches proved atheism and doubt are evil.
      (Silverman)
B. Mather believed New England had a special part
   in God's plan.
   1. Mather saw the New England Puritan colony
      as the place where Christ would return to
      Earth. (Levy)
      a. The Bible said the Millennium would be
         preceded by evil days.
      b. So, the witchcraft outbreak seemed to
         signal Christ's immediate return.
   2. Mather focused on the American Puritan
      church's special role in God's plan for the
      world. (Middlekauff)
      a. It was purer than the English Puritan
         church.
      b. It deserved to be the site of Christ's return.
   3. The witchcraft epidemic brought good and
      bad news. (Miller)
      a. It pained individual sufferers.
      b. It foretold Christ's Second Coming.

Conclusion

1. All the social perspectives have some merit, but the role of Mather's personal beliefs seems to have been the basic source of his attitudes toward witches.

2. Afterthought: Mather may have found the conflict between the Devil's agents and God's followers a "thrilling" spectacle to participate in. (Starkey)

Hutchins 1

Cotton Mather's Necessary Witches

In 1692, a series of trials held in Salem,

Introduction of topic

Massachusetts, resulted in the execution of twenty people for practicing witchcraft. Over the years, many historians have tried to explain both the outbreak of witchcraft hysteria at that time and the motives of certain community leaders who played important roles in hunting down and convicting people who were

Reference to source for background information

considered to be witches.[1] One such leader was Cotton Mather, a prominent Puritan minister and theologian, whose complex life and voluminous writings have provided historians with ample material for attempting to understand both the man and his times.

More background material

Early critics of Mather painted him as a cruel witch-hunter and tormentor of innocent people. And while this negative image of Mather has not entirely disappeared, modern historians have largely ruled out

Nature of sources for this paper

the interpretation that Mather's involvement in witch-hunting stemmed from a deliberate desire to inflict suffering upon innocent victims. Indeed, some historians have all but absolved Mather of any unusual responsibility for the trials. He was a person of the times, these writers argue, and in late-seventeenth-century America, it was a rare person who did not believe in and fear the existence of witches. Other historians see Mather's general support of the trials growing out of his desire to defend the authority of the civil judges and protect the Puritan social systems. Yet

Preparing the Manuscript

Hutchins 2

another interpretation views Mather's role as that of a champion of the patriarchal social order. This idea may explain why Mather supported the trials of accused witches, the overwhelming majority of whom were women.

Cotton Mather was a complicated human being, and there may be some truth in all of these ideas. However, the ultimate explanation for his behavior during this fascinating if terrible moment in American history may well lie in his unique view of himself and the Puritan colony. His belief in witches, along with his need to identify and punish them, seems to have supported both his belief that he enjoyed a special, personal relationship with God, and his view that the New England Puritan colony was destined to play the central role in God's plan for the future of humanity.

The commonly accepted description of Cotton Mather shows a "bloodthirsty persecutor" who fanned the flames of the witchcraft hysteria that swept through New England during the last half of the seventeenth century. However, historians today claim that this inaccurate picture of Mather was based upon early misinterpretations of Mather's role in the proceedings. Kenneth Murdock, for example, says that Mather's writings and recent research "prove him to have been not less but more humane than his contemporaries."[2] Murdock accepts that Mather believed in witches, and he attributes that belief to the simple fact that most of Mather's contemporaries believed in them.[3]

Narrowing of chief argument

Statement of thesis

Subtopic: mistaken views of Mather

Mixture of paraphrase and quotation

Preparing the Manuscript

In the same vein, Richard Hofstadter sees an anti-intellectual bias in the way Mather and other educated leaders of that era have been treated by the "modern liberal mind." The charge that intellectual ministers were the "prime movers" of the Salem witch-hunts does not take into account the social complexities of that period. According to Hofstadter, there is "ample evidence" that these ministers, including Cotton Mather, used their influence to "encourage greater tolerance" in the New England colony. In fact, in Hofstadter's view, these ministers wished to oppose the unenlightened actions of the civil judges who conducted the trials.[4]

The idea that Cotton Mather served as a moderating influence during the trials comes from a number of warnings he issued concerning the conduct of the trials. He said it was dangerous for a court to accept "spectral evidence" as decisive proof that a person was guilty of having made a contract with the Devil. Chadwick Hansen defines spectral evidence as "the appearance of the specter of a suspected person in the hallucinations of the afflicted."[5] People who claimed to be suffering from the torments of a witch would say in court that they could see the ghostly form of the person who was tormenting them. Although the form remained invisible to everyone else in the courtroom, at many trials this testimony was accepted as evidence against the accused. Mather reasoned that if spectral evidence

Further support for mistaken view of Mather

Summary with partial quotations

Quoted definition

Student's explanation of definition

Preparing the Manuscript

Hutchins 4

were accepted as proof that someone was "trafficking with the Devil," then the way was clear for anyone to be accused by a personal enemy or a dreamer, with very little chance of refuting such evidence. Mather trusted in the wisdom of the civil judges to minimize the value of spectral evidence when evaluating the total evidence against an accused. However, the judges were far more willing to accept spectral evidence than Mather had expected, and, as a result, the number of imprisonments and executions increased.[6]

Hansen's discussion of witchcraft revolves around the idea that witchcraft does exist in societies that strongly believe in it. As Hansen explains it:

> We must bear in mind that in a society which believes in witchcraft, it works. If you believe in witchcraft and you discover that someone has been melting your wax image over a slow fire or muttering charms over your nail parings, the probability is that you will get extremely sick. To be sure, your symptoms will be psychosomatic rather than organic. But the fact that they are obviously not organic will make them only more terrible, since they will seem the result of malefic and demonic power. So it was in seventeenth-century Europe, and so it was in seventeenth-century Massachusetts.[7]

From this point of view, Cotton Mather was a

Summary of source material related to note 6

Preparing the Manuscript

Long, direct quotation indented

Hutchins 5

product of his society; for Mather and the Salem community, the strange behavior of the people who claimed they were being attacked by witches could only be due to the influence of the Devil. And, as Babette Levy says, Mather would have taken seriously the warnings in the Bible against witches and recognized the need to put such sinners to death.[8]

It appears, then, that Cotton Mather's belief in witches reflected the commonly accepted beliefs of seventeenth-century New England. And, to the extent that he tried to influence people's attitudes toward the judgment of accused witches, he was more enlightened and humane than most Puritans of that time.

However, the evidence also indicates that Mather was not simply a person of his times who got caught up in a sudden awareness of the Devil's activity in New England. Kenneth Silverman, one of Mather's biographers, says that Mather may have contributed to the outbreak of witch-hunting. For many months before the witchcraft trials, Mather "kept calling public attention to the existence of devils and witches." As the leader of a large congregation, Mather preached frequently, and he was a prolific writer. The wide circulation of his ideas could have led to the general fear of an evil "invisible world" that threatened the very existence of the Puritan colony.[9]

Silverman suggests, however, that the persecution of witches stemmed from a number of factors. Such

---

Preparing the Manuscript

Student summarizes paper to this point

Subtopic: Mather heavily involved in witchcraft events

Hutchins 6

outbreaks were "distinctly community events," in that members of the community had to start accusing each other of being witches. And taking these accused witches to trial and punishing them could only occur with the consent of the community as a whole. Thus, the witchcraft mania might have broken out in New England at that time whether or not Cotton Mather had spoken out against the danger.[10]

David Levin, in another biography, offers a stronger criticism of Mather. Levin asserts that a study of Mather's role "will not allow even the most sympathetic biographer the pleasure of casting Mather as a defeated hero in this affair." Levin points out that even though Mather criticized the courts for relying on spectral evidence as grounds for convictions, he did not strongly oppose the witch-hunts, thereby allowing the hunts to continue with his apparent approval. Levin warns against viewing Mather as a noble hero challenging the established order over the issue of spectral evidence. Instead, we should realize that Mather's doubts about the conduct of the trials were clearly secondary to deeper religious beliefs that touched his personal sense of God and of the way God's will works in the world.[11]

Mather's involvement tended toward approval of the trials

In 1692 Cotton Mather wrote Wonders of the Invisible World, an account of five witchcraft trials. In this book, he expressed great concern for New England and its Puritan church, saying that his goal was "to countermine the whole Plot of the Devil against New

Preparing the Manuscript

England, in every Branch of it, as far as one of my darkness can comprehend such a work of darkness."[12] Without doubt, Mather showed concern for the colony and the Puritan church, but Chadwick Hansen senses

Subtopic: Mather as defender of Puritan social order

another purpose behind this book. He regards Wonders as a defense of the court, in which Mather went out of his way "to defend his friends," the judges of the court, from the increasing criticism of their methods. In this view, Mather becomes the "chief apologist" for a group of men whose methods he had earlier criticized.[13] Later in life, Mather acknowledged that the judges had made some mistakes that resulted in innocent people being hanged; however, as Levy explains, Mather attributed those errors to human weakness, not to "intentional evil." Yet, despite questioning the judges' methods and admitting their mistakes, Mather never repudiated his belief that the witchcraft peril had been substantial and that therefore the trials were fully justified.[14]

Another aspect of Mather's defense of social order

Carol Karlsen also sees Wonders as Mather's defense of the social order, but from a slightly different point of view. Calling Wonders Mather's "chief" justification for the witchcraft trials and executions,[15] Karlsen goes on to connect the events at Salem to the history of witchcraft, which she sees as "primarily the story of women." She places considerable emphasis on the fact that throughout history a great many more women than men were executed as witches.[16] Further, Karlsen traces a long tradition of female suppression in Christianity, starting

Preparing the Manuscript

Hutchins 8

with the concept of Eve as the "main symbol of woman-as-evil . . . in many ways, the archetypal witch."[17] Applying this view of history to her evaluation of Cotton Mather, Karlsen claims that he focused in Wonders on "women's complicity" in the Devil's plot to destroy the Puritan church.[18]

Karlsen regards the Salem trials as a symptom of problems growing out of the role of women in the New World. The growth of capitalism in the New England colony had led its leaders to call for a "new woman," one who would relieve her husband of most domestic responsibilities so he could direct his energies toward success in business. It was woman's duty to bolster her husband's sense of self-importance.[19] Back in England, and during the earliest days of the colony, women had come to assert that they were the spiritual equals of men, basing their argument on parts of the Puritan creed. However, once the Puritan church became established in New England, church leaders questioned this idea of spiritual equality because they feared it would spill over into the social order as well and call into question the tradition of male superiority, a tradition which, according to the male leaders, was divinely ordained.[20]

Mather, in his defense of the "true Church" against the Devil's assaults, was, according to Karlsen's interpretation, equally ready to defend the Puritan social structure against the Devil's wily attempts to use women

Summary of source material

Church and social order linked

Preparing the Manuscript

Hutchins 9

as tools for subversion of that social order. The divine order that began with God, the all-knowing, all-powerful father, established the model for men as fathers on earth, both within the family and within the church. This order had to be preserved at all costs, in Mather's view, and witchcraft, which was primarily a woman's crime, threatened that order.[21]

Surely the question of what role the fear of women's influence upon the social order played in the Salem witch trials will continue to be investigated, but Karlsen's study calls our attention to the close connection between the religious and the civil power structures in the Puritan colony. Along these lines, Carla Pestana shows how the Puritan leaders had "shaped all their social institutions—the church, the state, the family—into weapons to be used in the cause of good." The Puritans, says Pestana, "expected Satan to attempt to undermine their holy commonwealth in countless ways," and, as a result, they were constantly on the alert for his disciples and agents, who could appear in their midst at any time.[22]

These various interpretations of Cotton Mather's role in the tragic occurrence at Salem leave us with the fundamental question "How did Mather come to believe so strongly in the Devil and witchcraft?" Levin tells us that Mather's belief in the Devil was derived, through a kind of religious logic, from his belief in good supernatural entities. For Mather, "denial of the Devil's

Depths of Puritan regard for social order supported

Student's interpretation

Hutchins 10

power in this world implied the denial of other spirits, including angels. . . ."[23] Such denials would, of course, strike at the heart of Mather's religious beliefs and destroy the faith upon which his whole life was based. Kenneth Silverman expresses much the same idea in saying that Mather thought that a disbelief in witches "threatened to deny the reality of Spirit itself." As Silverman states: "No witches, no Spirit, no God."[24]

In fact, as Babette Levy points out, for Mather to deny the existence of witches, he would have to deny his "totality of faith." And that would mean denying that he had been visited by his "guardian angel" on a number of occasions following extended periods of fasting and prayer.[25] Mather needed to believe the angel's appearances were real because those visits assured him that he was predestined for salvation and that he was performing his clerical duties in a manner that was pleasing to God. Belief in angels compelled him to believe in witches, for both are part of the supernatural world in which good and evil spirits operate in inexplicable ways. Silverman notes that Cotton Mather looked upon instances of witchcraft as "Letters of Thanks from Hell"—signs of a supernatural order that disproved atheism and theories of religious doubt.[26]

To a large extent, then, Cotton Mather wanted to believe in witches. Their existence justified both his view of himself as a God-chosen person and the traditions of his Puritan faith. In addition, as part

Ellipsis in quotation

Support for thesis

Support for thesis

Subtopic: Mather's special relationship to God

Restatement of thesis

Preparing the Manuscript

of this system of belief, Mather had formed a concept of the Puritan colony's special role in God's eternal plan.

Further support for thesis

According to Levy, Mather believed that New England was a "likely site for the New Jerusalem," the place where "Christ would rule the Earth in a kingdom with his saints for a thousand years before the final Day of Judgment," as foretold in Revelation. This last book of the New Testament spoke of signs that would appear when the Millennium (Christ's thousand-year reign) was close at hand. The major sign would be a "period of deepening corruption . . . when the Devil would make

Mixture of paraphrase and quotation

more violent assaults than usual" on humankind. In the 1690s, Mather and other Puritan leaders thought the Millennium was about to begin, probably in the early 1700s. The outbreak of witchcraft fit neatly into this view.[27]

New England's special place in God's plan dominated Cotton Mather's thinking throughout most of his life, according to Robert Middlekauff. The Puritan church in New England was the "true church," having escaped from the corruption of the original Puritan church in England, as well as from the corruption that plagued all other religions. Mather believed it was his duty to "preserve the Church," and thus the "true faith," until Christ returned to make all things right and just.[28]

Further support for thesis

But if the Devil's assault on New England through witchcraft was painful to witness and called for a

Hutchins 12

courageous counterattack, the situation also offered opportunity for optimism, since it meant Christ would be returning soon. In analyzing <u>Wonders</u>, Perry Miller notes that "the discourse plunges into chiliastic ecstasy. The witches are signs of the times, of the death pangs of the Devil; mischievous powers prevail for the moment, but only because his rule is nearing extinction."[29] Thus, for Cotton Mather, the outbreak of witchcraft was bad news and good news at the same time.

It seems, then, that Mather was a complicated person, and that, in all likelihood, the beliefs of his time, his concept of social and religious order, and his view of women's place within that order all played parts in shaping his attitude toward witchcraft and the Salem trials. However, these factors seem to provide only secondary motives for his belief in witches and for his general support of the witchcraft trials. Looked at one way, the witches represented Satan's insidious plot to throw the Puritan church and its community into disorder. On the other hand, the witches' presence confirmed Mather's concept of a supernatural world populated with good and bad spirits, a concept that supported Mather's understanding of his personal relationship with God. From yet another viewpoint, the Devil's use of witches marked the final days before Christ's glorious return to Earth to reign in New England, the New Jerusalem.

Conclusion

Restatement of major points of paper

Student's summary of his research

Preparing the Manuscript

Hutchins 13

Interesting
afterthought
speculating
on Mather's
"dramatic"
view of the
witchcraft
events

In addition, recognizing that the Salem witchcraft

crisis provided a time of high excitement for the New

England colony, and that Cotton Mather was profoundly

involved in the event, intellectually, emotionally, and

spiritually, one might wonder, along with Marion

Starkey, about the poetically dramatic "thrill" that may

have been "unconsciously submerged" in this great

religious figure as he witnessed "a collision between

heaven and hell."[30]

Preparing the Manuscript

Hutchins 14

Notes

1. For an overview of a number of the more current interpretations of causes leading to the New England witchcraft outbreak, see David D. Hall, "Witchcraft and the Limits of Interpretation," New England Quarterly 59 (June 1985): 253-81.

2. Kenneth B. Murdock, ed., introduction, Cotton Mather: Selections, by Cotton Mather (1926; New York: Hafner, 1965), xv.

3. Murdock, xvi.

4. Richard Hofstadter, Anti-intellectualism in American Life (New York: Knopf, 1963), 62-63.

5. Chadwick Hansen, Witchcraft at Salem (New York: Braziller, 1969), 101.

6. Hansen, 101-04.

7. Hansen, 10.

8. Babette M. Levy, Cotton Mather (Boston: Twayne, 1979), 59-60.

9. Kenneth Silverman, The Life and Times of Cotton Mather (New York: Harper, 1984), 87-88.

10. Silverman, 89-90.

11. David Levin, Cotton Mather: The Young Life of the Lord's Remembrancer (Cambridge: Harvard Univ. Press 1978), 200.

12. Cotton Mather, Wonders of the Invisible World, in Narratives of the Witchcraft Cases 1648-1706, ed. George Lincoln Burr (1914; reprint, New York: Barnes, 1975), 211.

Preparing the Manuscript

13. Hansen, 171.

14. Levy, 64.

15. Carol F. Karlsen, The Devil in the Shape of a Woman: Witchcraft in Colonial New England (New York: Norton, 1987), 180.

16. Karlsen, xii.

17. Karlsen, 177.

18. Karlsen, 179.

19. Karlsen, 180.

20. Karlsen, 172.

21. Karlsen, 181.

22. Carla G. Pestana, "The City upon a Hill under Siege: The Puritan Perception of the Quaker Threat to Massachusetts Bay, 1656-1661," New England Quarterly 56 (Sept. 1983): 353.

23. Levin, 200.

24. Silverman, 92.

25. Levy, 59.

26. Silverman, 92-93.

27. Levy, 33-34.

28. Robert Middlekauff, The Mathers: Three Generations of Puritan Intellectuals, 1596-1728 (New York: Oxford Univ. Press, 1971), 200.

29. Perry Miller, The New England Mind from Colony to Provinces (Cambridge: Harvard Univ. Press, 1962), 203.

30. Marion L. Starkey, The Devil in Massachusetts: A Modern Inquiry into the Salem Witch Trials (1949; New York: Anchor, 1969), 239.

Bibliography

Hall, David D. "Witchcraft and the Limits of
Interpretation." New England Quarterly 59 (June
1985): 253-81.

Hansen, Chadwick. Witchcraft at Salem. New York:
Braziller, 1969.

Hofstadter, Richard. Anti-intellectualism in American
Life. New York: Knopf, 1963.

Karlsen, Carol F. The Devil in the Shape of a Woman:
Witchcraft in Colonial New England. New York:
Norton, 1987.

Levin, David. Cotton Mather: The Young Life of the
Lord's Remembrancer. Cambridge: Harvard Univ.
Press, 1978.

Levy, Babette M. Cotton Mather. Boston: Twayne, 1979.

Mather, Cotton. Wonders of the Invisible World. In
Narratives of the Witchcraft Cases 1648-1706,
edited by George Lincoln Burr. 1914. Reprint, New
York: Barnes, 1975.

Middlekauff, Robert. The Mathers: Three Generations of
Puritan Intellectuals, 1596-1728. New York: Oxford
Univ. Press, 1971.

Miller, Perry. The New England Mind from Colony to
Provinces. Cambridge: Harvard Univ. Press, 1962.

Murdock, Kenneth B., ed. Introduction to Cotton Mather:
Selections. 1926. Reprint, New York: Hafner, 1965.

Preparing the Manuscript

Hutchins 17

Pestana, Carla G. "The City upon a Hill under Siege:
    The Puritan Perception of the Quaker Threat to
    Massachusetts Bay, 1656-1661." New England
    Quarterly 56 (Sept. 1983): 323-53.
Silverman, Kenneth. The Life and Times of Cotton
    Mather. New York: Harper, 1984.
Starkey, Marion L. The Devil in Massachusetts: A
    Modern Inquiry into the Salem Witch Trials. 1949.
    New York: Anchor, 1969.

Solenopsis invicta: Destroyer of Ecosystems

by

David Perez

Current Issues in Ecology

Section 1F

Professor Kim Harris

May 12, 20_ _

Preparing the Manuscript

Abstract

Solenopsis invicta, a South American fire ant accidentally imported into the United States, is a notable example of the catastrophic destruction an aggressive alien species can cause when it invades an ecosystem. Since its appearance in Alabama in 1917, S. invicta has spread throughout the southern United States, outcompeting and outbreeding native ant species, as well as decimating other organisms. Ecologists are aware of S. invicta's threat to biodiversity, and they fear the ant will eliminate some native species before science can fully study them for the potential benefits they may yield for humankind. As a result, scientists are studying possible methods for controlling S. invicta, including the importation of its natural enemies from South America. However, it is unlikely that an effective and safe program for controlling this fierce invader will be initiated very soon.

Solenopsis 2

Solenopsis invicta: Destroyer of Ecosystems

History has shown us time and again the adverse effects suffered by people whose world is invaded by other people from an entirely different culture. Europeans came to the New World bringing death and destruction through their advanced technology and through diseases such as smallpox for which the native people had no defense. Later, industrial powers invaded less technologically advanced societies and turned them into colonies, debasing the lives and cultures of the natives in the process. But human beings are not alone in ravaging territories through forceful aggression and occupation. Destruction of an ecosystem by an invading species is fairly common throughout nature.

Right now in the United States we are seeing a dramatic example of an aggressive species causing cataclysmic destruction as it becomes a major factor in an ecosystem that it recently invaded. The culprit is a red fire ant named Solenopsis invicta, which, since moving to the United States from South America, has wreaked havoc on the southern part of this country, making life miserable or actually ending it for numerous species that are natives to the ecosystem (Mann, 1994).

In this paper, I will investigate how an aggressive alien species that becomes transplanted to a new ecosystem can do considerable damage to that system's native inhabitants and, in some cases, pose a serious

Example of territorial aggression by human beings to provide general introduction to paper

Subject limited to single example of aggression

Date of Mann's work given according to APA style; complete information on this source appears on References page

Statement of purpose

Preparing the Manuscript

Solenopsis 3

threat to biodiversity. My subject for this study will be the red fire ant known as Solenopsis invicta.

Background information   S. invicta came north accidentally just after World War I, entering the southeastern United States through the port of Mobile, Alabama. In the 1940s, according to B. Hölldobler, professor of zoology at the University of Würzburg, and E. O. Wilson, professor of science and curator of entomology at Harvard University (1990), the ant began a "rapid expansion that was to extend its **Page of book on which quotation appears** range over most of the United States by 1970" (p. 431). By the end of the century, "[i]solated colonies [had] been found as far west as California and as far north as Kansas City, Missouri" (California Department

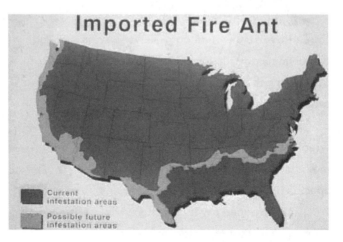

Figure 1.   Current and possible future infestation areas of S. invicta.

Preparing the Manuscript

Solenopsis 4

of Food and Agriculture [CDFA], 2000). Eventually, as shown in Figure 1, the ant may infest areas as far-flung as Puget Sound and Chesapeake Bay (CDFA, 2000).

Government agency as author; abbreviated in second reference

If S. invicta had simply blended into its new surroundings and thrived as just another ant species in a biosystem that was home to numerous ant species, scientists would not regard it today as a significant ecological problem. But about twenty years after its arrival, S. invicta showed it had no intention of peacefully blending into its new ecosystem. And just as Europeans drastically reduced the native peoples after they invaded this land, so this foreign ant species has managed to devastate most of the native ants who had lived in harmony in the southern United States for millions of years.

Analogy of human/ant aggression repeated to emphasize point

A remarkable population density has been achieved by S. invicta in the last few decades. This change was brought about by a fairly recent develop-ment in the ant's reproductive practices. Mann (1994) explains that when it first entered the new ecosystem, S. invicta was a "monogyne" species, which means that each colony had a single egg-laying queen ant. In the 1980s, however, the species "increasingly appeared in a non-territorial 'polygyne' form which creates interconnected 'super colonies' that may contain scores of egg-laying queens" (p. 1560). Obviously, when a colony includes multiple queens,

A reason for S. invicta's successful expansion

Preparing the Manuscript

Solenopsis 5

each producing a colony of ants, it can rapidly outbreed, and thus conquer, the native single-queen species of ants.

S. Lutz, a wildlife ecologist at the University of Wisconsin-Madison, points out a further threat of the multi-queen system. "Ants are less territorial in the multi-queen mound system," allowing individual colonies to establish their mounds fairly close to one another, which leads to a large number of mounds in relatively small areas. Usually, Lutz explains, a single-queen system will produce anywhere from ten to twenty colonies, or mounds, per acre. But a multi-queen system can create from 600 to 700 mounds per acre (cited in Department of Agricultural Journalism, 1996, p. 2).

It is not only its neighbor ants that are suffering from the aggressiveness of S. invicta. Recent findings show that creatures as large as birds are being devastated as well, as the invaders spread ever more forcefully across the land. Mann (1994) summarized an interview with S. D. Porter, an entomologist at the Insects Affecting Man and Animals Research Laboratory in Gainesville, Florida. Porter studied the effects of the polygyne S. invicta's invasion of seventy acres in Texas. He found that after the invasion, the numbers of other ants had decreased by about 75 percent; other creatures, such as spiders and ticks, had decreased by about half. Porter painted a rather grim picture of the destructive

Further support for point made in preceding paragraph

S. invicta's competitive dominance expanding threat to biodiversity

Solenopsis 6

potential of S. invicta: "The fire ants just seem to have outcompeted everything else. The monogyne form is a nuisance to people, but the polygyne form may pose a significant threat to biodiversity" (cited in Mann, 1994, p. 1561).

APA format for an author quoting another author

We might wonder why scientists are deeply concerned about, rather than merely interested in, the destructive activities of this hostile immigrant. After all, most of us are not overly fond of ants, spiders, ticks, or other arthropods. E. Royte (1995), reporting on the extinction and near extinction of flora and fauna native to Hawaii as a result of invasions by alien species, offers a practical reason for attempting to save species from extinction. "Conservationists . . . stress that the loss of even one species may contribute to the decline of entire ecosystems, and that native plants and animals contain genetic information that could lead to new food and medicines" (p. 14). Thus, S. invicta, by wiping out native species, might well deprive us of information that could enable us to lead healthier lives.

Reason for broad scientific interest in *S. invicta*

As the close scientific observation of S. invicta continues, the fear that these fire ants may seriously endanger biodiversity is becoming well justified. Lutz discovered that large species such as birds are also endangered. The northern bobwhite quail is one of the ant's latest victims. Lutz killed off large numbers of fire ants in some areas inhabited by the quail while

Support for biodiversity threat introduced earlier in paper

Preparing the Manuscript

Solenopsis 7

leaving other areas untouched. The quails quickly
increased in the areas where the S. invicta population
had been reduced, but no increase was seen in the
areas where the ants were left in command. Lutz
speculates that the fire ants either "sting chicks or adult
birds to death" or "deprive the birds of a major food
source when they eliminate the native insects upon
which the quails feed" (cited in Department of
Agricultural Journalism, 1996, p. 1).

Oi and Koehler (1996) found that S. invicta can
deliver a "burning sting" to human beings that leads to
a "pustule and intense itching, which can persist for ten

**Real and
possible
threats
to human
beings**

days." Some people with an allergy to the sting can
suffer everything from rashes to infectious shock, and
in rare cases an extreme allergic reaction can result
in death. Despite these possibilities, S. invicta seems
to pose no substantial threat to the quality of human
life in the United States. However, news from South
America is a little unsettling. Blount (1993) reported in
the Houston Chronicle of a nightmarish possibility.
An abstract of Blount's article states that nearly 7,000
people living in Elvira, Brazil, may be forced to leave
town due to severe fire ant infestation (p. A24). It would
seem, then, that S. invicta's territorial ambitions know
no limits.

An obvious question at this point concerns efforts
we should be making to control this destructive species.
Actually, the federal government sponsored a serious

Solenopsis 8

attempt to control S. invicta during the 1960s. Mann
(1994) tells us that the anti-fire-ant program included
bombing large areas infested by S. invicta. The bombs,
dropped by World War II bombers, consisted of a
mixture of ant bait and ant poison. At first, S. invicta
was stymied in its march across Dixie, but it soon
recovered and came back stronger than ever. However,
its victims, the native ant species, were permanently
decimated. The result of this misguided strategy only
made the world easier for S. invicta to conquer.

Attempts at
control

Less dramatic plans for control are now being
studied by scientists. Lutz tells of a fly species that
preys on fire ants in their original South American
habitat, thereby keeping the spread of S. invicta under
control (cited in Department of Agricultural Journalism,
1996, p. 2). Lutz implies that these flies could be imported
and turned loose in areas where S. invicta is spreading
rapidly because it has no serious enemies. In the same
vein, Mann (1994) discusses scientific interest in a
parasite found in Argentina that has been known to
reduce S. invicta populations drastically. However, it is
unlikely that any such programs of fire ant control will
be implemented in the near future, because scientists
must first make sure that by importing another alien
species in an effort to control S. invicta they are not
adding another, perhaps even greater, threat to the
native ecosystems they hope to protect.

Preparing the Manuscript

Solenopsis 9

Taking a long-range view, we may find that nature will eventually resolve the problems caused by S. invicta, or any other aggressive invaders, through its own processes. "It is entirely possible that, given enough time, evolutionary and ecological changes will result in the 'taming' of such species and in their increasingly harmonious assimilation into the indigenous faunas" (Hölldobler & Wilson, 1990, p. 400). If all else fails, then we can hope that Solenopsis invicta, the accidental immigrant, will someday conclude that it has done quite well in the United States. At that time it may, much to everyone's relief, decide to settle down and join the system.

Conclusion

Solenopsis 10

References

Blount, J. (1993, September 19). Brazilian village trying to stamp out fire ants. Houston Chronicle, p. A24. Retrieved January 31, 2000, from DNEW database.

California Department of Food and Agriculture. (2000). U.S. History. Retrieved January 31, 2000, from http://www.cdfa.ca.gov/pests/ fire_ants/new/ history.html

Department of Agricultural Journalism, University of Wisconsin-Madison. (1996). Fire ants create problems for native wildlife. [Press release]. Madison, WI: Author.

Hölldobler, B., & Wilson, E. O. (1990). The Ants. Cambridge, MA: Belknap-Harvard University Press.

Mann, C. C. (1994, March 18). Fire ants parlay their queens into a threat to biodiversity. Science, 263, 1560-1561. Retrieved January 31, 2000, from DPER database.

Oi, D. H., & Koehler, P. (1996). Imported fire ants on lawns and turf. Retrieved January 31, 2000, from University of Florida, Institute of Food and Agricultural Sciences Web site: http://edis.ifas.ufl.edu/LH059

Royte, E. (1995, September). Hawaii's vanishing species. National Geographic, 2-37.

Appendix I

Glossary of Internet Terms

access to connect to via computer. For example, you might access a database or an Internet site.

bookmark a software device for storing the address of a Web site you may want to revisit.

browser a computer program that allows you to access the Web and jump from site to site. Netscape Navigator and Microsoft Explorer are two popular *graphic* browsers. Lynx is a popular *text-based* browser.

bulletin board a network of computer users connected to a specific institution or interest group.

chat room the electronic equivalent of a private room, where a limited number of people are allowed to "chat" via computer at any given time. Chat rooms are maintained by the Internet and by various on-line services and can accommodate from two people to several dozen or even several hundred.

cyberspace the imaginary "space" you inhabit when you access documents or communicate with others by computer.

dial-up access access to an institution's computer resources via modem. You may be able to get dial-up access to your school's library or Internet resources.

discussion groups Internet forums that allow members to exchange ideas and opinions. The two main types of discussion groups are *mailing lists* (or *listservs*) and *newsgroups.*

download to copy material from another computer onto your own computer. For example, you can get a journal article into your computer's memory and then tell your computer to print it for easier note-taking.

e-mail (electronic mail) messages sent via the Internet. E-mail can be exchanged between people anywhere in the world as long as each person has Internet access and an e-mail address.

FAQs (frequently asked questions) a term most often used in connection with discussion groups. A group's FAQ posting answers basic questions that users might have about the group and its rules.

file the electronic format in which a document (text, art, or sound) is stored on computer.

free-net a community computer network established to give more people access to communicating by computer.

FTP (file transfer protocol) a method for downloading (copying) files from other computers linked to the Internet.

gopher software that searches the Internet for sites related to a specific keyword and organizes the information at the site into layers of menus.

home page the main page of a Web site. The home page introduces the site and shows what materials can be accessed at the site. *Home pages* are sometimes called *Web pages*.

hyperlink a fast route between two destinations on the World Wide Web. Web sites use hyperlinks, represented by graphics or text, to give their visitors access to other parts of a site and to related sites.

hypertext a group of documents connected by *hyperlinks*.

hypertext link See *hyperlink*.

icon an image on a computer display that you can click on with a mouse to make the computer perform a command. Icons function as *hyperlinks*.

Internet a worldwide computer network connecting tens of thousands of smaller networks.

Internet service provider a company that simply connects you to the Internet without offering its own software to make using the Internet easier.

listserv See *mailing list*.

mailing list a discussion group in which postings are delivered to your e-mail address.

modem a device that connects your computer to the telephone system, carrying information between your computer and other computers.

netiquette Internet etiquette; accepted rules and standards for online behavior.

newsgroup a discussion group whose postings are accessible to anyone using a browser.

online service a commercial provider of Internet access that offers its own software to make using the Internet easier.

post to send a message to a bulletin board or discussion group. (The message is called a *posting*.)

protocol a set of steps that need to be performed for moving information along the Internet. Different protocols perform different functions.

real-time communication Internet communication that happens in "real time," like conversation in person or over the phone. Tools like TALK and CHAT let you see what another person is typing to you while he or she is typing it.

search engine a World Wide Web tool that looks for information on the Web and elsewhere on the Internet by keyword and/or subject.

site a place (information center) on the Internet.

surf (the Net) to look at various sites and resources on the Internet just to see what's there.

telnet an Internet tool that lets you access another computer from your own computer. (The activity is called *telnetting*.)

URL (uniform resource locator) the address of an Internet site. Most URLs begin with the prefix <http://>.

Web browser See *browser*.

Web page   the amount of hypertext that appears as a single unit on a Web browser. The entire contents of a Web page can be viewed by scrolling up and down within a single window. Sometimes used to mean *home page* or *Web site*, especially when a site consists of only one page.

Web site   a Web page or collection of Web pages. *Web site* is mainly used to refer to the Web pages of institutions and companies, which tend to offer more complex collections of data than pages created by private individuals, with more of their own material as well as more links to other Internet resources.

World Wide Web   a system that makes the Internet easier to navigate by creating hypertext links between different places on the Internet and enabling users to move quickly and easily from one site to another.

Appendix 2

Reference Sources

A Note on Using This Appendix: In the first section of this appendix, you will find general reference sources — encyclopedias, periodical indexes, and biographical sources. In the second section, you will find the most important sources within a wide range of disciplines. Because these reference works are more often known by their titles than by their authors or editors, we have listed them all by title. Within each discipline, we list first the major reference books and then, in a combined section, the main indexes and databases you might explore. Note that many titles are available in more than one format (for example, print, microfilm, CD-ROM, or online). Conversion from one format to another is occurring continually, and accessibility will vary considerably among libraries.

General Sources

Encyclopedias and General Reference Sources

Academic American Encyclopedia. 21 vols. Revised annually.

Acronyms, Initialisms and Abbreviations Dictionary. Ed. Jennifer Mossman. 20th ed. Detroit: Gale, 1995. Revised annually.

Dictionary of the History of Ideas. Ed. Phillip P. Wiener. 4 vols., plus index. New York: Scribner's, 1973.

Encyclopaedia Britannica. 32 vols. Updated annually.

Encyclopedia of Associations. Separate editions for regional, national, international data. Revised frequently. Also available online.

Facts on File. Weekly news summary in a loose-leaf format with a cumulative index. Also available on CD-ROM.

Van Nostrand's Scientific Encyclopedia. Ed. Douglas M. Considine. 8th ed. 2 vols. New York: Van Nostrand, 1995.

General Periodical Indexes and Databases

Academic Index. Scholarly and general-interest publications.

Alternative Press Index

American Statistical Index (ASI)

AP News (Associated Press)

Arts and Humanities Index

Bibliographic Index. Lists bibliographies containing 50 or more titles of books and periodicals.

Book Review Digest

Book Review Index

Dissertation Abstracts

Humanities Index. Online version is *Humanities Abstracts.*

Magazine Index. Widely available on microfiche or CD-ROM. Also online.

National Newspaper Index. Indexes five major papers on microfiche or CD-ROM.

New York Times Index. 1913–.

Newspaper Abstracts

Periodical Abstracts

ProQuest Direct. A full-text periodical service found in many libraries. Utilizes microfiche, CD-ROM, and electronic ordering for less accessible journals.

Social Scisearch. Multidisciplinary index covers 4,500 journals.

UnCover. A full-text online periodical service found in many libraries. Provides faxed copies of articles for a fee.

Biographical Sources

Chambers Biographical Dictionary. Ed. J. O. Thorne. Rev. ed. T. C. Collocott. 5th ed. New York: Two Continents, 1994.

Contemporary Authors. Various editions. Detroit: Gale, 1967–. Also available on CD-ROM.

Current Biography. New York: Wilson, 1940–. Monthly, with annual accumulations. Portraits and brief biographies of contemporary figures.

Dictionary of American Biography. 17 vols., plus supplements. New York: Scribner's, 1927–. Also available on CD-ROM. Includes only deceased Americans.

Dictionary of American Negro Biography. Ed. Rayford W. Logan and Michael R. Winston. New York: Norton, 1983.

Dictionary of Literary Biography. Various editions, with frequent supplements. Detroit: Gale, 1978–.

Dictionary of National Biography. Ed. Leslie Stephen and Sidney Lee. 22 vols., plus supplements. New York: Oxford UP, 1882–. Also available on CD-ROM. Includes only deceased Britons.

Dictionary of Scientific Biography. 8 vols., plus supplements. New York: Macmillan, 1981–.

Great Lives from History. Ed. Frank N. Magill. Englewood Cliffs, NJ: Salem, 1987–91. Includes six sets of 5 vols. each: *Twentieth Century, Renaissance to 1900, Ancient and Medieval, American Women, American Series,* and *British and Commonwealth Series.*

Who's Who. Many editions, various publishers.

Indexes and Databases

Biography Index. Indexes books as well as periodicals.

Sources in the Disciplines

Art and Architecture

Art through the Ages. Horst de la Croix and Richard G. Tansey. 9th ed. New York: Harcourt, 1992. A revised edition of Gardner's *Art through the Ages.*

Contemporary Artists. Ed. Amanda Hopkinson. 4th ed. Chicago: St. James, 1995. A biographical dictionary revised every five years.

Encyclopedia of American Art. New York: Dutton, 1981.

Encyclopedia of Architecture. Ed. Joseph A. Wilkes and Robert T. Packard. 5 vols. New York: Wiley, 1988–90.

Encyclopedia of World Art. 17 vols. New York: McGraw, 1959–87.

Macmillan Encyclopedia of Architects. Ed. Adolf K. Placzek. 4 vols. New York: Free, 1982.

McGraw-Hill Dictionary of Art. Ed. Bernard S. Myers and Shirley D. Myers. 5 vols. New York: McGraw, 1969.

Oxford Companion to Art. Ed. Harold Osborne. New York: Oxford UP, 1970.

Indexes and Databases

Art Index Online version is *Art Abstracts.*

ARTbibliographies Modern

Artist Biographies Master Index

The Grove Dictionary of Art Online

Astronomy

Astronomical Almanac. Nautical Almanac Office. Washington, DC: GPO. Annually.

Astronomy and Astrophysics Encyclopedia. Ed. Stephen Maran. New York: Van Nostrand, 1992.

Encyclopedia of Astronomy and Astrophysics. Ed. Robert A. Myers. San Diego: Academic, 1989.

Facts on File Dictionary of Astronomy. Ed. Valerie Illingworth. 3rd ed. New York: Facts on File, 1994.

Indexes and Databases

Astronomy and Astrophysics Abstracts

Inspec

Biological Sciences

Atlas of Human Anatomy. Frank H. Netter. West Caldwell, NJ: CIBA-Geigy, 1989.

Cambridge Encyclopedia of Life Science. Ed. Adrian Friday and David S. Ingram. New York: Cambridge UP, 1985.

Facts on File Dictionary of Biology. Ed. Elizabeth Tootill. Rev. and exp. New York: Facts on File, 1988.

Oxford Companion to Animal Behavior. Ed. David McFarland. 1982. New York: Oxford UP, 1987.

Indexes and Databases

American Men and Women of Science

Biological Abstracts

Biological & Agricultural Index

BIOSIS Previews

Zoological Record

Business and Economics

Biographical Dictionary of American Labor. Ed. Gary M. Fink. Rev ed. Westport, CT: Greenwood, 1984.

Business Information Sources. Lorna M. Daniells. 3rd ed. Berkeley: U of California P, 1993.

Dictionary of Business and Economics. Christine Ammer and Dean S. Ammer. Rev. and enl. ed. New York: Free, 1986.

Encyclopedia of Economics. Ed. Douglas Greenwald. 2nd ed. New York: McGraw, 1994.

VNR Dictionary of Business and Finance. David M. Brownstone et al. New York: Van Nostrand, 1980.

Indexes and Databases*

ABI/Inform

American Banker

*Standard business sources such as Dun's, Thomas, and Moody's offer many of their directories and publications as databases.

Business Abstracts
Business Dateline
Business Periodicals Index
Company Intelligence
Economic Literature Index
Management Contents

Chemistry

Facts on File Dictionary of Chemistry. Ed.
John Daintith. Rev. ed. New York:
Facts on File, 1988.
Hawley's Condensed Chemical Dictionary.
Ed. Richard J. Lewis. 12th ed. New
York: Van Nostrand, 1993.
How to Find Chemical Information: A
Guide for Practicing Chemists, Teach-
ers, and Students. Robert E. Maizell.
2nd ed. New York: Wiley, 1987.
VNR Encyclopedia of Chemistry. Ed.
Douglas M. Considine. 4th ed.
New York: Van Nostrand, 1984.

Indexes and Databases

Analytical Abstracts
Chemical Abstracts
Chemical Engineering and Biotechnology
Abstracts
Chemical Industry Notes

Computer Sciences

Computer Dictionary. Donald B.
Spencer. 4th ed. Ormond Beach,
FL: Camelot, 1993.
Encyclopedia of Artificial Intelligence. Ed.
Stuart C. Shapiro. 2nd ed. New
York: Wiley, 1992.
McGraw-Hill Encyclopedia of Electronics
and Computers. Ed. Sybil P. Parker.
2nd ed. New York: McGraw, 1988.

Indexes and Databases

Applied Science & Technology Index
Computer Database
Microcomputer Index

Dance

Bibliographic Guide to Dance. 2 vols.
New York: New York Public Li-
brary. An annual supplement to
the library's Dictionary Catalog of
the Dance Collection.
Concise Oxford Dictionary of Ballet. Ed.
Furst Koegler. 2nd ed. New York:
Oxford UP, 1987.
The Dance Handbook. Allen Robertson
and Donald Hutrea. Boston: Hall,
1990.
Encyclopedia of Dance and Ballet. Ed.
Mary Clarke and David Vaughn.
New York: Putnam's, 1977.

Drama

A Guide to Critical Reviews. 4 vols. plus
updates. Metuchen, NJ: Scarecrow,
1979–91. Includes American and
foreign drama, musicals,
screenplays.
Major Modern Dramatists. 2 vols. New
York: Unger, 1984–86.
McGraw-Hill Encyclopedia of World
Drama. Ed. Stanley Hochman. 5
vols. 2nd ed. New York: McGraw,
1984.
Modern World Drama: An Encyclopedia.
New York: Dutton, 1972.
The Oxford Companion to the American
Theater. Ed. Gerald Martin Bord-
man. 2nd ed. New York: Oxford
UP, 1992.
The Oxford Companion to the Theater.
Ed. Phyllis Hartnoll. 4th ed. 1983.
New York: Oxford UP, 1993.

Indexes and Databases

Dramatic Criticism Index: A Bibliography
of Commentaries on Playwrights
from Ibsen to the Avant Garde.
Detroit: Gale, 1973.
Play Index

Earth Sciences

Cambridge Encyclopedia of Earth Sciences.
Ed. David G. Smith. New York:
Cambridge UP, 1981.
McGraw-Hill Encyclopedia of Geological
Sciences. 2nd ed. New York:
McGraw, 1988.
McGraw-Hill Encyclopedia of Ocean and
Atmospheric Sciences. Ed. Sybil P.
Parker. New York: McGraw, 1980.

Indexes and Databases

Geophysical Abstracts. Online version is
GeoRef.

Education

Dictionary of Education. Ed. Carter Vic-
tor Good. 3rd ed. New York:
McGraw, 1973.
Education: A Guide to Reference and In-
formation Sources. Englewood, CO:
Libraries Unlimited, 1989.
Encyclopedia of Education. Ed. Lee C.
Deighton et al. 10 vols. New York:
Macmillan, 1971.
Encyclopedia of Educational Research.
American Educational Research
Association. Ed. Marvin C. Alkin.
6th ed. New York: Macmillan, 1992.
The Facts on File Dictionary of Education.
Jay M. Shafritz et al. New York:
Facts on File, 1989.

Indexes and Databases

A-V Online (nonprint educational
materials)
Education Abstracts
ERIC (U.S. Dept. of Education Resources
Information Center)
Exceptional Child Education Resources

Environmental Science

Grzimek's Encyclopedia of Ecology. Ed.
Bernhard Grzimek. New York:
Van Nostrand, 1976.

McGraw-Hill Encyclopedia of Environ-
mental Science and Engineering. Ed.
Sybil P. Parker. 3rd ed. New York:
McGraw, 1993.

Indexes and Databases

Environmental Bibliography
EPADOC: EPA Documents (U.S. Envi-
ronmental Protection Agency)
Pollution Abstracts

Ethnic Studies

African American Encyclopedia. 6 vols.
North Bellmore, NY: Marshall
Cavendish, 1993.
Asian American Studies. Ed. H. Kim.
Westport, CT: Greenwood,
1989.
Ethnicities and Nations: Processes of
Inter-ethnic Relations in Latin Amer-
ica, Southeast Asia and the Pacific.
Ed. Remo Guidieri et al. Austin,
TX: Rothko Chapel–U of Texas P,
1988.
European Immigration and Ethnicity in
the United States and Canada: A
Historical Bibliography. Ed. David
L. Brye. Santa Barbara, CA: ABC-
CLIO, 1982.
Guide to Multicultural Resources, 1995.
Ed. Alex Boyd. Ft. Atkinson, WI:
Highsmith, 1995.
Sourcebook of Hispanic Culture in the
United States. Chicago: ALA,
1982.

Indexes and Databases

Black Newspapers Index
Ethnic NewsWatch
Hispanic American Periodicals Index. Los
Angeles: UCLA Latin American
Center, 1974–. Also available on-
line.
Index to Black Periodicals. Boston: Hall,
1950–. Annually.
Index to Literature on the American

Indian. San Francisco: Indian Historian, 1970–. Annually.
Sociological Abstracts. La Jolla, CA: Sociological Abstracts, 1952–.

Film

Chambers Concise Encyclopedia of Film and Television. Ed. Allan Hunter. Denver: Chambers, 1992.
The Complete Film Dictionary. Ira Konigsberg. New York: NAL-Dutton, 1989.
The Film Encyclopedia. Ephraim Katz. 2nd ed. New York: HarperCollins, 1994.
Magill's Survey of Cinema. Ed. Frank N. Magill. Englewood Cliffs, NJ: Salem. An ongoing series that includes American films from 1927 and foreign films. Complete cast, technical credits, and critical essay.

Indexes and Databases

International Film Archive

Health and Medicine

American Hospital Association Guide to the Health Care Field. Chicago: American Hospital Assn. Annually.
American Medical Association Family Medical Guide. Ed. Charles R. Clayman. 3rd ed. New York: Random, 1994.
Introduction to Reference Sources in the Health Sciences. Ed. F. Roper and J. Boorkman. 2nd ed. Chicago: MLA, 1984.
The Nutrition and Health Encyclopedia. David F. Tyer. New York: Van Nostrand, 1994.

Indexes and Databases

AIDSline (U.S. National Library of Medicine)

Consumer Drug Information
Health Periodicals Database
Index Medicus. Online version is *MEDLINE* (U.S. National Library of Medicine).

History

Cambridge Ancient History. Ed. J. B. Bury et al. 3rd ed. 19 vols. New York: Cambridge UP, 1923–91.
Cambridge Medieval History. Eds. H. M. Gwathin et al. 9 vols. New York: Cambridge UP, 1911–36.
Dictionary of American History. Rev. ed. 8 vols. New York: Scribner's, 1978.
An Encyclopedia of World History: Ancient, Medieval, and Modern, Chronologically Arranged. Ed. William Leonard Langer. 5th ed. Boston: Houghton, 1973.
Guide to Historical Literature. Ed. George F. Howe et al. 3rd ed. New York: American Historical Assn., 1995.
Harvard Guide to American History. Ed. Frank Freidel and Richard K. Showman. Rev. ed. 2 vols. Cambridge, MA: Belknap–Harvard UP, 1974.
International Bibliography of Historical Sciences. New York: Saur, 1930–. Annually.
New Cambridge Modern History. Ed. G. R. Potter. 14 vols. New York: Cambridge UP, 1979.

Indexes and Databases

America: History & Life
American Memory
Historical Abstracts

Language and Linguistics

The ABC's of Languages and Linguistics. Curtis W. Hayes, Jacob Ornstein, and William W. Cage. 2nd ed. Lincolnwood, IL: NTC, 1987.

Dictionary of Linguistics and Phonetics.
3rd ed. Cambridge, MA: Black-
well, 1991.
International Encyclopedia of Linguistics.
Ed. William Bright. 4 vols. New
York: Oxford UP, 1992.
*The Origins and Development of the
English Language.* Thomas Pyles.
4th ed. New York: Harcourt, 1993.
The World's Major Languages. Ed.
Bernard Comrie. New York:
Oxford UP, 1987.

Indexes and Databases

Linguistics Abstracts
*Linguistics and Language Behavior Ab-
stracts (LLBA)*

Literature

*Annual Bibliography of English Language
and Literature.* Modern Humanities
Research Assn. New York: Cam-
bridge UP, 1921–.
*Black American Literature: A Critical His-
tory with a 1,520-Title Bibliography
of Works Written by and about Black
Americans.* Chicago: Nelson Hall,
1973.
*Black American Writers, Past and Present:
A Biographical and Bibliographical
Dictionary.* Theresa G. Rush et al.
Metuchen, NJ: Scarecrow, 1975.
*Cassell's Encyclopedia of World Litera-
ture.* Ed. J. Buchanan-Brown. Rev.
ed. 3 vols. New York: Morrow,
1973.
*Columbia Dictionary of Modern European
Literature.* Ed. Jean-Albert Bede
and William Edgerton. 2nd ed.
New York: Columbia UP, 1980.
*A Concise Bibliography for Students of
English.* Rev. by William E.
Coburn. 5th ed. Stanford, CA:
Stanford UP, 1972.
Contemporary Literary Criticism. Detroit:
Gale, 1973–.

*Crowell's Handbook of Classical Litera-
ture.* Ed. Lillian Feder. New York:
Crowell, 1964.
Dictionary of Literary Biography. Series.
Detroit: Gale, 1978–.
The Literary History of the United States.
Ed. Robert E. Spiller et al. 4th ed. 3
vols. New York: Macmillan, 1974.
*New Cambridge Bibliography of English
Literature.* 5 vols. New York: Cambridge UP, 1969–77.
Nineteenth-Century Literary Criticism.
Detroit: Gale, 1981–. Excerpts
from critical articles in books and
periodicals. A separately bound
index cross-references all Gale literary series, including *Contemporary Authors* and *Dictionary of
Literary Biography.*
*The Oxford Companion to American Liter-
ature.* Ed. James David Hart. 6th
ed. New York: Oxford UP, 1995.
*The Oxford Companion to English Litera-
ture.* Ed. Margaret Drabble. 5th rev.
ed. New York: Oxford UP, 1995.
The Oxford History of English Literature.
15 vols. New York: Oxford UP,
1947–90.
*The Penguin Companion to World Litera-
ture.* 4 vols. New York: McGraw,
1971. Includes European, American, Asian, and African literature.
*A Research Guide for Undergraduate Stu-
dents: English and American Literature.* Nancy L. Baker and Nancy
Huling. 4th ed. New York: MLA,
1996.

Indexes and Databases

Essay and General Literature Index
MLA Bibliography

Mathematics

CRC Handbook of Mathematical Sciences.
Ed. William H. Beyer. 6th ed.
West Palm Beach, FL: CRC, 1987.

Encyclopedic Dictionary of Mathematics.
Ed. K. Ito. 2nd ed. 4 vols. Cambridge: MIT P, 1987.
VNR Concise Encyclopedia of Mathematics. Ed. W. Gellert. 2nd ed. New
York: Van Nostrand, 1989.

Indexes and Databases
MathSciNet

Media

Broadcasting Yearbook. Ed. Donald V.
West. Washington, DC: Broadcasting, 1982–.
Encyclopedia of American Journalism.
Donald Paneth. New York: Facts
on File, 1983.
*Mass Media: A Chronological Encyclopedia of Television, Radio, Motion Pictures, Magazines, Newspapers and
Books in the United States.* New
York: Garland, 1987.
*Webster's New World Dictionary of
Media and Communications.* New
York: Webster's, 1990.

Indexes and Databases
Communications Abstracts
Gale Database of Publications and Broadcast Media
National Newspaper Index
Newsearch
Newspaper Abstracts

Music

Baker's Biographical Dictionary of Musicians. Nicolas Slonimsky. 8th ed.
New York: Schirmer, 1992.
*International Cyclopedia of Music and
Musicians.* Ed. B. Bahle. 11th ed.
New York: Dodd, 1985.
*Music Reference and Research Materials:
An Annotated Bibliography.* Vincent
Duckles and Michael A. Keller. 4th
rev. ed. Boston: Schirmer, 1994.

New College Encyclopedia of Music. Rev.
by Conrad Wilson. Rev. ed. New
York: Norton, 1981.
*New Grove Dictionary of American
Music.* Ed. H. Wiley Hitchcock
and Stanley Sadie. 4 vols. New
York: Grove's, 1986.
New Grove Dictionary of Music and Musicians. Ed. Stanley Sadie. 20 vols. 6th
ed. New York: Macmillan, 1980.
New Oxford Companion to Music. Ed.
Denis Arnold. New York: Oxford
UP, 1983.

Indexes and Databases
International Index to Music Periodicals
Music Index
Music Literature International (RILM)

Philosophy

Dictionary of Philosophy. Ed. A. R. Lacey.
New York: Paul/Methuen, 1987.
Encyclopedia of Philosophy. Ed. Paul Edwards. 4 vols. New York: Macmillan, 1973.
A History of Philosophy. Frederick Copleston. New York: Image, 1993.
History of Western Philosophy. Bertrand
Russell. 2nd ed. New York: Routledge, 1991.
*Women Philosophers: A Bio-Critical
Source Book.* Ethel M. Dersey.
Westport, CT: Greenwood, 1989.
*World Philosophy: Essay-Reviews of 225
Major Works.* Ed. Frank Magill.
5 vols. Englewood Cliffs, NJ:
Salem, 1982.

Indexes and Databases
The Philosopher's Index

Physics

Encyclopedia of Modern Physics. Ed.
Robert A. Meyers. San Diego:
Academic, 1990.

Encyclopedia of Physics. Ed. Robert M. Besancon. 3rd ed. New York: Chapman, 1990.

Encyclopedia of Physics. Ed. E. Fluegge. 54 vols. New York: Springer-Verlag, 1956–74.

The Facts on File Dictionary of Physics. Ed. John Daintith. Rev. and exp. ed. New York: Facts on File, 1989.

Indexes and Databases

Inspec

Physics Abstracts

SPIN (Searchable Physics Information Notices)

Political Science

American Political Dictionary. Jack C. Plano and Milton Greenberg. 9th ed. New York: Holt, 1993.

Congressional Voting Guide. Comp. Victor W. Bosnich. 5th ed. Washington, DC: CVG Press. Voting records of 535 members of Congress, 1982–92.

Encyclopedia of Crime and Justice. Ed. Sanford H. Kadish. 4 vols. New York: Macmillan, 1983.

Oxford Companion to Politics of the World. Ed. Joel Krieger. New York: Oxford UP, 1993.

The Statesman's Yearbook. New York: St. Martin's, 1964–. Statistical and historical summary of all nations of the world.

Worldmark Encyclopedia of the Nations. 8th ed. 5 vols. Detroit: Gale, 1995. Frequently updated.

Yearbook of World Affairs. London Inst. of World Affairs. Boulder, CO: Praeger. Annually.

Indexes and Databases

ABC Pol Sci

CIS (Congressional Information Service)

International Political Science Abstracts

U.S. Political Science Documents

Psychology

Baker Encyclopedia of Psychology. Grand Rapids, MI: Baker, 1985.

Encyclopedia of Occultism and Parapsychology. 3rd ed. 3 vols. Detroit: Gale, 1991.

Encyclopedia of Psychology. Ed. Raymond J. Corsini. 2nd ed. 4 vols. New York: Wiley, 1994.

Indexes and Databases

Psychological Abstracts

PsycINFO

Religion

Dictionary of Philosophy and Religion, Eastern and Western Thought. William L. Reese. Rev. ed. Atlantic Highlands, NJ: Humanities P, 1996.

Dictionary of Religion and Philosophy. Geddes MacGregor. New York: Paragon, 1989.

Encyclopedia of Religion. Ed. Mircea Eliade. 16 vols. New York: Macmillan, 1987.

Encyclopedia of Religion and Ethics. Ed. James Hastings. 12 vols. New York: Scribner's, 1961.

Encyclopedia of the American Religious Experience: Studies of Traditions and Movements. Ed. Charles G. Lippy and Peter Williams. 3 vols. New York: Scribner's, 1987.

Encyclopedic Dictionary of the Bible. 2nd rev. ed. New York: McGraw, 1963.

The Interpreter's Dictionary of the Bible. Ed. George Arthur Buttrick et al. 4 vols. New York: Abingdon, 1962. Identifies all proper names and significant terms in the Bible, with attention to archeological discoveries and the life of ancient times.

A Reader's Guide to the Great Religions. Charles Adams. 2nd ed. New York: Free, 1977.

Indexes and Databases

Religion Index (American Theological
Library Association)
Religious and Theological Abstracts

Social Work

Encyclopedia of Social Work. 18th ed.
New York: National Assn. of Social Workers, 1990. Frequent
supplements.

Sociology

Encyclopedia of Sociology. Ed. Edgar F.
Borgatta. 4 vols. New York:
Macmillan, 1992.
Encyclopedic Dictionary of Sociology. Ed.
adviser Richard Lachmann. 4th
ed. Guilford, CT: Dushkin, 1991.
International Encyclopedia of Sociology.
Ed. Michael Mann. New York:
Continuum, 1984. Also published
as *The Macmillan Student Encyclo-
pedia of Sociology.*

Indexes and Databases

Child Abuse and Neglect (National Cen-
ter on Child Abuse)
Criminal Justice Periodical Index
Family Resources (National Council on
Family Relations)
Social Sciences Index
Sociological Abstracts

Women's Studies

*An Annotated Bibliography of Twentieth-
Century Critical Studies of Women
and Literature, 1660–1800.* Paula R.
Backscheider and Felicity A.

Nussbaum. New York: Garland,
1977.
*Black Women in White America: A Docu-
mentary History.* Gerda Lerner.
New York: Pantheon, 1972.
*Index to Women of the World from An-
cient to Modern Times: Biographies
and Portraits.* Norma O. Ireland.
Westwood, MA: Faxon, 1970. Sup-
plements available.
*Notable American Women, 1607–1950: A
Biographical Dictionary.* Ed. Ed-
ward T. James and Janet W.
James. 3 vols. Cambridge, MA:
Belknap–Harvard UP, 1973.
Women and History. Gerda Lerner. New
York: Oxford UP, 1986.
*Women Today: A Multidisciplinary Ap-
proach to Women's Studies.* M. A.
Baker et al. Monterey, CA: Brooks,
1979.
*The Women's Rights Movement in the
United States, 1848–1970: A Bibliog-
raphy and Sourcebook.* Albert Krich-
mar. Metuchen, NJ: Scarecrow,
1972.
Women's Studies Encyclopedia. Ed.
Helen Tierney. 3 vols. New York:
Greenwood, 1989–91.
*Women's Thesaurus: An Index of Informa-
tion Used to Describe and Locate In-
formation by and about Women.* Ed.
Mary Ellen S. Capek. New York:
Harper, 1987.

Indexes and Databases

Contemporary Women's Issues. A full-
text resource of periodical articles
and research reports about
women in over 190 countries.
Women's Resources International
Women's Studies Index

Acknowledgments (continued from page vi)

William K. Stevens. "Study of Cloud Patterns Points to Many Areas Exposed to Big Rises in Ultraviolet Radiation." From *The New York Times*, November 21, 1995. Copyright © 1995 by The New York Times Company. Reprinted by permission.

Malcolm W. Browne. "Russian Spy Plane Is Turning Its Sights from U.S. to Ozone." From *The New York Times*, October 17, 1995. Copyright © 1995 by The New York Times Company. Reprinted by permission.

Roger D. McGrath. "The Myth of Frontier Violence." Excerpt from *Gunfighters, Highwaymen, and Vigilantes: Violence on the Frontier* by Roger D. McGrath. Copyright © 1984 University of California Press. Reprinted with permission from the author.

Natalie Angier. "Gene Hunters Pursue Elusive and Complex Traits of Mind." From *The New York Times*, October 31, 1995. Copyright © 1995 by The New York Times Company. Reprinted by permission.

"Mary Cassett" entry. From *The New Columbia Encyclopedia*, fourth edition. © 1975 Columbia University Press. Reprinted by permission of the publisher.

Emily Dickinson, "Poem 1475." Reprinted by permission of the publishers and the Trustees of Amherst College from *The Poems of Emily Dickinson*, Ralph W. Franklin, ed., The Belknap Press of Harvard University Press. Copyright © 1998 by the President and Fellows of Harvard College. Copyright © 1951, 1955, 1979, 1983 by the President and Fellows of Harvard College.

Emily Dickinson. "Poem 406." From *The Complete Poems of Emily Dickinson*, edited by Thomas H. Johnson. Copyright © 1929 by Martha Dickinson Bianchi; copyright © renewed 1957 by Mary L. Hampson. By permission of Little, Brown and Company.

Index

Points to Consider as You Plan and Write Your Research Paper

- Do you understand the difference between a subject and a topic?
- What methods can you use to develop possible topics and to select one for your paper?
- Is your topic neither too limited nor too broad to satisfy the requirements of your research project?
- Have you thought of a preliminary hypothesis to guide your early research and to focus your thoughts?
- Have you learned how to take advantage of the various research opportunities in your library, including computerized facilities?
- Have you investigated the Internet as a possible source of material for your paper?
- Have you acquired an adequate number and variety of sources for your paper?
- Have you evaluated your sources?
- Have you developed an efficient method for taking notes from your sources? Are you able to record direct quotations correctly? Can you paraphrase and summarize adequately?
- Do you understand what constitutes plagiarism? Can you distinguish between general knowledge and material that must be documented?
- Has your hypothesis evolved into a thesis statement? Is the thesis clearly stated in your paper? Does it appear early in the manuscript?
- Have you provided yourself with an outline or a statement of purpose to guide the organization of your paper?
- In your preliminary drafts, have you worked at integrating your sources into a smooth and coherent presentation? Have you revised sentences and paragraphs to improve the clarity and effectiveness of your writing?
- Have you carefully applied the documentation style appropriate for your paper?
- Have you proofread your final manuscript to catch and correct any remaining writing or documentation errors?
- Have you followed your instructor's specifications for preparing your final manuscript?

CONTENTS